Cecil H Page

The Spirit of American Christianity

The Spirit of
American Christianity

by
RONALD E. OSBORN

Harper & Brothers Publishers, New York

to the congregations which have nurtured me

First Christian Church, Douglas, Arizona
University Place Christian Church, Enid, Oklahoma
Pleasance Church of Christ, Edinburgh, Scotland
Hanover Avenue Christian Church, Richmond, Virginia
First Christian Church, Lynchburg, Virginia
Webster Groves Christian Church, Webster Groves, Missouri
First Christian Church, Eugene, Oregon
University Park Christian Church, Indianapolis, Indiana

the congregations which called me as their minister

First Christian [now United] Church, Lahoma, Oklahoma
First Christian Church, Geary, Oklahoma
First Christian Church, Jonesboro, Arkansas
The Church of Christ, Creswell, Oregon

and the Christian Churches in Indiana
which I have served as ad interim *preacher*

West Park (Indianapolis), Morocco, North Liberty, Roachdale,
Pendleton, Whitesville, Union (Franklin), Cayuga, Edinburg,
Mishawaka, and Richmond

this book is gratefully dedicated

Contents

Preface

The purpose of this book is to set forth, within the unity of the universal faith, the peculiar characteristics of Christianity in the United States. This is not a systematic treatise on American theology or church history. It is an exposition of the spirit of a people, undertaking to discover the reasons for the distinctive quality of their religion and to suggest its ecumenical significance. The effect of social and cultural factors on the ideas and practices of the American churches is a recurring theme, setting this book in the context of discussions now going on in the Faith and Order movement.

Since this work was addressed first to an audience outside the United States, European Christianity sometimes appears in it as a foil for exhibiting the peculiarities of American religion. The original purpose of the frequent comparisons was to illustrate our distinctive traits, so that they might stand out sharply in the minds of hearers who were predominantly English, Continental, Asian, and Latin-American. The reader is asked to remember the real subject of the book and not to expect a coherent picture of European church life; if some judgments seem unjust to the faith of the Old World, the purpose of the comparison must be borne in mind. Besides bringing an interpretation to outsiders, it is hoped that the book will help readers in the United States to understand the peculiar features of their own religion and to view it in a larger perspective. In trying to explain ourselves to others we may see ourselves more clearly.

The book may seem, at points, less critical than it might well be. But the duty imposed upon me was to interpret the faith of our churches, not my own personal views; to report what American Christianity is, not primarily to contend what it ought to be. Hence I found it necessary to take seriously, and even sympathetically, elements of American church life of which I have been highly critical and to seek the underlying unity in our various expressions of Christianity. To a group which was understandably suspicious of Americans corporately, though most gracious to us individually, I sought to interpret our people and our faith.

My approach is not that of mere academic analysis, but rather of testimony. My effort is to bear witness to the *spirit* of our people as I have known them in all sorts of Christian groups, from the "Bible Belt" to the campus of the University of Chicago, from the unpainted frame meetinghouse on the wind-swept prairie to the marble magnificence of the National City Christian Church in Washington, D.C. In my ministry I have had associations with believers of many professions, both in work and in worship, and reflections arising from these encounters form the basis for my many generalizations. Generalizing is always treacherous, but a book like this must run the risk.

My title is not intended to be presumptuous. I must apologize for sometimes using the term "American Christianity" in less than a fully inclusive sense. For example, I have not treated Roman Catholicism in the United States in any systematic fashion. Such a witness as I am trying to bear must come from *within* a faith; yet surely much that is said here throws light on the Roman Church in America, while revealing my own Protestant convictions. Even many Protestants may feel that I have claimed too much and have set up as typical of American Christianity a point of view which is held by only some of our churches. I admit the justice of such criticisms. Still, a writer ought not complicate every paragraph with a qualifying clause conceding important exceptions.

The reader will hardly need to be told that I am a "free churchman" and a Westerner. If the views here expressed appear provincial, a look at a map of the United States will reveal the extensive area in which many of them are held; my earliest religious associations were in Arizona, Virginia, and Oklahoma, my ministry has been in Arkansas, Missouri, Oregon, and Indiana. I confess a lack of intimate association with churches in the Deep South, in New York, and New England, and I have never been to Hollywood! A Universalist from Boston or a Southern Baptist from New Orleans would have written a different book from this one. Yet I have made an honest effort to transcend the limitations of my confession and personal experience; and I have tried to present American Christianity integrally, rather than fractionally after the manner of those authors who deal with our major communions one by one.

My sincere gratitude goes to many friends whose generosity and insight have entered into this work. I mention particularly those who had a part in the Third Graduate School of Ecumenical Studies. My service there was a contribution of Disciples of Christ in America; to all my colleagues who helped work out the arrangements for this ecumenical exchange, especially to Dean O. L. Shelton of the School of Religion, Butler University, and to Dr. George Walker Buckner, Jr., of the Council on Christian Unity, I express appreciation. While writing the lectures I recalled many conversations with President Ross J. Griffeth of Northwest Christian College; I received important help in planning them through discussions with J. Edward Moseley of Indianapolis, with my colleague, Professor Robert Tobias, with my father, Professor G. Edwin Osborn of Phillips University, and with my wife, Naomi, who also typed the first two drafts. Several friends gave me the benefit of discriminating comment on the manuscript, especially the Rev. Dr. Robert S. Paul of the Ecumenical Institute, Mrs. Mae Yoho Ward of the United Christian Missionary Society, the Rev. Richard Dickinson of Boston, the Rev. William G. Baker of Edinburgh, and the Rev. Dr. William G. West of Chattanooga. Professor Hendrik Kraemer was persistent in urging that I prepare the lectures for publication.

We hear much today of the Lord of history. In recent ecumenical gatherings, those Europeans who have suffered for their faith have spoken frequently of what God has revealed to them in their experience, and we have listened with respect and gratitude. This book asks, "What has God revealed in the experience of the American churches?" I have no desire to preach a "gospel according to the U.S.A.," knowing full well that any partial apprehension of the Christian message is not the gospel. But I ask that the Christianity of the United States be taken seriously and its ecumenical significance considered along with that of European theology and of the life of the younger churches.

In all the great conferences of the twentieth-century ecumenical movement, the participants have felt a tension between the Christians from Europe and those from America. It was so at Edinburgh, 1910, and still at Evanston, 1954. Half a century of theological discussion has not relaxed the strain; perhaps it will continue for a long time to come. Yet a respectful understanding of one another by Christians on both sides of the Atlantic is essential to that reconciliation which may lead to a deeper unity. My hope for this book is that it may make some contribution to such a strengthening of the ecumenical spirit.

RONALD E. OSBORN

The Spirit of American Christianity

I.

The American Spirit

At the Evanston Assembly of the World Council of Churches, the five presidents of that body, resplendent upon their lofty dais, moved constantly in the public eye. Each was an eminent Christian leader, symbolizing allegiance to an ecumenical faith, yet each was a memorable individual, colorfully embodying a particular culture. Archbishop Athenagoras, the Metropolitan of Thyatira, incorporated in his presence the magnificence of the Greek Orthodox tradition. Bishop Eivind Berggrav exuded a salty Norwegian humor, which emphasized a rugged strength of spirit. Pastor Marc Boegner personified French courtliness and devotion. The Archbishop of Canterbury manifested the parliamentary gifts and genial mediating skill of a true Englishman. Bishop G. Bromley Oxnam demonstrated the vigor and administrative prowess of a two-fisted American executive. Every one of these five ecumenical figures typified the character of his own culture, yet none of them was the less Christian for that.

Every nation has a spirit of its own, and that ethos, although it is profoundly affected by the faith of its people, imparts certain distinctive traits to the religion of the country. Contrast, for example, the worship of the Russian Orthodox Church, the Church of Sweden, the Church of Scotland, and a Southern Baptist church. All these have received common elements of Christian tradition, but each has incorporated them into the life of its own culture and given them liturgical utterance in its own idiom. The so-called younger churches, no longer subservient to missionary direction, are now telling forth the marvelous works of God in their own way; the liturgy of the Church of South India or the worship of the Church of Christ in Congo differs from anything known in Europe.

Christianity early became indigenous in the United States and developed there qualities peculiar to the New World. Certain characteristic traits have derived from the ethos of our people. This chapter does not undertake a full and impartial delineation of our character; whole books are constantly being written on that subject. But certain peculiar experiences of our relatively brief history are suggested as having given rise to those qualities of spirit which observers from abroad consider typically American, and the significance of these traits to our type of Christianity is noted.

THE EUROPEAN HERITAGE

Our cultural roots go back to Europe. The preponderance of early settlement was British, with German, French, Dutch, and Swedish minorities. We are heirs of the great cultural and religious tradition of Western Christendom. To maintain it our churchmen very early began to found institutions of higher learning; in 1636, only sixteen years after coming to New England, they established Harvard College in a town to which they gave the name of Cambridge. One of our hymns sung especially at our season of national Thanksgiving praises the divine providence which brought our fathers to the New World:

> O God, beneath Thy guiding hand
> Our exiled fathers crossed the sea;
> And when they trod the wintry strand,
> With prayer and psalm they worshiped Thee.

The hymn likewise recalls the precious cargo which they carried with them:

> Laws, freedom, truth, and faith in God
> Came with those exiles o'er the waves.

The faith in God was overwhelmingly Protestant. As an effective influence on the common life and national character, Roman Catholicism came much later. Moreover, the Protestantism transplanted to our soil was that which had been defined within the first century of the Reformation. Once this hardy shoot had been set in the good soil of the New World it began to develop in its own right; our Old World roots came from Europe as it was before 1630, certainly before 1776. The new plant has been repeatedly fructified by cross-pollination from the other side of the Atlantic, and in intellectual circles major ideological developments have been brought over for grafting. Nevertheless, in its popular expression, our Christianity has been pruned and trained by American, not European, conditions; and in the new environment it has undergone important mutations.

Once they had ventured across the Atlantic, our immigrants and their children began to conform to a new type. So we ask in the words of Crèvecœur, who wrote about us early in the nineteenth century: "What then is the American, this new man?" And what made him that way?

THE UNPOSSESSED FRONTIER

A major factor in changing the European into an American was the existence of the unpossessed frontier.[1]

From 1607 to 1890 an immense tract of arable land lay to the west, waiting to be possessed. If it was held by Indians for a hunting ground, the opinion of the Scotch-Irish settlers ultimately prevailed: it was "against the laws of God and Nature, that so much land should be idle while so many Christians wanted it to labour on." One of the stupendous achievements of human history is the settlement of the continental United States. In 1790 the frontier line was marked by the Appalachian Mountains, except for a few incursions into Tennessee and Kentucky; a century later—after moving 2,500 miles

---

[1] In Europe, frontier usually means military or political boundary. In America it meant the edge of advancing civilization. Territory inhabited by not more than two persons per square mile was considered beyond the frontier.

—it was gone. Within so short a span of time an eager race of pioneers and immigrants subdued a continent, beating back savage tribes, felling forests to make way for fields, breaking sod that had never yielded to the plow, bringing the raw prairie under cultivation, spawning cities that grew like young giants, throwing bridges across primeval rivers, laying highways and railroads where herds of buffalo still roamed the plains, going down into mines to bring up long-hidden riches and the sinews of industry, building factories and markets, rearing towers of churches and universities, framing charters and institutions of government for an area larger than Europe, rising from colonialism to world power. Because all this happened in a hundred years it profoundly affected the spirit of our people. In the Old World a similar work had begun with the Romans, but suffered setback under the barbarian invasions. Requiring long centuries of feudal and monastic toil and of exploits by the rising national monarchs for even its nonindustrial phases, it affected the ethos of the European peoples in quite a different fashion.

The cutting edge of American civilization was the advancing frontier, the belt of newest settlement that lay between the "old" country to the east and the unclaimed west, between land already reduced to cultivation and government and a wilderness harboring wild beasts and Indians where only the trapper and the trader had dared to intrude. Constant pressure from the land-hungry children of the East kept pushing the frontier farther toward the Pacific with the passing of every decade. Editors wrote of the roads to the west being white with covered wagons. In 1854, during a single month, 1,743 of the slow-moving prairie schooners passed a point beyond Peoria, Illinois, all bound for Iowa. When at last a family came to unclaimed ground, they selected the site of their future home. The federal government surveyed all the public lands and established the price at $1.25 per acre. After the Homestead Law of 1862 public land was free; a man could claim a "quarter section" (160 acres) by living on it for five years and making improvements.

On that frontier, in the generation when civilization was

imposed on the wilderness, the settler found himself as an American. The situation demanded a certain type of man and produced that type; the frontier was our first "melting pot." The process lasted from the day the English touched foot on the bank of the James River (1607) until the last decade of the nineteenth century, when the director of the census announced that the frontier line could no longer be traced on the map. The cities on the Atlantic seaboard maintained commercial and cultural contacts with the Old World, but beyond the mountains men's faces were turned to the west. Emerson coined a famous aphorism: "Europe extends to the Alleghenies; America lies beyond."

What sort of spirit characterized the frontiersman, and what did it mean for the peculiar quality of Christian faith in America?

Self-reliance. To strike into the unknown, like Abraham "not knowing whither he went," to locate in the wilderness a place suited for settling down, to put up a shelter and get a crop into the virgin ground, to live through the first winter on what one could take by hunting or fishing and the dwindling provisions that one had brought overland, to make and repair the tools and clothing for a whole family, to protect family and stock against wild animals or Indians, to sustain the religious life in such a remote situation—all this called for the utmost courage and self-reliance on the part of the frontiersman and his wife. Because of the government's land policy, each family on the prairie lived alone on its own farm, not in villages as in agricultural Europe. For years one might have no near neighbors. Even when the country was fully settled, a rural family was essentially alone. With only four houses to a square mile, one's closest neighbor might well be half a mile away. So the frontiersman was "on his own." And he was proud of his achievement. One western motto runs: "The cowards never started, the weaklings fell by the way." The experience of the pioneers fostered American individualism, in politics, in business, and in religion. Self-reliance is still a notable trait, as evidenced in the custom of "working one's way through college." A recent survey of university seniors in the United States revealed that 72 per cent of them had earned at least part of the expenses of their education. Many poor boys have gone through college depending entirely on income from their own labor.

Egalitarianism. One of the "self-evident truths" to which Thomas Jefferson gave sonorous utterance in the Declaration of Independence was the proposition "that all men are created equal." The frontiersman put it even more bluntly: "One man is as good as another." This was a fundamental article of our early democratic faith, and conditions in the West underlined it with convincing proof; if a man had the strength, the courage, the self-reliance, and the resourcefulness to wrest a farm from the wilderness, he had all the qualities that counted. Name, ancestry, wealth, station, all were irrelevant. Nobody belonged to a special class. If a man was "free, white, and twenty-one," he was as much a man as any other. Few verses of Scripture were quoted more often or with greater conviction than Simon Peter's perception that "God is no respecter of persons." Neither was the frontiersman.

In politics, Western egalitarianism won its first great victory with the election of General Andrew Jackson to the Presidency in 1828. For the first time since the establishment of the republic, a president had come to office without previous apprenticeship as vice-president or secretary of state. Washington, Adams, Jefferson, Madison, Monroe, and John Quincy Adams had all sprung from distinguished Eastern families. Jackson was a rough-and-ready Westerner, untutored in polite culture, an Indian fighter who had won a famous victory over the British at New Orleans in 1815. For his inauguration a multitude of frontiersmen tramped into Washington. They crowded into the executive mansion—now christened the "People's Palace"—and clad in buckskin jackets and coonskin caps stood on chairs and sofas to get a better view of their hero and to raise a cheer for Andy Jackson. One of the watchwords of Jacksonian democracy was rotation in office. In days when there was little cash and a regular salary was a rare privilege, no one should be allowed more than a "fair share at the public trough." One man was as good as another.

From Jackson's day onward a real or affected "folksiness" became the politician's stock in trade. (Witness Franklin D. Roosevelt's "fireside chats" and Harry Truman's "off-the-cuff" speeches.) It was a priceless political asset to have been born in a log cabin; a few candidates for minor office in quite recent years have still claimed this advantage. One of our most amazing presidential elections was the famous "Hard Cider Campaign" of 1840. The Whig party nominated an aging military hero, General William Henry Harrison, who had won a frontier battle against the Indians at Tippecanoe in 1811; the candidate for vice-president was John Tyler, and the slogan became "Tippecanoe and Tyler too." An opposition editor, attempting to dismiss Harrison with a slighting remark, observed that the old general would really be happier if he were allowed to retire to a log cabin with a pension and a barrel of cider. Immediately the West, which now possessed an impressive number of electoral votes, was up in arms, and the offended Whigs were delighted. They put out log-cabin badges, served hard cider at every party rally, and won the election.

One aspect of early egalitarianism was a fear of the specialist. A man ought to work for his living like everyone else. If he concentrated on a line requiring a particular education, the suspicion arose that he was unwilling to do a real man's work and was trying to take advantage of ordinary folks. A constitution drawn up by a group of frontiersmen in 1784 for the abortive state of Frankland (in the region that is now eastern Tennessee) excluded "ministers of the gospel, attorneys at law, and doctors of physics" from eligibility for the legislature. The laws were to be kept simple, for plain people, and the advantages which the learned professions had created for themselves by technicalities and a special education were to be eliminated. The suspicion extended to all the occupations which might be found on the frontier in which a man did not work with his hands. A teacher or a preacher was as despicable as a lawyer if he remained a specialist. First he had to show that he could split as many rails or carry as heavy a load or break as mean a horse as any man around. As likely as not he had to beat the village bully in a fair fight. If he could do all these things and teach or preach besides, then he was admired and listened to with respect. His learning came out of strength, not weakness.

The idea of equality persists, though considerable social and economic stratification has taken place since the simpler days of the frontier. But the effect of earlier thinking is still apparent: by hard work or good luck a man may readily change his status. And there remains considerable moral uneasiness about either assuming or granting that one man is intrinsically better than another. Here is the basis for the American practice of calling another by his first name. It quickly cuts away the pretensions of formality, though at times it may be in itself a pretense of informality, and places everyone on the same level. Men meet as men and, it is assumed, as friends.

Frontier egalitarianism had important implications for religion. Communions which interpreted the doctrine of the priesthood of all believers in terms of lay responsibility for the work and worship of the church or which developed a ministry close to the people—often their preachers were farmers or miners or storekeepers, with little pretension to formal learning—grew rapidly in the West. Notable among these were Baptists, Methodists, Disciples of Christ, Cumberland Presbyterians. By contrast, those churches whose sacramental life depended on a separate order of priests or a learned ministry with advanced theological education did not flourish until a later generation. The point will be discussed in Chapter IV.

Direct action. If a grainfield caught fire, the frontiersman and whatever neighbors could be quickly summoned must take immediate action. In case of an accident to himself or his family, he must administer first aid and, except in the most severe injuries, whatever treatment followed. When a strange sound broke the silence of the night, he must creep out of bed to kill a wolf with his musket or perhaps to face an attack by Indians. If his neighbor fell ill at harvesttime, he and a few others would join to save the crop. In the struggle to stay alive the Westerner became accustomed to making quick decisions, and usually they involved action. When a problem arose, he was sure to ask, "Well, what are we going to *do* about it?" Short on theory, he was long (and quick) on deeds. It became a typical trait of American behavior, whatever the problem, to assume that there must be some simple solution and that we are the ones to see it through.

In the complexities of international relations, the frontiersman's propensities for hasty action did not always lead to felicitous results. The War of 1812 was a good example. Fought ostensibly for "the freedom of the seas," it was precipitated not by the maritime state of Massachusetts, but by the young "war hawks" in Congress, representing the Western states. Most of their constituents had never seen the ocean, but the British impressment of American sailors on the high seas offended their national pride. More serious was the British provision of firearms to the western Indians, through Canada. Something had to be done, and the "war hawks" forced a declaration of war. Part of their strategy was a march on Canada. With a well-founded confidence in Kentucky marksmanship they expected to expel the British from North America in short order. Their plans were sadly confounded when they learned that the Canadians were not seeking liberation from the supposed tyranny of the English crown.

The impetuosity which some Americans show in affairs of state is, therefore, no recent development. Rather it expresses a streak in the national character. The long patience of India is a quality we have not learned. In our past there were simple and obvious solutions to our most pressing problems. We seized them, and the result was usually good. The famous pioneer hero of Texas, Davy Crockett, put it in a simple formula: "Be sure you're right, then go ahead." Now, an expert on foreign policy tells us, we must revise that counsel to read as follows:

Be as sure as you reasonably can of the rightness of your premises. Take care as best you can to see that the conclusions which you draw from them are tolerably right. . . . After you have done your best to meet these obligations, go ahead as far as the circumstances taken as a whole warrant, getting others to go along as far as you can.[2]

Americans are learning restraint in dealing with the new complexities. But the tentativeness of the procedure just recommended leaves them decidedly uncomfortable, almost with a sense of guilt.

The tendency toward direct action expresses itself in our religious life. It has been a factor in the rise of new denominations. A situation arose, needing to be remedied. What did our fathers do? They did not discuss the theory of the matter. They did not wait long for higher authorities to deal with the problem, especially if there was official reluctance. They started a movement. Perhaps it resulted in a new denomination, but the need was met. In the earlier decades of the twentieth century many Americans talked boldly of "building the Kingdom of God." The phrase is not so popular today as it was a generation ago. It is scarcely heard in the seminaries. In our pulpits it is a convenient synonym for "doing the work God has given us to do." It was natural that such a phrase, expressing the liberal theology that we learned from Europe, should have appealed to our people. Though we now describe our service more modestly, we still believe in Christian action. The millions of dollars which American churches have given in cash and commodities for Interchurch Aid and material relief are not merely the foam spraying off the wave of national prosperity. Nor must such contributions be dismissed merely as evidence of a peculiar popular bent toward generosity. They are expressions of this fundamental trait, a determination, when a problem arises, to do something about it. In the face of obvious need, not to do anything about it strikes us as an act of disobedience to the will of God.

Localism. Most of the problems which the frontiersman faced were local in character. An important exception was the building of roads, and there was constant pressure from the West on the federal government to appropriate funds for this

[2] Charles Burton Marshall, *The Limits of Foreign Policy* (New York: Holt, 1954). Quoted in *Time*, Nov. 1, 1954.

purpose. Another exception was defense against the Indians.
The pioneer often had to take on the job in an emergency,
but he wanted United States troops to do the job. Otherwise
he wished to deal firsthand with the issues affecting his welfare. He often resented the federal policy for the disposition
of the public lands, especially the plotting of homesteads in the
arbitrary pattern of the quarter section. He would have much
preferred to choose for himself a site following the contours of
the ground or embracing such natural advantages as a spring,
a stream, an expanse of rich "bottom land," or a grove of trees.
Some families in the vanguard of Western expansion held on
to such irregular claims in defiance of the government, appealing to "squatter's rights." Why should a man who knew a
good farm-site when he saw it and had put out the labor to
develop it give it up years later because it did not coincide
with a surveyor's map back in Washington?

The frontiersman's attitude was simple: the men here on the
ground should deal with the problem. He joined with his
neighbors in "committees of safety" to combat lawlessness.
The less government the better, as far as he was concerned; he
tended to resist all authority, more especially that which
resided across the sea or even across the mountains. He constantly agitated to get self-government in the West. He experienced a sense of triumph when the population had grown
to the point of establishing a territorial government, even more
when there were enough citizens to adopt a state constitution.
There was a rapid growth in the West of the "democratic
churches." The congregational polity commended itself to
many, and churches with a connectional structure were under
constant pressure to create new conferences or synods. In
religious matters most of all the pioneers resented being
governed by the East.

Today this tendency is changing. Both the government and
the churches are centralizing, but the inheritance of localism
is a powerful brake on the process. Sometimes it blinds ecumenical vision: a contemporary pastor trying to awaken his
congregation to their missionary duty was distressed by the
constant tendency of his officers to speak of "building the

Kingdom here at Sixth and Main" (the corner on which their church was located). Throughout whole denominations there is an inclination to think of the church primarily in local terms, and some of these communions remain outside the World Council of Churches on that account, in spite of an awakening ecumenical concern among many of their leaders. The localist attitude is not, however, an unmitigated evil. It reflects a wholesome realization that the thing which really counts in the Christian movement is what goes on in the lives of men and women where they live, not decisions which are taken by the denominational or the ecumenical bureaucracy. Here is the real basis for Christian action "at the grass roots." Here is the reason for that healthy resentment against the tendency of ecclesiastics to talk about "getting *down* to the local level." The local community is not some inferior region, the last stop on a descending scale of wisdom and grace. It is the place where men live and work and pray and serve and give, where the lost are saved, where the saints suffer and die and triumph. The localism of the congregation needs to be redeemed by the concept of the one holy, catholic, and apostolic church. But the resistance which runs through a large section of the American churches against ecclesiastical centralization will remain a fact to be reckoned with for a long time to come and may be a wholesome reminder to the developing ecumenical movement that the church is nowhere if it is not local.

Restlessness. The son or grandson of immigrants who had left the Old World in search of a new life, the pioneer went west "to better himself." The struggle with the wilderness and the promise of a brighter future lured the backwoodsman ever deeper into the unknown. He was the most primitive of the settlers, living in a lean-to or a three-sided cabin open to the south; the area was too crowded for him when he could see the smoke from another man's fire. After him came the genuine settlers who really established farms with houses and outbuildings, but even they did not always stay permanently. Many a pioneer went west three times during his life—as a child with his parents, perhaps at the time of his marriage to take up a claim of his own, and in mature years when he could sell his farm and improvements at a profit to some less venturesome latecomer and strike out for virgin territory to begin the process all over again. The typical American of today, like his frontier ancestors, is not rooted in one place. He too goes where he can better himself as to income or living conditions. Families follow a job halfway across the continent. Others move miles across a city to build a new house in a more desirable location.

Such fluidity presents the church with difficult problems. "How do you evangelize a procession?" our home mission workers ask. Pastors are constantly lamenting the loss of leadership as some dependable family leaves for another community. One minister of a congregation with fewer than 800 members found that his church must add 97 new members each year just to compensate for losses by death and removal. And, although our population has been in flux for so many years, the problem of getting people to enter actively into the religious life of their new communities has not yet been solved. Many cherish an emotional attachment to the old home church which they hesitate to break by affiliating with another congregation. Because of our lack of the parish concept a family does not regard itself as belonging automatically to the church in its neighborhood. Membership is "transferred" by a formal act, and one of the constant chores of pastors is to find the new residents in their communities and persuade them to identify themselves with the church where they are before their Christian commitment grows cold.

The break with tradition. Many of the pioneers left Europe or our own East to get away from conditions they disliked. Not a few avowedly utopian communities were planted in the West, and all the settlers carried with them a sense of doing something new. It still quickens one's imagination to pass through a prairie town named Athens or New Palestine. Walt Whitman catches the spirit in his "Pioneers! O Pioneers!" a moving poem which deserves to be read in its entirety: "All the past we leave behind us." The frontier was an area of experimentation in both government and religion, especially the latter. To the departing Pilgrims, Pastor John Robinson gave the assurance, "The Lord hath more truth and light yet to break forth out of his holy Word." Increase Mather explicitly formulated the negative aspect of the idea:

There never was a generation that did so perfectly shake off the dust of Babylon, both as to ecclesiastical and civil constitution, as the first generation of Christians that came to this land for the Gospel's sake.

The consciousness of our earliest generations of settlers that they were breaking with tradition has profoundly affected our Christian life and institutions. A foremost historian of the church in the New World has written of the situation at the time of the Revolution:

The people of America possessed a larger degree of freedom in religion than was to be found among any other people. They had carried on the freest debate on all religious questions without regard to bishops, priests, councils or creeds, thus encouraging an individualism in religion such as existed nowhere else.[3]

If our present generation of churchmen and theologians is sometimes at variance with those in Europe, it is perhaps because our spiritual fathers made a deliberate break with the immediate past. In the virgin setting of the New World, with a clear messianic consciousness, they initiated a novel effort to reconstitute church and society in accordance with the will of God.

Faith in the future. The whole American venture has been posited on a belief in a better tomorrow. An immigrant or a pioneer might be destitute of possessions, but abundant land stretched to the west and the future lay ahead. Men wasted little effort dreaming of the past; their visions glorified a time yet to come. The experience of countless individuals, of many families, and of the nation itself seemed to corroborate the popular faith in the future. The New World was a land of plenty. During the generations when the national character

[3] William Warren Sweet, *The Story of Religion in America* (New York: Harper, 1950), p. 3.

was being formed, any family could strike out for the frontier and "homestead" a farm. Ours is still an expanding economy, as our population grows. Businessmen expect their markets to increase year after year, and financial faith in the future has created a credit structure which allows common citizens to buy everything from houses to automobiles on the installment plan—a small down payment and a fraction of the balance each succeeding month.

Expansion became a major virtue. As long as a city was increasing in population, a business in volume of trade, a university in enrollment (or, alas, it would seem, the government in debt), it was considered a success. I remember passing through a small Western town and seeing from the window of the train a sign which read: WATCH US GROW! That was the slogan of the West. Like the hymnboards in a European church, an American congregation displays a register with attendance figures for its Sunday school, showing gains over last Sunday and over last year. The vitality of congregational life is to a large extent measured by the number of "additions" (conversions) during a given period of time.

The popular faith in the future is hard to shake; even the atomic bomb has failed to stifle it. The individual American may harbor many personal anxieties, but he still proceeds on the assumption that things in general will be "bigger and better" tomorrow. In such a setting, millennialism has flourished chiefly among the dispossessed. To other American Christians the popular interpretation of the social gospel in terms of corporate moral and spiritual progress "made sense." Even in the more sober mood of our own time, American interest in eschatology is slight. The tendency is to dismiss the European concern with this emphasis as temporary, the result of wartime disaster. If pressed, the average Christian among us would concede that someday the earth will pass away and that God will still reign; he believes deeply in the gospel of eternal life. But right now the future looks bright. Even Evanston failed to inject a strong concern for eschatology into the main stream of American religious interest. The optimistic inheritance of the Golden West is still with us.

An aspect of romance pervades our memory of the frontier. It is our heroic past, and it is celebrated in that most stylized of American art forms, the "western" movie or novel. (In my boyhood, children crowded the local theater every Saturday morning to see another "horse opera"; now there are daily performances on television.) A greatly oversimplified and highly optimistic morality play, the western presents the struggle and the victory of right against wrong. Distorted as its picture of actual frontier life is, it celebrates the characteristics we have been discussing. And these traits are deeply ingrained in our character as a people and in our institutions. They remain a part of the American self-image, even in a radically changed society where some of them have little relevance and perhaps have actually ceased to exist. Just as many customs and ideals persist in contemporary Europe from the days of chivalry, so the present-day American who has never sat a horse or wielded an ax or seen a wild bear (much less had to shoot one) still thinks of himself in the tradition of the hardy frontiersman.

Yet the frontier has receded at least two generations into our past. Other factors have emerged to recast the American character, and in some instances to alter it radically. Still certain of the frontier "values" persist in institutional form, especially in the life of our churches and in politics.

But what of these newer factors? They also require mention.

THE GROWTH OF THE CITIES

The rapid urbanization of the nation during the past century changed the quality of our life and the work which the churches must undertake. In 1860 only one-sixth of our population lived in cities; by 1890 the proportion had risen to more than one-third; in 1950 only one-sixth of the people were left on the farms. Urbanization was a tremendous cultural stimulus, perhaps more to music and the arts than to letters. It has made for a higher degree of popular sophistication. The effect on preaching, church architecture, sacred music, and worship has been profound, as well as upon an increased Christian concern for social questions. Some of the practices which rural life had impressed upon the churches gradually gave way to the different demands of the city. The old midweek prayer meeting on Wednesday or Thursday night is almost forgotten, and the Sunday evening service has dropped out of the calendar of many urban congregations; these events no longer compete with the attractions of the radio and television and the desire of people to spend a quiet evening at home. Most urban congregations are unable to draw a crowd of the unconverted to evangelistic meetings, once the chief means of enlisting members in the church (see Chapter III), although huge city-wide revivals in great public arenas are beginning again to have some success. The kind of leisurely pastoral visiting which bound a rural congregation to its minister becomes increasingly difficult; it is hard to find people at home, and there are so many demands on their time that an innocently ill-timed call by the pastor may cause annoyance. A major problem of the churches has become the adaptation to the city of those methods which won the country or the devising of new methods.

Yet old rural traditions linger. In many a city church one still hears a congregation, whose members were born in hospitals and grew up in apartment houses, singing a song that expresses nostalgia for a simpler day:

> There's a church in the valley by the wildwood,
> No lovelier place in the dale.
> No spot is so dear to my childhood
> As the little brown church in the vale.
>
> Come to the church in the wildwood,
> Oh, come to the church in the dale. . . .

In congregations influenced by the liturgical revival such a song would not be sung. But for many it recalls values identified with the "old-time religion." When a church becomes too "citified" it often loses touch with large numbers of people more recently come from rural areas and with the less sophisticated class of city-dwellers. Then someone comes along to minister to them after the traditional formula of revivalism.

The appeal of many of the fundamentalist churches would seem to be not so much their explicit theology, although it is traditional; certainly not their constant attacks on modernism; but rather their deliberate folksiness and warm-heartedness, their continuation of familiar patterns, their maintaining of the mood and spirit of the old evangelistic meeting even in services where everyone present has been a Christian for years. It is no easy matter for an urban church, caught in a changing cultural situation, to minister to all the people whom it ought to be reaching with the gospel of Christ.

THE PATTERN OF IMMIGRATION

The changing nature of immigration affected both the American spirit and the prevailing faith. Our earliest settlers were predominantly British, with some other Western Europeans, and predominantly Protestant. In the 1820's the Irish began coming in force, and after the potato famine in 1846 their numbers vastly increased. Destitute upon arrival, many found work in the great cities of the Atlantic coast, although some went west in labor gangs and helped to lay the rails that first spanned the continent. For the first time in our history we had a sizable body of Roman Catholics in our population. Boston, New York, Philadelphia, Baltimore grew into mighty centers of Roman strength, where divided Protestantism is overshadowed in both numbers and influence. The Irish policeman became a fixture on the American scene, and so did the Irish priest. For a time antiforeign and anti-Roman prejudice asserted itself in ugly fashion. The Native American party flourished briefly and without honor. Industrial establishments posted signs reading "No IRISH NEED APPLY."

Late in the same decade and increasingly through the 1850's a new flood of Germans streamed into the country. The numerous German settlers of the colonial period were concentrated in the Middle Atlantic states; marked by their piety and, in some quarters, by sectarian peculiarities of dress and custom, they were good-humoredly dubbed "Pennsylvania Dutch." But the mid-nineteenth-century wave of Germans inundated the West, which until then had remained the almost exclusive preserve of Protestants in the Reformed tradition. While many of the newcomers settled in the rural areas, others converged upon the inland cities. Cincinnati, St. Louis, Chicago, Minneapolis received sizable German colonies, which greatly augmented Roman Catholic influence in the heartland of America. Many of the Germans and Scandinavians, however, were Lutheran. But no more than the Roman believers from Europe were they accustomed to the Puritan way of looking at life. They greatly offended the sensibilities of the older American Protestants by introducing beer gardens and the Continental Sabbath; their merrymaking on Sunday was a scandal to Christians in the Calvinist tradition, who frowned on any sort of frivolity on the Lord's day. The Germans also brought a taste for good music, an art which had until then been woefully undeveloped in our country. Symphony orchestras and grand operas began to be heard in our cities, and the concert became an institution. The cultural life of the nation took on a new dimension, and of course the churches were affected.

Toward the end of the century the most abundant sources of immigration shifted to Southern and Eastern Europe, introducing new ethnic groups. Hardly any of these people were Protestant. They were overwhelmingly Roman Catholic, with two sizable new elements, Jews and Eastern Orthodox. The changing nature of immigration so alarmed those older-type Americans who preferred to have fellow citizens like themselves that restrictive laws were passed, the legislation of 1924 setting quotas based on proportions prevailing in the population in 1890. Meanwhile the churches were busy among the newcomers, ministering to both spiritual and social needs. Many of the ex-Europeans had left their homeland in protest against the prevailing religion and others had no strong confessional roots, so that the old-line Protestant communions were reasonably successful in winning numbers of them. Nevertheless, the proportionate strength of Roman Catholicism increased. The American spirit became less Puritan and more complex. The old religious mores, while persisting into the twentieth century among Christians of the Reformed tradition, ceased to dominate social behavior, even among respectable people. The battle for prohibition (legislation forbidding the manufacture, transportation, and sale of alcoholic beverages), which was won on a national scale by the "Christian forces" of America in 1919 and lost again in 1933, has been called the last stand of Protestantism against the non-Puritan pluralism that has come to dominate our society. But in many communities, especially in the South, where "local option" elections may be held to establish prohibition within the limits of a city or a county, the "forces of righteousness" have not yet given up the fight.

From the standpoint of political ideology and of our "way of life," the children of these diverse sorts of immigrants and of the older families have been cast into remarkably similar molds; the melting pot has done its work. But the common culture is less distinctively Protestant than it once was, less Christian and more secular. The advent in large numbers of Roman Catholics, Jews, and (to a lesser extent) Orthodox shattered that unity of faith by which old-line American Protestantism, for all its denominational separatism, was able to give guidance to the spiritual life of the nation. Even though Protestant and Orthodox forces have achieved a degree of consolidation in the National Council of Churches, American religion is more parochial than it was a century ago. Protestantism is strong. Romanism is strong. Judaism is by no means weak, and is growing in vigor. But because none is in a position to dominate, secularism has grown in effective power. In Europe there are some signs of rapprochement between Protestantism and Roman Catholicism in relation to their common witness to a "post-Christian" civilization.[4] In the United States, each is too weak to achieve dominance now, but strong enough to strive for it as a realistic possibility. The two are therefore caught up in an intense rivalry to decide which of

[4] The term "post-Christian" has been used by various European authors to describe the situation on the Continent. See "Evangelism in France" (Information Bulletin published by the Secretariat for Evangelism, World Council of Churches, Geneva: 2nd ed., May, 1952), pp. 21, 54.

f American Christianity

among Christians of the F
minate social behavior, ever
battle for prohibition (legislat
e, transportation, and sale of a
won on a national scale by the
a in 1919 and lost again in 19.
and of Protestantism against the
has come to dominate our society
especially in the South, where '
be held to establish prohibition w
a county, the "forces of righteousr
the fight.

nt of political ideology and of our "v
of these diverse sorts of immigrants a
have been cast into remarkably simi
pot has done its work. But the commo
ctively Protestant than it once was, le
secular. The advent in large numbers o
Jews, and (to a lesser extent) Orthodox
y of faith by which old-line American
all its denominational separatism, was able
to the spiritual life of the nation. Even
and Orthodox forces have achieved a degree
the National Council of Churches, Ameri-
re parochial than it was a century ago. Prot-
g. Romanism is strong. Judaism is by no
is growing in vigor. But because none is in a
ate, secularism has grown in effective power.
are some signs of rapprochement between
d Roman Catholicism in relation to their com-
a "post-Christian" civilization.[4] In the United
o weak to achieve dominance now, but strong
e for it as a realistic possibility. The two are
nt up in an intense rivalry to decide which of

st-Christian" has been used by various European authors
uation on the Continent. See "Evangelism in France" (In-
n published by the Secretariat for Evangelism, World
hes, Geneva: 2nd ed., May, 1952), pp. 21, 54.

cern for social questions. Some of the practices which rural life had impressed upon the churches gradually gave way to the different demands of the city. The old midweek prayer meeting on Wednesday or Thursday night is almost forgotten, and the Sunday evening service has dropped out of the calendar of many urban congregations; these events no longer compete with the attractions of the radio and television and the desire of people to spend a quiet evening at home. Most urban congregations are unable to draw a crowd of the unconverted to evangelistic meetings, once the chief means of enlisting members in the church (see Chapter III), although huge city-wide revivals in great public arenas are beginning again to have some success. The kind of leisurely pastoral visiting which bound a rural congregation to its minister becomes increasingly difficult; it is hard to find people at home, and there are so many demands on their time that an innocently ill-timed call by the pastor may cause annoyance. A major problem of the churches has become the adaptation to the city of those methods which won the country or the devising of new methods.

Yet old rural traditions linger. In many a city church one still hears a congregation, whose members were born in hospitals and grew up in apartment houses, singing a song that expresses nostalgia for a simpler day:

> There's a church in the valley by the wildwood,
>   No lovelier place in the dale.
> No spot is so dear to my childhood
>   As the little brown church in the vale.
>
> Come to the church in the wildwood,
>   Oh, come to the church in the dale. . . .

In congregations influenced by the liturgical revival such a song would not be sung. But for many it recalls values identified with the "old-time religion." When a church becomes too "citified" it often loses touch with large numbers of people more recently come from rural areas and with the less sophisticated class of city-dwellers. Then someone comes along to minister to them after the traditional formula of revivalism.

The appeal of many of the fundamentalist churches w
seem to be not so much their explicit theology, although
is traditional; certainly not their constant attacks
modernism; but rather their deliberate folksiness and warm
heartedness, their continuation of familiar patterns, their
maintaining of the mood and spirit of the old evangelistic
meeting even in services where everyone present has been a
Christian for years. It is no easy matter for an urban church, ev
caught in a changing cultural situation, to minister to all the
people whom it ought to be reaching with the gospel of
Christ.

THE PATTERN OF IMMIGRATION

The changing nature of immigration affected both the
American spirit and the prevailing faith. Our earliest settlers
were predominantly British, with some other Western Europeans, and predominantly Protestant. In the 1820's the Irish
began coming in force, and after the potato famine in 1846
their numbers vastly increased. Destitute upon arrival, many
found work in the great cities of the Atlantic coast, although
some went west in labor gangs and helped to lay the rails that
first spanned the continent. For the first time in our history
we had a sizable body of Roman Catholics in our population.
Boston, New York, Philadelphia, Baltimore grew into mighty
centers of Roman strength, where divided Protestantism is
overshadowed in both numbers and influence. The Irish
policeman became a fixture on the American scene, and so
did the Irish priest. For a time antiforeign and anti-Roman
prejudice asserted itself in ugly fashion. The Native American
party flourished briefly and without honor. Industrial establishments posted signs reading "No IRISH NEED APPLY."

Late in the same decade and increasingly through the 1850's
a new flood of Germans streamed into the country. The
numerous German settlers of the colonial period were concentrated in the Middle Atlantic states; marked by their piety
and, in some quarters, by sectarian peculiarities of dress and
custom, they were good-humoredly dubbed "Pennsylvania
Dutch." But the mid-nineteenth-century wave of Germans

these radically different types of Christianity will become the determining faith of the nation, as the Reformed tradition was in the nineteenth century. Perhaps they are blindly struggling to turn back the clock. It may well be that Romanism will never dominate American life and culture as it once dominated Europe, that Protestantism will never regain the ascendancy it once enjoyed in our land. But each strives to realize the vision.

THE MECHANIZATION OF LIFE

The increasing role of technology in our civilization is imprinting new marks on the American character. Our life is more and more mechanized. Even among families of moderate income nearly every household has its automobile and electrical appliances, the number increasing as wages and salaries go up. Our great cities boast more television sets than bathtubs. In offices stenographers and bookkeepers work with an increasing array of equipment for calculating, dictating, transcribing, recording, and duplicating. Modern agriculture requires such a variety of mechanized equipment that the farmer has become a capitalist on a sizable scale. A host of workers are engaged in the manufacture, demonstration, sale, and service of all these mechanical devices for home, office, factory, and farm.

The effect of all this mechanization on the inner life is difficult to assess. The visitor to our shores frequently jumps to the conclusion that Americans are gadget-crazy. There is some evidence for the judgment: our luxury automobiles, for example, provide not only automatic gearshift, power brakes, and power steering, but also electrically operated devices for opening and closing windows and for adjusting the height and position of the driver's seat at the touch of a button. Our inventors and manufacturers are constantly bringing forth some new device for doing work formerly done by hand. But foreigners who stay in America for a while soon begin to acquire and enjoy the conveniences which they at first scorned.

There is little evidence that a world whose labor is lightened by mechanical appliances is necessarily a spiritual jungle. It is true that the desire to possess new gadgets and the compulsion of meeting installment payments on those already acquired may occupy the mind with worldly concerns, but these are probably no more distracting than the bodily pain and weariness of less complex cultures. It may be that some Americans easily become so preoccupied with the pleasures of this life that they have little concern for things of the spirit and thoughts of eternity. If so, they fall into the snare that threatens all rich men—and not the wealthy alone. Gadgets cannot be proscribed on that account, as certain fiery preachers a generation ago assailed the automobile, attributing its invention to the devil because some people went motoring on Sunday instead of going to church. (Most well-to-do urban Negroes today dream less of the joys of heaven than did their ancestors a century ago, but that fact is no argument for the restoration of slavery as a spiritual discipline.) Doubtless the modern city-dweller, or even the farmer plowing fifty acres a day with his tractor, is less aware of his dependence upon nature, or providence, than was the medieval serf or the Asian peasant. But the feeling after God is not dead; life still moves amid the wonders of birth and love and death, of dreams and sin and redemption. Science and technics have not banished the mystery from life. Indeed, one important factor in the return to religion now apparent in the United States is a dawning realization of the limits of science. Research, experimentation, invention have not yet exhausted themselves; there will doubtless remain new worlds for them to conquer as long as the race endures. But the soul of man abides, unsatisfied by gadgets, hungering for the bread of life and not satisfied by the stone of knowledge, still crying out for the living God.

It is in this situation that we Americans find ourselves most commonly misunderstood today. In a recent book, for example, the European journalist Robert Jungk paints a disconcerting picture of the future, under the title *Tomorrow Is Already Here*. His analysis of certain trends in the applied sciences, and particularly of the totalitarian demands made by military research, deserves consideration by thoughtful men.

But his underlying assumption that a Promethean, or even demonic, principle dominates our science, that in pride we have set ourselves to master the ultimate mysteries and to wrest from the hands of God the sovereignty over his universe, must be seriously challenged and modified, if not repudiated. Science, like love or labor or any other human endeavor, may be perverted by sin. But do the instances cited by Jungk justify his dark conclusions? Why is it blasphemous to undertake the watering of the desert by seeking to control the rainclouds, any more than by building dams to control rivers? To improve a breed of cattle by artificial insemination? To describe in a school of "aviation medicine" the limitations of the human body for space navigation? Were not earlier efforts —to master the plagues that devastated continents or to fly a heavier-than-air machine—also called blasphemous, and with no better reason? Many an American scientist, in the spirit of George Washington Carver, has worked in humble companionship with God.

Unfortunately many Europeans have formed a distorted picture of life in the United States and of the spirit of our people by reading Jungk's book. From the examples he has given we would all seem to be hopelessly materialistic, inwardly consumed by the passion of power, dazzled by our technical achievements. Yet we Americans who have yielded to the Lordship of Christ are under no illusions about our technical accomplishments. We are proud of them. We would not want to give them up. But neither do we want to make technology our golden calf. Doubtless we too often make invidious comparisons to the disparagement of peoples and cultures that lack our "advantages." And our problem is by no means easy—living as children of God in a "sensate culture." Many of us do not succeed at all, and all of us fail at times. But we are aware of the problem; it is not apparent only to foreign eyes. The late American dramatist, Eugene O'Neill, confronted us with it in *Marco Millions*, bringing the brash and aggressive young Marco Polo, a personification of Western commercialism and pride in its own superiority, into encounter with the ancient wisdom and the spiritual hunger of the East. O'Neill did not solve the problem, and we confess that we have not done so, even in our churches. But we know that it exists. We do not think that heaven will be illuminated with neon lights; we do not expect to bring in the kingdom of God by pushing a button. At the same time we know that there is no easy way out of our difficulty. However alluring the visions of romantic or reactionary critics, we cannot reverse the process of history and go back to some simpler, more mystical, pretechnical era. We must come to terms with the Eternal in our own age. And, though there is much secularism among us, this book has been written to witness to a spirit in contemporary America, behind the façade of gadgets and glamour, a spirit which bows in humility and need before the presence of God.

Our life is noisy. We are assailed on all sides by the hum of motors, the clatter of machines, the blare and the squawk of radio and television. We have less solitude than our rural forebears. But we have more leisure. Instead of physical drudgery from dawn to dusk, our housewives find their work greatly lightened and enjoy frequent afternoons and evenings free from toil. Instead of a six- or seven-day week, ten hours a day, our workingmen now put in forty or forty-four hours a week, and the imminent advent of automation in industry will doubtless reduce that period as much as one-half. The organized power of the labor unions is a factor in the better conditions, but so is the greater productivity brought about by technical advance. The result is that families have far more free time than ever before—to devote to the improvement of their homes, to active outdoor recreation, to cultural pursuits, and to religious activities. Not all Americans spend every evening looking at television or going to the movies. An amazing amount of time is given over to serious endeavors in adult education (many of them in the churches), to sponsoring wholesome activity for young people, to social welfare, to meeting for Christian fellowship and service. Our sociologists tell us that our people will have an increasing amount of free time at their disposal. The churches are helping to serve them by providing constructive activities and are gaining in strength by the additional service that many are able to render in the name of Christ.

Even our churches, however, impress many foreign observers as having been overwhelmed by the national obsession with techniques and organization. We admit that "program" and "administration" hold a large place in our religious institutions. Since the 1890's there has been much talk of bringing "business efficiency" into church work. Many of our courses offered in theological seminaries and many of the books published for ministers are concerned with procedure—how to organize a congregation, methods of stewardship and finance, techniques of evangelism, publicity, and promotion. There are even sizable firms with large staffs which deal exclusively in conducting financial campaigns for churches. We are self-deceived if we do not recognize the danger of losing the Spirit in the machinery; some of our ministers doubtless score higher as executives than as saints. But again we cannot solve the problem merely by stating it. Our churches are made up of, and attempt to serve, people living in an age of organizational revolution. The faith of the psalmists and the prophets found expression in the familiar pastoral and agricultural terms of their time; ours must find expression in the forms of an institutional era. It is still the ancient faith. So in our modern mechanized society stands the church of Christ, organized for the sake of its mission, but determined to keep its soul.

We cannot go back to the supposedly simpler days of the preindustrial age. Every nation on earth is moving toward a more complex technical development. Even India is repudiating Gandhi's spinning wheel. The question before mankind is not a choice between God and machines. Machines are doubtless here to stay, and God certainly is. Our problem is to maintain the life of the spirit in an age when it may be so easily lost and when it is desperately needed. If the United States has been launched on the sea of technology rather in advance of some other peoples, and if to the eye of the stranger the waters look dark and foreboding, we have not left the eternal God on the shores of the agricultural past. We who have heard his voice are convinced that he goes before us, and because we follow him our course is not unknown.

II.

A Free Church and a Free State

The distinctiveness of American Christianity arises only in part from the peculiarities of the American spirit. The character of religious life in the United States also has been affected, and that most profoundly, by a political principle—the separation of church and state.

It is true that most of the nations of Western Europe guarantee religious liberty to their citizens, and that in some of them there is complete separation of church and state. But these are comparatively recent developments in the long history of European Christianity; many of its characteristic ideas and practices arose in the earlier era of establishment and enforced uniformity. By contrast, church and state in America have been separate since the achievement of nationhood (1789); the settlement of the whole country west of the Appalachian Mountains took place after that time. (Even earlier, several of the seaboard colonies were without an ecclesiastical establishment.) Religious life and institutions developed among us under strikingly different circumstances than in Europe.

What do Americans mean by the separation of church and state, and how do they justify it?

THE THEORY OF SEPARATION

Our fundamental law, the Constitution of the United States, seeks to guarantee the existence of a free church along-

27

side a free state within a free society.[1] Neither the church nor the state exercises legal authority over the other, and each leaves the other institutionally free. The basic guarantee of this freedom is the First Amendment to the Constitution, the primary assurance in our Bill of Rights:

Congress shall make no law respecting an establishment of religion, or prohibiting the free exercise thereof; or abridging the freedom of speech, or of the press; or of the right of the people peaceably to assemble, and to petition the government for a redress of grievances.

This first article in the Bill of Rights protects the church against the state, the state against the church, and the people against both; freedom of religion is inextricably linked with the other civil rights. This freedom is conceived as beneficial to the church as well as to the body politic. Separation of church and state in America implies no antipathy of the government or the people against religion; rather it is regarded as one of the "blessings of liberty" secured by the Constitution.

The provisions of the First Amendment at first applied only to the federal government, and some of the states retained religious establishments for a generation after 1789. But by the Fourteenth Amendment, adopted in 1868 during the era of reconstruction following the Civil War, the constitutional guarantees were made binding upon the states. Throughout the length and breadth of the land it is contrary to law for any agency of government to collect or appropriate funds for the use of any church or to interfere with the religious beliefs of any citizen. No ecclesiastical leader, however important, is entitled on account of his status in the church to any governmental position or privilege. He may take his chances in running for public office, or he may make representations

---

[1] I am indebted to Charles Clayton Morrison for his illumination of the concept that the church is not "within" the state, but that both are "within" society. In the American understanding of constitutional government, the state and society are not coterminous, but the state has limited functions. A free church and a free state, therefore, exist side by side within a social order that is also free because it includes no totalitarian institution.

to the government like any citizen. But the only authority which the churches can exercise upon the state is through the common mind of their members expressed in their civil capacity as voters. No bishops automatically sit in the United States Senate or the president's cabinet; no act of Congress is necessary in order for a church to revise its doctrinal standards or forms of worship. No man convinced that he is called of God need apply to any civil official for authority to organize a new church. Both church and state must leave each other free.

This constitutional liberty is an American *political* achievement (although other nations practice it also); it is not an explicit principle of historic Protestant doctrine. Freedom of religion is so much a part of our life and system of values that many American Protestants assume it has always been taught by their communions. The fact is that this freedom was won against the opposition of the established churches in the new nation. At the same time, certain Protestant doctrines, especially of churches in the Reformed tradition, contributed powerfully to its realization.

During the colonial period there was no uniform practice respecting the establishment of religion. In Virginia, the oldest of the permanent English colonies, the Church of England was established; later it received the support of the colonial governments in Maryland, North Carolina, South Carolina, Georgia, and certain counties of New York. Puritanism was established in Massachusetts (Quaker missionaries were imprisoned there and four of them were hanged) and Connecticut. But other colonies were founded on a basis of religious freedom.

The first of these was Maryland, chartered in 1634, the first haven of conscience in the New World. It was not Lord Baltimore's church, however, which inspired him to write religious toleration into the fundamental order of his colony: he was a Roman Catholic proprietor receiving a charter from a Protestant king, and the potential immigrants, upon whom the prosperity of his colony depended, were nearly all Protestants. In such circumstances it was neither possible nor desirable to secure a charter establishing the Roman faith.

Two years later Rhode Island was founded by Roger Williams as "a shelter for persons distressed in conscience." In 1676 the Quaker proprietors of West New Jersey inscribed in their charter: "No person to be called in question or molested for his conscience, or for worshipping according to his conscience." William Penn looked upon free Pennsylvania (1681) as "an Holy Experiment" and advertised its blessings of religious liberty far and wide among the oppressed minorities of Europe.

A major influence toward the freedom of religion guaranteed in the Bill of Rights was the struggle for disestablishment in Virginia, after the Revolutionary War. The fight was led by Thomas Jefferson, George Mason, and James Madison, foremost leaders in developing the American structure of liberty and the shape of our government; Madison's *Memorial and Remonstrance*, a tract issued during the debate in the state legislature, is a powerful summation of the political thinking which repudiated establishment. The efforts of these great political liberals were seconded by many Presbyterians in Virginia, and more enthusiastically by the Baptists and the Quakers. The crucial law gained final approval in 1786:

No man shall be compelled to frequent or support any religious worship, place, or ministry whatsoever, nor shall be enforced, restrained, molested or burthened in his body or goods, nor shall otherwise suffer on account of his religious opinions or belief; but . . . all men shall be free to profess, and by argument to maintain, their opinion in matters of religion, and . . . the same shall in no wise diminish, enlarge, or affect their civil capacities.

The importance which these framers of the American system attached to the struggle was expressed by Thomas Jefferson when he composed his own epitaph. One may read it today over his grave at Monticello: "Here was buried Thomas Jefferson, Author of the Declaration of Independence, of the Statute of Virginia for Religious Freedom, and Father of the University of Virginia." He did not mention his two terms as president of the United States.

The reasons for writing religious freedom into our system were not merely pragmatic. Some authors have observed that no one church was strong enough throughout the new nation to demand special privileges, implying that disestablishment was a matter of necessity rather than of principle. The fact is that when the established churches saw that they were about to be stripped of their peculiar advantages, which they desperately wanted to maintain, they then proposed that *all* the churches be established. Various plans were drawn up for assessing a religious tax and distributing it according to a particular ratio or the instructions of the taxpayer. But the architects of American freedom rejected establishment on principle. The government would impose disabilities for religious opinions upon no one—orthodox, dissenter, heretic, or infidel.

There was a sound religious reason for granting freedom of conscience in some of the early colonies: the principle of spiritual integrity. Worship or faith that is coerced by the power of the state is unprofitable to the individual and displeasing to God. Both dissenters and political liberals made use of the argument. "Religion, or duty which we owe to our Creator and the Manner of discharging it, can be directed only by reason and conviction, not by force or violence," wrote Madison in his *Memorial and Remonstrance.*

The founders of the republic believed that the best interests of the people, of government, and of the churches demand freedom of religion. Madison penned a withering charge:

During almost fifteen centuries, has the legal establishment of Christianity been on trial. What have been its fruits? . . . Pride and indolence in the Clergy, ignorance and servility in the laity: in both, superstition, bigotry, and persecution.

The champions of popular liberty feared an alliance between church and state as a threat to the people's freedom. In some instances, Madison charged, ecclesiastical establishments

have been seen to erect a spiritual tyranny on the ruins of Civil authority; in many instances they have been seen upholding the thrones of political tyranny, and in no instance have they been the guardians of the liberty of the people.

So, from the beginning, freedom of religion has been an abiding principle of "the American way." In various decisions across the years the Supreme Court has sought to maintain the "wall of separation between church and state."

In the light of this long tradition a strange development recently took place. In the Eighty-third Congress (which adjourned in the summer of 1955) Senator Flanders introduced a proposed constitutional amendment, which read: "This nation devoutly recognizes the authority and law of Jesus Christ, Savior and Ruler of nations, through whom are bestowed the blessings of Almighty God." The suggested revision in our fundamental law was not intended to abridge any of our present freedoms, and perhaps, if adopted, it would not. The intent rather was to bring the Constitution into line with the Declaration of Independence, which specifically affirms that it is "by their Creator" that "men are endowed with certain unalienable rights." Some sincere citizens have expressed concern that our Constitution makes no similar reference to the divine "Author of Liberty."

Yet it must be admitted that such "devout recognition" of Jesus Christ, as the proposed amendment asserts, cannot be compelled. In the life of the nation there would seem to be little value in an affirmation which must be a source of offense to our five million Jewish citizens, to the not inconsiderable number adhering to other non-Christian faiths, and to many free thinkers, and which might well be an occasion of false pride in our alleged national piety. What is really to be desired is the actuality, a government by the people which in both domestic and foreign affairs follows such policies as are most in accord with "the authority and law of Jesus Christ." Difficult as that goal is of attainment, a nation might well exercise some reticence in proclaiming its devout character.

Should the Flanders amendment be resubmitted to the Congress and come up for serious discussion (as now seems unlikely), the Protestant churches generally might well follow the line of argument advanced in the previous paragraph. But one cannot predict with assurance. It is difficult to imagine the churches, in the interests of religious freedom, actively opposing a national affirmation of faith, although many thoughtful churchmen would undoubtedly do so. On the other hand, the proposal might carry as a sentimental concession to religion and to what politicians think the "church vote" might be.

It should be emphasized that the separation of church and state in America is a positive principle; it involves no hostility toward religion. But our Founding Fathers feared great and irresponsible institutions of power and the selfish ambition of men who gain control of them. Nearly every writer on America quotes Lord Bryce's famous remark about our Constitution: "It is the work of men who believed in original sin, and were resolved to leave open for transgressors no door which they could possibly shut." [2] To guard against tyranny, they provided for separation of the powers of government—legislative, executive, and judicial. And for the same reason they separated the power of the church from that of the state. They wanted both church and state to be free.

RECENT ISSUES

It is one thing to enunciate a principle, it is another to work it out. Various issues involving the relation of church and state have arisen in recent years because of misconceptions of the principle of separation, or difficulties in applying it, or reservations with respect to it.

The place of religion in public education.[3] In the current decade the sorest point in the whole area of church-state relations is the question of religious teaching for children in the public schools.

Religion was the mother of education in America. During the colonial period, the primary schools were conducted in close alliance with the churches. Until the turn of the present century, secondary education, especially in more recently set-

---

[2] James Bryce, *The American Commonwealth*, 2nd rev. ed. (New York: Macmillan and Co., 1891), Vol. I, p. 299.

[3] In the United States, "public schools" are those supported by tax funds.

tled parts of the country, was largely provided in academies taught by ministers or operated under religious auspices. A majority of our colleges and universities, including some of our most honored institutions—Harvard, Yale, Columbia, Chicago, Kentucky, Vanderbilt—were established by churchmen. The ministry of teaching has been one of the major contributions of Christianity to American culture; it resulted in a tradition of spiritual concern and of public service which characterized an educated man in the nineteenth century. The tradition has by no means vanished.

Yet, for a hundred years and more, education has been growing more secular and at the same time more comprehensive. In the first half of the nineteenth century the states took over the elementary schools: early in the twentieth century public high schools became available to nearly all our young people; now state-supported colleges and universities serve the large majority of students seeking a higher education. In no instance has the state ejected the church from the field of teaching; it has merely offered an education to all young people at no charge (or, in the universities, at a nominal fee); working with limited resources and compelled to charge tuition, the church schools have been largely eliminated by the competition. Today the state universities enroll tens of thousands while the church colleges enroll hundreds.

At the same time that the state has become the chief patron of our schools educational theory has announced its concern for "all of life." Its goal is "education for living." Young pupils are pleasurably introduced to all the activities of the common life—buying and selling, music and the arts, cooking and mechanics, sports and politics, banking and philanthropy, to every concern of the community—except religion. For just as this philosophy of education was assuming dominance the growing complexity of our urban populations and an increasingly secular interpretation of the principle of separation have led to the virtual elimination from the classroom of such exercises as Bible reading or the recitation of the Lord's Prayer, which were once common in the more homogeneous Protestant communities. Both educators and churchmen now recognize the unintended effect of these concomitant developments: the inference by the pupils that religion is an incidental concern, irrelevant to the life of the community.

The churches, committed for the most part to the principle of separation from the state, have sought various ways of solving the problem. For a time noncompulsory classes in religion were given during school hours and in school buildings by teachers in the employ of the churches, but in the McCollum case (1948) the Supreme Court of the United States declared this plan, as conducted at Champaign, Illinois, to be unconstitutional. In many communities the churches now offer a similar program on "dismissed time," the pupils going for an hour a week from the school building to a nearby church for religious instruction. While thousands of children are enrolled under this scheme, the sheer process of the physical transfer emphasizes the segregation of religion from the rest of the curriculum.

Believing that religion must not be a mere subject that is taught but a determining factor in the entire educational program, some churches have refused to relinquish the field of elementary education and have undertaken to conduct their own system of parochial schools parallel to the public schools. At great expense, Roman Catholicism in America has embarked on a thoroughgoing program of this sort so that every child of the church may receive his education in schools of the church. Many Lutheran congregations maintain parochial schools, and in recent years a number of fundamentalists also have entered the field. Most American Protestants hesitate to commit themselves to such a program. We believe that religion should be a unifying, not a fractionalizing, element in society. We have long supported the public schools as the common training ground for enlightened citizenship in a democracy which derives, in large measure, from Christian principles and which we hope will continue to operate in accordance with them.

Yet our present situation has resulted in a degree of ignorance about the religious roots of our culture which was surely not intended by the authors of the First Amendment and which is not required by it. Our fundamental law restrains the state from the establishment of religion but there is no intent to establish irreligion. Recently, respected Protestant leaders such as George A. Buttrick and Henry P. Van Dusen have written books to urge upon educators their responsibility for teaching children about God.

It is difficult to see how the public schools can undertake to inculcate religious devotion without violating the principles of disestablishment and (in our heterogeneous communities) of religious freedom. But there is no sound reason why they cannot deal with religion as a formative element in our culture and a major concern in our common life. History, art, music, literature, and the social studies may all be taught much more honestly and vitally if religious implications are made clear. Society has the right to expect the *schools* to inform the on-coming generation as to their whole cultural heritage, including the formative ideas of the Hebrew-Christian faith; under the American system it is the duty of the *churches* to bring the young to salvation and to religious commitment. This view has been advocated by F. Ernest Johnson and C. C. Morrison and has received the endorsement of a commission appointed by the American Council on Education. The suggested procedure lends itself most readily to studies on the high school and college levels. Indeed, a number of state universities have actually instituted departments of *religion*, supported by tax funds, as part of their regular program; obviously the approach is academic and "scientific" rather than evangelical. But in the general program of public education, especially in the primary schools, the place which may rightfully be given to religion remains an unsolved problem.

The use of public funds for parochial schools. Parents who send their children to private schools, which charge tuition, or to parochial schools, for which sizeable assessments are made through the church, complain that they are burdened by a "double tax," since they are subject also to local levies for public education. The answer of the state is that every property owner pays public school taxes, and every child is entitled to attend: if some persons want to maintain other schools for particular reasons, they are at liberty to do so but must bear the cost themselves. Our laws have remained unequivocal at this point.

Nevertheless, as the expanding program of parochial education becomes an increasing financial burden, Roman Catholic opinion in America increasingly decries our system as unjust and looks with longing toward the public treasury. In some localities, where the board of education was dominated by a Roman Catholic majority, parochial schools have actually been operated with public funds, or nuns wearing the distinctive garb of Dominican sisters and subject to the discipline of their order have been employed as teachers in the public schools. Parochial schools throughout the nation have benefited in the case of free hot lunches paid for from federal funds (a contribution to the child and not to the school), and in many states their pupils have won the right to free textbooks and school bus transportation financed by state or local taxes. Frequent court cases over such issues reveal that we are still attempting to define just where "the wall of separation" runs.

The appointment of an ambassador to the Vatican. In 1939 President Franklin D. Roosevelt appointed Myron C. Taylor as his "personal representative to His Holiness the Pope, with the rank of ambassador." There was a general outcry on the part of Protestants, but opposition was mitigated by the plea that Mr. Taylor's appointment was only temporary and that he was conferring with the Pope in the interests of world peace. Furthermore, his appointment as the President's "personal representative" was an executive action not subject to Congressional review.

In the autumn of 1951 President Truman announced that he would send to the next session of Congress for approval by the Senate the name of General Mark Clark in nomination as ambassador to the Vatican. This time it was not a question of a personal representative but of full-fledged open and official diplomatic relations between Washington and the Holy See. In the weeks that followed, an avalanche of protesting mail descended on Washington and senators found themselves facing the uncomfortable prospect of either offending a large bloc of Protestant and liberal opinion against the embassy or of seeming to cast a vote against the Roman Church. The dilemma was so painful that most of the newspapers across the country refused to discuss it in the realm of principle, but opposed the move on grounds of expediency: it was unwise at the time, the editors said, because of the sharp division of public opinion on the question. Many members of the Senate must have been greatly relieved when Senator Tom Connally of Texas, then chairman of the Foreign Relations Committee, announced that he had no confidence in General Clark. Because of a military operation under the general's command, during which many Texans had lost their lives in World War II, the senator was prepared to oppose him. General Clark subsequently requested that his name be withdrawn from consideration, and President Truman made no further nomination for the post. There has been no subsequent official talk of an ambassador to the Vatican.

During the whole episode consistent and increasing opposition came from American Protestants and Jews on grounds of principle. While some conceded that such an appointment, technically considered, might not violate the specific wording of the First Amendment (Congress would be making no law respecting an establishment of religion), opponents of the move saw it as opening a breach in the wall of separation. The proposed embassy, they said, involved relations with the Vatican either as a church or as a state. If it was considered a relationship with the Vatican as headquarters of the Roman Catholic Church, it meant an obvious interlocking of the institutional functions of church and state in clear denial of the principle of separation. It would give the Roman Church an official tie with, and access to, the American government which no other religious group in the United States would accept for itself or tolerate for others. If, on the other hand, the relationship was interpreted as establishing diplomatic ties with a foreign state, it seemed ludicrous and inappropriate. The Vatican is not a secular power of the magnitude to demand diplomatic relations through an ambassador. Further, the logic of this position would seem to cast all the representatives of the Vatican in America in a questionable role. When the argument was advanced that the embassy would strengthen co-operation between our government and the Vatican in the cold war against communism, it seemed to place the Roman Church throughout the rest of the world in the position of a political institution and its priests in that of intelligence agents.

Thoughtful Protestant leaders regretted the "anti-Catholic" position in which their opposition to the embassy appeared to put them. They desired no revival of the religious bigotry which has marred American life at certain unhappy periods in our history. But they were firm in their insistence on the principle of separation of church and state and regard the outcome of the incident as a victory in the continuing battle to maintain that principle.

Tax exemption for religious and charitable bodies. The statutes of the various states (not the federal Constitution) exempt from taxation property held by schools, colleges, and hospitals not conducted for private profit, by charitable institutions, and by churches. (In some states the exemption is now limited to property used in fulfilling the actual charitable or religious purpose; taxes must be paid on income-producing properties held as endowments.) The federal government also allows deductions up to 30 per cent of personal income, for gifts to charities and churches, before computing the income tax. All these concessions acknowledge the service which religious, charitable, and educational institutions render to society and lighten somewhat the burden of maintaining them. But at this juncture the line of separation is not clear. Does tax exemption constitute establishment? Or would the taxation of churches infringe on religious freedom, especially since our Supreme Court has declared, "The power to tax is the power to destroy"? The question is not much debated, although raised now and then by the *Christian Century*. That influential religious journal holds that Protestants should voluntarily renounce tax exemption in order to clarify their witness to the principle of separation.

Loyalty oaths for tax-exempt bodies. The issue of tax

exemption was sharpened for the churches in 1954 when the legislature of California, as an anti-Communist measure, enacted a law requiring the officials of all bodies exempted from taxes to sign annually an oath of loyalty to the government. Some church groups signed but issued statements resenting the inference of disloyalty. The American Friends Service Committee announced that it would not sign the oath and the First Methodist Church of San Leandro challenged its constitutionality before the state Supreme Court. If a church must swear its loyalty to a government, can religious freedom remain, especially the freedom to maintain a loyalty transcending all earthly loyalties?

The military chaplaincy. Chaplains in the armed forces of the United States are commissioned as military or naval officers. They must have ecclesiastical endorsement to secure and to hold their commissions, but they are ultimately responsible to the Department of Defense, which pays their salaries. Before World War II numerous questions about this situation were raised by Christian leaders who were reluctant to identify the church with the war system. The reluctance was heightened by the pacifist views widely prevalent at that time, but appeal was frequently made to the principle of separation of church and state.

With the coming of World War II and the induction of millions of young men into the armed forces, the arguments ended. The people want an adequate religious ministry for our troops, and there seems no other feasible way of providing it. The Defense Department has carefully drawn its regulations to protect the integrity of the chaplain's religious ministry against any inappropriate demands of his commanding officer.

Yet the precarious position of the church in this situation is illustrated by an event which occurred during the closing months of World War II. The advance of General George S. Patton's famed divisions had been delayed for days because of heavy rains which mired down his tanks. At length he ordered his chaplain to compose a prayer for dry weather which could be published to all of his troops. The chaplain hesitated to invoke the aid of God in the slaughter of the enemy, observing that such a task seemed hardly fitting for a minister of religion. Patton responded with a spontaneous question which summarizes the whole issue: "Are you teaching me theology or are you the Chaplain of the Third Army?"

The theological difficulty was hardly clarified by the upshot of the story. A prayer was published and the rains ceased.[4]

The investigation of church leaders by legislative committees. The important legislative function of investigation by committee in private and public hearings is sometimes exploited by politicians as a means of gaining personal publicity. In the months before the McCarthy censure it was particularly abused by those seeking to build up reputations as opponents of communism. Very few actual investigations of clergymen took place, but allegations against Protestant ministers in general and some of our most respected leaders in particular emanated from the offices of Congressional committees. The impression was created either that these men had been investigated and found disloyal or that they would be investigated soon. A blanket charge against the Protestant clergy brought about the dismissal of J. B. Matthews as an employee of Senator McCarthy's committee. Early in 1953, when a congressman from Illinois suggested that his own committee might investigate alleged subversion on the part of churchmen, Methodist Bishop G. Bromley Oxnam, then a president of the World Council of Churches, assailed the idea. A few days later the bishop's patriotism was impugned in a speech delivered to the House of Representatives. Bishop Oxnam replied by demanding a public hearing before the House Committee on Un-American Activities; at the time and subsequently he courageously denounced abuses of the investigative procedure.

Now that the furor seems to have subsided, at least for a time, a constitutional question may well be raised concerning the propriety of a Congressional investigation of the churches. In our governmental theory investigation is a preliminary

[4] George S. Patton, Jr., *War As I Knew It*, annotated by Col. Paul D. Harkins (Boston: Houghton Mifflin Company, 1947), pp. 184–186.

phase of the legislative process. But what sort of legislation is contemplated respecting religion? Can any statute, applying specifically to religious bodies, be conceived which is not a violation of the First Amendment?

If new legislation is not the intent, the motives for an investigation of churchmen may well be examined. Is the threat of investigation designed to discredit or intimidate religious leaders who have been outspoken on social issues? The question gains credibility from the obvious prominence of a few fundamentalists in consulting with Congressman Velde during the Oxnam hearing. Any churchman who would resort to intrigue in the processes of government in order to discredit his religious rivals is playing with fire.

Other issues. Our survey can only hint at a number of additional problems. For more than a decade the Supreme Court has heard various cases involving Jehovah's Witnesses, and most of the decisions have firmly upheld the principle of civil and religious liberty, even in the case of a minority whom many consider a nuisance. Our legislation imposing military conscription provides alternative service for conscientious objectors, attempting to safeguard freedom of conscience, though it has not removed all the problems; some citizens are uneasy about the status of ministers, who have been exempted from the draft. Our legislatures and courts have had to deal on occasion with practices, ordinarily considered immoral or dangerous, carried on in the name of religion—polygamy, snake handling, drinking of poison, flagellation. The restraints imposed in the name of the general welfare have been handled in such a way as to apply only to overt acts, not to deny freedom of belief. Questions are now being raised in opposition to the practice of turning over to religious bodies the title to hospitals built with public funds.

Our experience in the United States reveals that the principle of separation is not always easy to interpret. The seriousness with which the American people have taken many of these issues in recent months also indicates the vitality of the concept of religious freedom and the determination of our people to maintain both a free church and a free state.

RELIGION IN THE LIFE OF THE NATION

The great social function of religion, beyond the transformation of individuals, has been the integration of the common life about a spiritual center. One of the strong arguments advanced for an establishment is the service of the chosen faith in binding the community together. We in the United States have repudiated the idea of any unifying ecclesiastical structure. Yet the religion of our people has to a large degree rendered such a service, without interlocking the functions of church and state. This religion is, in a broad sense, the historical faith of a free Protestantism, allowing for individual differences and recognizing the spiritual contribution of Roman Catholicism and Judaism. (A recent observer of the American scene has commented that even our Roman Catholics and Jews are more Protestant than they realize.)

To the extent that a general Christian world view serves as a unifying and even sanctifying faith in the life of the nation, a potential danger must be recognized. American Christianity may allow the lines of its distinctive character to be blurred and may unconsciously begin to act like an established religion, even becoming subservient to nationalism. It would not be difficult to name instances when these possibilities have actually occurred. Yet the religion of the American people has informed the life of the nation with principles of right and with an idealism that has often redeemed our policies from cynicism and ruthlessness.

How has a nonestablished religion diffused itself so extensively through our society? We must consider first of all the religious roots of our life as a nation.

In the era of settlement—an age of romance and of heroism now celebrated in our schoolbooks, children's tales, and the contemporary folk media of radio and television—the faith of the pioneers was a determining factor in their actions. Even though the gentlemen who first came to Virginia were engaged primarily in a commercial venture, they were loyal members of the Church of England. Impressive among the few monuments at Jamestown, the site of their first settlement

in 1607, are the restored tower of the old brick church and
the bronze memorial to the Rev. Robert Hunt, their first
minister. The latter depicts in bas-relief the first communion
in the colony: the men kneel before an altar set up under the
shelter of a sail to receive the sacred bread and wine. In the
popular imagination the Pilgrims who came to Plymouth in
1620 take on something of the spiritual stature of Old Testament prophets; because of their connection with our national
feast of Thanksgiving, they are often mistakenly regarded as
the real founders of our nation, and the Virginia colony drops
out of mind. Lord Baltimore, Roger Williams, William Penn,
and other less celebrated proprietors desired, among other
things, to establish in the New World havens for religious
refugees; the courage of faithful minorities who made the
perilous passage across the dark sea and ventured into the unknown wilderness in order to keep the faith is a precious element of our common heritage. So a nimbus of sanctity glows
in the popular impression of our national origin.

Contrary to the notion created by our "western" movies,
the frontier was not the exclusive preserve of Indians, cowboys, and badmen. It was settled for the most part by families,
and among the meager possessions that many of them took
west by raft or covered wagon was a copy of the Holy
Scriptures.

The famous statue of the Pioneer Mother at Ponca City,
Oklahoma, is a heroic bronze of a sturdy woman in full stride,
marching into the future, one hand clasping that of her young
son and the other holding a Bible. The church went with the
pioneers, one of the familiar figures of the frontier being the
Methodist circuit rider. All these symbols of the early faith
are cherished among us, even if the response of our people to
them is primarily emotional and not always well informed
concerning the ideological content of the faith thus represented.

In the establishment of a free nation, the religion of the
colonists also played an influential role. They appealed to
Christian sanctions for the free institutions they sought to
establish. The rights which they demanded were rights "to

which the laws of nature and of nature's God" entitled them. (The members of the Continental Congress insisted on adding the religious assertion to Thomas Jefferson's original draft of the Declaration of Independence.) The metaphysical base for the philosophy of the American Revolution was not provided by the Deists alone, but also by the Puritans. Out of the Covenant theology came the colonist's concept of the contract theory of government, expounded to them periodically from the pulpits in election sermons.

Furthermore, popular piety soon began to recount legends of crucial hours in our early history when our leaders were upheld by prayer. George Washington is said to have knelt in the snow at Valley Forge, and is so depicted in a well-known bas-relief. Our preachers tell of a desperate hour in the proceedings of the Constitutional Convention when discussions had reached an impasse. Then the venerable Benjamin Franklin arose and suggested that an appeal for wisdom be made to the Almighty. Thus the effort to establish a federal government was saved. The incident is not recorded in John Adams' Journal, the chief source for the history of the convention, but the event may have happened. Whether it did or not, the mythology which represents the national heroes as sustained by communion with God points to a widely held concept of our common life as rooted in religion.

Without an established church, Americans have long given a religious interpretation to their history. The Congregationalists who settled New England believed firmly in Providence, and it was not difficult for them to trace the movement of the divine hand in their own experience. Their situation was like that of the Israelites entering the Promised Land, including the necessity of dispossessing the heathen. The events of their life day by day brought many passages of the Bible stirringly to life, and the prosperity gained by hard labor in the New World seemed to them the blessing of God. The same experience came to their children and grandchildren as they pushed farther and farther into the abundant land of the West.

But there was more to this religious interpretation of American history than belief in God's providential care for his own; there was a sense of national mission which in the nineteenth century was expressed by the phrase "Manifest Destiny." Different concepts of the national destiny were manifest to different users of the phrase; but if it most commonly appeared in political addresses it had for many primarily a religious reference: the United States was called of God to create a land of freedom as a demonstration to the rest of mankind and as a haven for the oppressed from other parts of the world. The inscription at the base of the Statue of Liberty reflects this sentiment:

> "Keep, ancient lands, your storied pomp!" cries she
> With silent lips. "Give me your tired, your poor,
> Your huddled masses yearning to breathe free,
> The wretched refuse of your teeming shore,
> Send them, the homeless, the tempest-tossed to me,
> I lift my lamp beside the golden door."

Explicitly the poem reflects mere humanitarianism; but implicit in it are religious overtones, to which its Jewish authoress was surely sensitive and which characterized the concept of Manifest Destiny.

Such a doctrine of national election is easily perverted. It was used to justify the plunder of the War with Mexico and in the effort to stir up enthusiasm for an American empire at the end of the nineteenth century. Restricted to Anglo-Saxon Protestantism, it found demonic expression in the terrorism of the Ku Klux Klan. Even sincere and upright American Christians are in constant danger of assuming an attitude of moral superiority over the rest of mankind because of our secular abundance. Such are the perils of any "chosen people." However divine the mission to which they are called, they may forget that the mission is the reason for their election. Even the ancient Hebrews kept thinking of themselves as God's favorites.

Yet, taken at its best and in the light of a true realization of the nature of God, a religious interpretation of history is the only adequate basis for a nation's understanding of itself. Two of our most mature Christian social thinkers, Reinhold Niebuhr and Paul Tillich, have explored the validity inherent in the concept of Manifest Destiny.[5] If one really wishes to comprehend the American mind, he must take into account this tradition of viewing our history in moral and spiritual terms. It sometimes strikes others as presumptuous, irrelevant, or hypocritical to hear an American president or secretary of state discussing an international issue as a problem of morality. Europeans must remember that, even if his ethical view seems distorted, it is natural for an American statesman to speak thus, and the chances are that he does so in all sincerity. Religion was not established among us institutionally, but it was planted in the popular mind.

So there have emerged through the years various religious expressions of our national life. These are not the prerogative of any church, nor are they nationalism concealing itself under the cloak of piety. They are the reverent acknowledgment of a people that their help comes from the Lord who made heaven and earth.

Our day of national Thanksgiving is a striking example of common religious expression. Going back to a feast kept by the Pilgrim Fathers in 1621 after an abundant harvest, it was observed throughout the young nation during Washington's term as president. In 1789 he issued a proclamation recommending

that we may . . . all unite in rendering unto him our sincere and humble thanks for his kind care and protection of the people of this country previous to their becoming a nation; for the signal and manifold mercies, and the favorable interpositions of his providence, in the course and conclusion of the late war; for the great degree of tranquility, union, and plenty, which we have since enjoyed; for the peaceable and rational manner in which we have been enabled to establish constitutions of government for our safety and happiness, and particularly for the national one now lately instituted; for the civil and religious liberty with

[5] Reinhold Niebuhr, *The Irony of American History* (New York: Scribner, 1952), pp. 4, 24–29, 65–88; Paul Tillich, *Love, Power, and Justice* (New York: Oxford University Press, 1954), pp. 103–104.

which we are blessed, and the means we have of acquiring and diffusing useful knowledge; and, in general, for all the great and various favors, which he has been pleased to confer upon us.

From time to time succeeding presidents published a call to national penitence, or thanksgiving, but the observance did not take a regular place in the calendar until 1863, when Abraham Lincoln renewed the custom. Thanksgiving has been observed annually since that time, long being appointed by presidential proclamation and now fixed by statute on the fourth Thursday of November. It is a national holiday, when people repair to the churches to express gratitude for the fruits of the earth and when families or friends come together to feast on the traditional fare of roast turkey, cranberry sauce, and pumpkin pie. The unthinking doubtless fall into self-congratulation on this occasion, but it has abiding value in calling upon the people to "praise God from whom all blessings flow."

The proclamation issued by President Truman in 1947 is a fair sample of the mood to which the nation is called:

Older than our nation itself is the hallowed custom of resting from our labors for one day at harvest time and of dedicating that day to expressions of gratitude to Almighty God for the many blessings which He has heaped upon us. Now, as the cycle of the year nears completion, it is fitting that we should lift up our hearts again in special prayers.

May our thanksgiving this year be tempered by humility, by sympathy for those who lack abundance, and by compassion for those in want. As we express appreciation in prayer for our munificent gifts, may we remember that it is more blessed to give than to receive; and may we manifest our remembrance of that precept by generously sharing our bounty with needy people of other nations.

Now, therefore . . . I proclaim Thursday, November 27, 1947, as a day of national thanksgiving; and I call upon the people of the United States of every faith to consecrate that day to thoughts of gratitude, acts of devotion, and a firm resolve to assist in the efforts being made by religious groups and other bodies to aid the undernourished, the sick, the aged, and all sufferers in war-devastated lands.

Prayer is normally offered on public occasions—civic events, political conventions, and days of memorial. The sessions of Congress and of our state legislatures are opened by daily prayer; if it sometimes becomes a perfunctory act, the service of the late Peter Marshall as chaplain of the Senate revealed that it might be a meaningful, even an exciting experience. At presidential inaugurations clergymen of the major faiths are invited for invocations and petitions, and in 1953 Dwight D. Eisenhower prefaced his inaugural address with a simple prayer of his own, beseeching in part:

We pray that our concern shall be for all the people, regardless of station, race, or calling. May co-operation be permitted and be the mutual aim of those who, under the concept of our Constitution, hold to differing political beliefs—so that all may work for the good of our beloved country and for Thy glory.

Two of our great national hymns conclude with prayer. The closing stanza of "America" intercedes for the nation:

> Our fathers' God, to Thee,
> Author of liberty,
> To Thee we sing:
> Long may our land be bright
> With Freedom's holy light;
> Protect us by Thy might,
> Great God, our King.

Another hymn, "America the Beautiful," is appropriately sung in the churches on patriotic occasions. The conclusion of each stanza is a prayer:

> America! America! God shed His grace on thee,
> And crown thy good with brotherhood
> From sea to shining sea.

> America! America! May God thy gold refine,
> Till all success be nobleness
> And every gain divine.

> America! America! God mend thine every flaw,
> Confirm thy soul in self-control,
> Thy liberty in law.

On occasion the American religious tradition rises to noble utterance in the state papers of our presidents. The news services of the world gave considerable attention to the appearance of Mr. Eisenhower before the Second Assembly of the World Council of Churches at Evanston, Illinois, in 1954, featuring especially his appeal for prayers for peace. Perhaps even more significant was his simple identification of himself as a member of one of the churches in the World Council and his subsequent plea to the assembly:

We hope that you will touch our imagination, remind us again and again of the vision without which the people perish. Give us criticism in the light of religious ideals. Kindle anew in us a desire to strive for moral greatness and . . . show us where we fall short. We shall listen if you speak to us as the prophets spoke in the days of old.

For the head of a great and powerful nation to address the representatives of the Christian faith in such terms indicates that even though the churches are not established they are expected to bear their witness to the common life.

The supreme interpretation of our history in religious terms came from the tragic days of the Civil War. In March, 1865, when the Union and the Confederacy had already been locked in battle for four years, Abraham Lincoln delivered his second inaugural address. Most of the oration was devoted to a Christian philosophy of history. It was the effort not of a theologian or a priest, but of a prairie lawyer, now the nation's elected leader, to discern the hand of God in the tragic events of the time. He spoke of the two sides in the bitter conflict:

Both read the same Bible, and pray to the same God; and each invokes his aid against the other. It may seem strange that any men should dare to ask a just God's assistance in wringing their bread from the sweat of other men's faces; but let us judge not, that we be not judged. The prayers of both could not be answered—that of neither has been answered fully.

The Almighty has his own purposes. "Woe unto the world because of offenses! for it must needs be that offenses come; but woe to that man by whom the offense cometh." If we shall suppose that American slavery is one of those offenses which, in the providence of God, must needs come, but which, having continued through his appointed time, he now wills to remove, and that he gives to both North and South this terrible war, as the woe due to those by whom the offense came, shall we discern therein any departure from those divine attributes which the believers in a living God always ascribe to him? Fondly do we hope —fervently do we pray—that this mighty scourge of war may speedily pass away. Yet, if God wills that it continue until all the wealth piled by the bondsman's two hundred and fifty years of unrequited toil shall be sunk, and until every drop of blood drawn with the lash shall be paid by another drawn with the sword, as was said three thousand years ago, so still it must be said, "The judgments of the Lord are true and righteous altogether."

With malice toward none; with charity for all; with firmness in the right, as God gives us to see the right, let us strive on to finish the work we are in; to bind up the nation's wounds; to care for him who shall have borne the battle and for his widow and orphan—to do all which may achieve and cherish a just and lasting peace among ourselves and with all the nations.

RELIGION, STANDING BY HER OWN STRENGTH

The purpose of the foregoing section has not been to argue that the American people are especially virtuous; we are not and, to the extent that our faith is honest, we know that we are not. But the evidence indicates that religion, left absolutely free and without benefit of establishment, may profoundly influence the common life of a nation. One need not naïvely assume that a patriot who goes to worship on Thanksgiving Day and thrills to the story of the Pilgrim Fathers or a president who offers a public prayer has thus fulfilled all righteousness. But cynicism may also be naïve: it is a mistake to dismiss the evidences of popular piety in America with a hasty judgment and not to discern the elements of genuine faith.

Unlike some other nations which have written disestablishment into their constitutions, we seldom speak of ours as a secular state. The separation of state and church, as we conceive it, is in no sense a matter of hostility between the government and religion, but is instead a means of assuring freedom for each. Though our system is not without its problems, it has worked well for the American churches and for the spiritual life of the nation. It is appropriate to quote Lord Bryce once again: "So far from suffering from the want of State support, religion seems in the United States to stand all the firmer because, standing alone, she is seen to stand by her own strength."[6]

There would seem to be considerable significance for the doctrine of the church in this fact. We have not failed to notice that for the first three centuries of its life the Christian church was wholly separate from the state, living and growing as a voluntary association within, but by no means identical with, the whole society. It appears to us—on grounds of New Testament teaching, of apostolic practice, of the history of the early church, and of experience in our own situation—that the separation of church and state is better justified, ecclesiologically, than is the practice of establishment.

When Congregationalism was disestablished in Connecticut a generation after the United States became a nation, Lyman Beecher supposed than an irreparable injury had been done to the cause of Christ. But he lived to change his opinion, concluding that it was "the best thing that ever happened in the State of Connecticut." So today Protestant Christians in America, almost without exception, would commend the separation of church and state as a practice which has made for health in our churches and for spiritual vitality in our common life.

[6] *Op. cit.* (New York: Macmillan, 1891), Vol. II, p. 584.

III.

Profile of a Free Church

In the course of European Christianity, religious liberty came late. For dissenters it brought release from coercion and the opportunity to win a place in society, yet the "free churches" have remained relatively small, overshadowed by the traditional position, the resources, and the prestige of the state churches. Where disestablishment has occurred, it was part of a program of anticlericalism, and the forces of religion have continued in retreat; ecclesiastical patterns formed through centuries of alliance with government have been adapted with great difficulty to newer circumstances. While European churchmen of the established traditions chafe at some embarrassments in their relationships with the state, what they have seen of disestablishment inclines them to regard it as a calamity. Even some free churchmen have begun to ponder the possibilities of their own churches being brought also within the framework of establishment.

American Christianity, by contrast, has grown up in an atmosphere of religious liberty. All the churches have been free churches. No communion has enjoyed prestige as *the* church of the nation. All have had to make headway in the same stream. Nearly two centuries of this sort of environment have left characteristic marks on our churches. One of our historians has observed that the various Protestant bodies of the New World are "closer to each other than to their European counterparts." [1] This chapter will sketch the predominant features of the church in America which have resulted from its separation from the state.

PERSONAL RESPONSIBILITY FOR THE SUPPORT OF THE CHURCH

Life in the United States has left the church standing entirely on its own. In the new nation and on the advancing frontier there were no church buildings coming from public funds or from royal gifts, save for a few in those colonies which had known establishment. Our fathers inherited no cathedrals from the long past. If there was to be a house of worship in a new community, it must be built at the time out of the current resources of the Christians there, who were a minority of the population. (In almost every instance, the Christian minority was divided among several denominations, so that the burden of church-building was made even heavier.) The struggling new churches received no current income from public funds or endowments. There were no "livings" to guarantee a young clergyman a comfortable or even a modest income. Some congregations that came to birth in the West received aid from missionary societies either in the Old World or in the American East, but significant as such help was, it was small in the total picture.

Wherever there is a church in the United States, outside the small area of the colonial establishment, it is there because someone gathered a group of Christians together and because they cared enough for their faith to put up a building and to support a minister. This process was not something that happened in the early Middle Ages; it has been going on in fairly recent times. A good many of our churches in the Midwest, priding themselves on their history, have been celebrating their centennial anniversary in the years just past, but far more have a much briefer record. It is not hard to find a congregation of a thousand members which has been in existence for less than thirty years. Because of our expanding population, new churches are being established all the time; while there

[1] Jerald C. Brauer, *Protestantism in America* (Philadelphia: Westminster, 1953), p. 8.

is often some help from general denominational funds in launching a new venture today, the burden of responsibility falls on the members of the congregation.

The other side of this picture is that a church declines and goes out of existence when it fails to get current support. If a neighborhood deteriorates (the process is sometimes quite rapid, especially when a residential area is re-zoned for business or industry) or if the lines of a rural community change (the introduction of the automobile was one cause, the consolidation of public schools another), a congregation faces a difficult struggle. The problem may arise on the side of the church itself: an evangelist, carried away by an unrealistic optimism, establishes a "new congregation" where potential resources are insufficient to maintain its life. In some instances sheer spiritual debility may contribute to the death of a congregation. At any rate, it is not unusual to see an old boarded-up church, or a former house of worship converted to business or agricultural use.

This utter dependence of the church upon the current support of its members for its very life has produced a strong sense of personal responsibility at the heart of American churchmanship. Because we so often quote the text "We are workers together with God" we have been accused of *synergism*, the heresy of believing that God needs our help. We actually believe that he does—not that we can save ourselves, but that God requires the service of faithful men to do his work on earth. A popular story, told many times by our preachers, illustrates the point. A minister was admiring a farmer's garden and, thinking to make an edifying remark, observed: "That's a fine garden you have there. It's wonderful what God and man can do together." Whereupon the farmer replied: "You should have seen it when God had it by himself."

Perhaps there are spiritual dangers in such an attitude, but there is also a basic truth: God works through persons. A strong emphasis in Christian theology lays stress on the saving operation of the Holy Spirit through the preaching of the Word and the administration of the sacraments, but in this ministry the Spirit works through men. Every missionary knows this; it is not a peculiarly American notion. It was explicit in the work of William Carey, David Livingstone, Albert Schweitzer. But the fact that the American churches have no hidden resources in the form of allotments from public funds or ancient endowments has required them to emphasize the necessity of material support by their members. They live by the generous and conscientious giving of believers in whom there has been awakened a sense of personal responsibility to the Lord of all the earth. A slogan we hear often runs as follows: "You need the church, and the church needs you."

It should be clear why the element of "challenge" is so strong in American religion. When a layman in one of our churches becomes especially concerned about his faith, he does not usually exhaust his concern in formal prayer nor in the study of theology; he wants to *do* something for God. His deeds become acts of devotion. Quite typical was the insistence of an American layman in the sessions of the World Council of Churches at Evanston in 1954, during the discussion on the main theme, "Christ the Hope of the World." He was not an anti-intellectual; he was dean of a major college in a university known around the world. But he was frustrated by the fine balancing of doctrine in the Report on the Main Theme and by the theoretical aspect of the discussions. He wanted a stronger emphasis for laymen, a clear, urgent statement of "what we can do about it."

A characteristic expression of the American sense of personal responsibility for the support of the church is the practice of Christian stewardship. The word derives from the various parables of our Lord which teach that we are not owners of what we possess, but stewards or trustees under God; and the doctrine is found throughout the Bible. In discussions of stewardship the emphasis usually falls on the obligation to give a portion of our income—the tithe is often mentioned—to the work of the church. But our doctrinal formulations and much of our preaching have also explored what the stewardship of life and possessions means in other respects such as the dedication of time and talent to the service of God and man, the ministry of daily work as a "calling," the recognition of responsibility to God in decisions involving the welfare of other persons, the virtues of sobriety and restraint, the obligation toward future generations to ensure the conservation of the soil and other natural resources.

It may be admitted that the "bite of necessity" has been a major factor in keeping the doctrine of stewardship to the forefront of our thinking and practice, rather than any peculiar insight into the Bible or any special devotion on our part. But stewardship is preached, various groups (men, women, youth, church boards) study the doctrine, and earnest church members take the matter seriously. To refer to Evanston once more, an American delegate in the Section on the Laity urged the inclusion of a statement as to the need for stewardship. The Europeans present did not know the doctrine by this name, nor did they see the value of inserting such an idea in their document. The American could not understand their reluctance. In his thinking, as in the general religious life of the country, a major Christian obligation of the layman is considered to be his responsibility for the support of the church.

The churches must keep their members aware of this responsibility. Most congregations adopt an annual budget and expect their members to make a financial pledge in order that the budget may be underwritten. The practice is widespread of assigning to each family or individual in the church a box of offering envelopes, one for each Sunday in the year, and a new member is often presented such a box along with his certificate of church membership. New pledges are taken annually in an endeavor to secure commitments from every person on the church roll.

The seriousness with which American Christians take this responsibility may be judged by the average annual contribution per member; in 1955 it was $48.81 (approximately £ 17/8 or Sw. fr. 208.90). Considering the comparative wealth of the United States, this figure falls far short of the biblical standard of stewardship. The average is, of course, pulled down by many nominal members who give little, if anything at all, and by large numbers of children and of the aged whose resources are limited. Nevertheless, many families set aside at least 10 per cent of their income for religious and charitable giving, and do it out of conviction. Nearly every pastor can recount experiences of sacrificial giving by persons in his parish. During hard times in congregations of limited means it has not been unusual for a devoted deacon or elder to mortgage his house or farm to keep the church from being foreclosed for debt.

In prosperity also some give sacrificially. In the industrial city of South Bend, Indiana, one of the churches, in a program of building expansion, was engaged in a drive for $100,-000. At the formal launching of the campaign the minister urged the people to give generously and said that he had been praying for one gift of $10,000 to ensure the success of the effort. That afternoon the minister's phone rang. The man calling had been received into church membership, along with his family, less than a year before; they were people of comfortable income, but not of wealth. Now he was saying, "At dinner today we decided to answer the minister's prayer and be the ones to give $10,000. Instead of building a house for ourselves, we decided to help build a house for the Lord."

Personal responsibility for the support of the church has not always been expressed through the giving of money. In pioneer days when a new congregation had been formed and needed a meetinghouse, one farmer would contribute a plot of ground, another the logs, and all the members would turn out to help in the construction. Still today much of the work on new church buildings, as well as the labor of repairs on older structures, is done by the men of the congregation. Recently at Glenwood, Oregon, the men of one communion throughout a whole county joined together to erect "a church in one day." On such occasions the Christian women are usually present also to bring hot coffee and to serve the meals, even to lend a hand with hammer or paintbrush.

In seeking to enlist the support of their members the churches face certain dangers. As money-raising becomes a large-scale enterprise, it may seem in a few congregations to be an end rather than a means to an end, and the minister's work may become largely promotional: he must lead his people in underwriting the budget for current expense, the budget for missions and benevolence, the building fund, and various special campaigns within the denomination or community. The temptation also arises to resort to easier methods than asking people to give. Now, there is a point at which it has seemed legitimate for church groups to earn money by various projects—bazaars, chicken dinners, ice-cream socials, fish fries—and these produce desirable by-products in opportunities for wholesome fellowship. In a few congregations, however, such activities demand the major attention of the members. The inclination of some Roman Catholic parishes to raise funds by means of Bingo games, raffles, and other forms of lottery embarrasses the witness which most of the Protestant churches bear against gambling and causes tension between the two faiths. Some church members feel that they have discharged their duty toward God when they have written an occasional check for some Christian cause. A more searching criticism than any of these may reside in the question: Is the money raised by generous giving and by hard work spent in the best way? But to raise the question does not imply that the answer must always, or even in most cases, be negative.

The basic fact remains that every church and religious institution in the United States (the latter category includes hundreds of colleges, seminaries, hospitals, and charitable homes) exists because somebody cared enough for the work of Christ to start it and others have cared enough to maintain it, entirely by voluntary gifts. One evidence of the sense of responsibility engendered by freedom of religion is the large number of foundations set up by men of wealth to administer sizable funds given for religious and benevolent purposes. These large gifts are not explained by the desire to lower income taxes; it would be cheaper to pay the tax and make no gift. But separation of church and state has contributed, in the providence of God, to the development of a sense of stewardship in American churchmen.

Not only among rich men has this sense of responsibility been significant. A humble worker whom I knew is typical of many faithful stewards in the ranks of labor. He was married about the turn of the century and went to work for the railroad. Soon he found himself in a village in northern Indiana which had no church of his persuasion. He gathered together a few persons of like mind, invited an evangelist to the community, and helped to organize a congregation. For more than fifty years he served in that church as an elder, Sunday-school superintendent, and leader in other capacities, all the time bearing witness also in his daily work. He was a layman who founded a church, and that is not unusual in America. His pastor during the closing months of his life was a man who, years before, had worked with him on the railroad and whom he had turned to the ministry of the gospel.

The ecumenical significance of the American churches is more than a matter of their size and wealth: it derives also from the characteristics which have made them strong. Chief among these is the widespread sense of personal responsibility for the support of the church and the consequent commitment on the part of many Christians to faithful stewardship of their time, talents, and financial means. It would appear that too much of this devotion is directed toward maintaining the church as an institution rather than ministering to the world—a weakness which will be mentioned again in other connections. But ours is not the first or only situation in which the church has turned its concern inward upon itself instead of outward upon mankind. Still, a great mission demands a vigorous church. And our churches learned a long time ago that their strength is not in the esteem of the state, in prestige before the world, or in inherited wealth, but in the dedicated support of their members. Some of our colleges and benevolent institutions, sizable Christian enterprises, operate with virtually no endowment, but derive their income entirely from current giving; a sudden depression might prove disastrous, but they depend utterly on the faithfulness of Christian stewards.

Thus it turns out that in the wealthiest and, some would say, most materialistic nation on the face of the globe many Christians are giving significant portions of their income to sustain their local congregations, church colleges and theological seminaries, homes for the orphaned and the aged, and the world-wide task of mission and of mercy. When we look at ourselves we know that most of us are keeping too much for ourselves; our standard of living includes many luxuries, and a large proportion of our church members have never begun to take the task of stewardship seriously. Every pastor can tell with despair of well-to-do parishioners who rarely miss a service and never contribute more than a dollar. But stewardship is never easy, and our most generous contributors did not wait until they became wealthy to start giving. Many of them learned to tithe when they were poor.

The casual critic who dismisses the giving of American Christians as mere charity on the part of the affluent has not seen to the heart of the matter. Nor must the observer from abroad be misled by the common use of promotional procedures which seem to him secular in tone. Advertising is part of the American idiom, and our churches employ its techniques to let all their members—the indifferent as well as the dedicated—know of the needs which must be met. Our people realize that the support of the church is up to them. A slogan often used in parish papers and in addresses to laymen poses the question: "What kind of church would this church be, if every member were just like me?" The sense of individual responsibility is one of the spiritual fruits in America of the separation of church and state. And it has ecumenical significance.

THE NECESSITY OF EVANGELISM

In a land without an established church no one becomes or remains a member of a religious communion except by his own volition. At the beginning of our national history, less than 10 per cent of our population belonged to any church. The situation presented the Christian forces of the United States with a tremendous missionary responsibility. But more than that: evangelism confronts the churches in an environment of religious freedom as a "fact of life." "Evangelize or die" is not merely a spiritual truth; it is an institutional reality for every congregation and denomination in America. We have heard it said often, and know from our experience, that "the church is only one generation from extinction."

This pressure partially accounts for the concern of the American churches with evangelism and the large place which it holds in their total life. They have long been preoccupied with the work of conversion and have given attention to various methods by which it may be accomplished.

"Mass evangelism" began in the colonial era with the preaching of the great revivalists—Jonathan Edwards, George Whitefield, their associates and successors. It remained the classic method in the successive "awakenings" which swept the population when the nation was young. An important center of mass evangelism in pioneer days was the "camp meeting." People from miles around would drive in with a supply of food sufficient for several days and take up temporary residence in tents or wagons at the appointed place. Part of the appeal of the camp meeting was the mere fact that "lots of folks" were there—often hundreds, sometimes thousands—an important ministry in itself to the loneliness of the frontiersman. In this scene of camaraderie and relaxation from the toil of the year religion was the main attraction. Sometimes several preachers held forth simultaneously on various parts of the grounds; people sang much and prayed, usually with considerable emotion and at times with violent feeling. Out of it all came dramatic conversions, as well as renewal of the believers' faith. Some camp meetings retained their popularity well into the twentieth century. The late George W. Truett of First Baptist Church, Dallas, Texas, held his famous annual camp meetings for the cowboys of West Texas as late as the 1930's. The Assemblies of God and some of the Holiness churches maintain camp grounds for the purpose of evangelism even today. But the automobile, radio and television, and the general tenor of life in modern cities have produced a new mood in our people. They must be led to Christ in other ways.

As more settlers filled up the country, the protracted meeting became the means of appealing to the people of a particular community. Every night for a week—or a fortnight or six weeks or longer—the pastor or some visiting minister would preach in an effort to bring about conversions. The "revival" might be held in the church building. But often, to make it less embarrassing for the sinner to attend, it was held on "neutral ground," under a brush arbor in the rural areas or a tent on a vacant lot in town. Some itinerant evangelists drew such crowds in the cities toward the end of the nineteenth century that huge temporary frame buildings—"tabernacles"—were erected to hold them. Instead of flooring, the ground was covered with sawdust, and persons wishing to make a Christian profession "hit the sawdust trail" as they made their way down the long aisle to the front of the tent or tabernacle to clasp the evangelist's hand and affirm their faith in Christ as their Savior. Dwight L. Moody, "Billy" Sunday, Charles Reign Scoville, "Gypsy" Smith (an example of the British evangelist who achieved marked success on our shores), and others preached to tremendous throngs and won thousands of decisions. Cities were stirred, communities were changed.

Before the advent of large-scale commercialized entertainment, evangelistic meetings brought a big splash of color into the drabness of life. The preachers themselves were dynamic men; often they were accompanied by entertainers who had dedicated their talents to the Lord—singers, trombonists, magicians—and who helped bring out a crowd. Even with less famous evangelists a pair of Swiss bell ringers or a brother playing a gospel tune on a "musical saw" could be counted on to put the audience in a receptive mood before the preacher got down to the serious business of the evening.

The protracted meeting was an important means of Christian education in the two generations before World War I. The evangelist who every night for a month or six weeks faced a congregation comprising most of a community had an unparalleled opportunity for systematic doctrinal preaching. Sermons dealt with the great themes of Christian life and thought—the divine "plan of salvation," the love of God, the person of Christ, the nature of the church, the missionary journeys of Paul, the practice of prayer, love for Jesus, the Ten Commandments. The didactic portion of a sermon might take an hour or more, and the preachers made use of charts, blackboards, and other devices of "visual education." The audiences were often drawn into systematic Bible study as they looked up the proof-texts quoted by the evangelists. When a preacher came toward the close of his sermon and began to plead with sinners to accept the gospel, the appeal shifted from head to heart. But authors who overdraw the raw emotionalism of the revivals would do well to consider their significant contribution to Christian education.

During the two decades after World War I mass evangelism seemed to have lost its effectiveness. Even some of the "old masters" among the revivalists failed to draw the crowds and to win the numbers of converts they had secured in earlier days. People no longer needed to go to church for entertainment, many thoughtful Christian people were ashamed of the circus atmosphere and blatant emotionalism which had become the hallmark of some professional revivalism, and the general mood of the country lacked interest in religion. Many observers concluded that mass evangelism was dead.

In 1936 the Federal Council of Churches launched a series of National Preaching Missions in an effort to make an evangelistic impact on our cities. Teams of distinguished preachers visited schools, civic clubs, factories, and women's groups and spoke to mass meetings each evening for a week. The missions attracted large crowds and, although most of the persons who attended were already church members, new decisions were won. University Christian Missions and Missions to the Armed Forces made a similar ecumenical approach to the evangelism of young people on the campuses and in the military camps.

During the years of World War II the older type of mass evangelism began to exert an appeal once again. "Youth for

Christ" organizations sprang up in cities all over the country, sponsoring meetings for young people every Saturday night. Out of Youth for Christ came such celebrated evangelists as Charles Templeton and Billy Graham, who have demonstrated anew the power of the mass meeting to impress upon a community the claims of the gospel.

One qualifying word should be added. Though called "mass evangelism," this method has always proceeded by seeking individual decisions. The effect of crowd psychology (even its exploitation in many instances) cannot be denied, but each individual convert has nevertheless been called upon to make his own response to God.

"Educational evangelism" arose in part as a corrective against the emotionalism and unstable decisions often associated with mass evangelism as well as the poor taste and offensive tactics which some of the evangelists employed. During the thirties many congregations abandoned revivalism altogether and still remain suspicious of it. The church school was made to carry the burden of winning new converts. A large group of our churches, it must be remembered—Baptists, Disciples, Churches of Christ, the Church of God, the Church of the Brethren, and others whose members constitute about one-third of American Protestants—practice believer's baptism only; hence the conducting of confirmation classes for adolescents and the memorization of catechisms are unknown in these communions. In some other churches which practice infant baptism at parental request there is no universal observance of the rite, and the Methodists insist that there must be a personal decision to "join the church" after reaching the age of accountability. Furthermore, 40 per cent of our population still has no formal church connection whatever. Hence there may be found in all our Sunday schools a large number of children and young people who have not received baptism in infancy and who, if they become members of the church at all, will do so on their own initiative.

The curriculum for our church schools includes considerable instruction in discipleship and the meaning of church membership, especially in the lessons for young people from eleven to sixteen or eighteen years of age (even for much younger children in some fundamentalist groups). Teachers are made to feel their evangelistic responsibility toward their pupils, and the youth organizations and adult classes also seek to lead their members to a Christian profession. Increasing numbers of ministers conduct a "pastor's class" once a year, or more frequently, to prepare interested persons for confession of faith and membership in the church. But the decision to accept Christ as Savior and Lord is not regarded as an automatic outcome of a course of lessons; it is left to the free choice of each individual. Some Sunday schools observe a "decision day" two or three times a year when, after appropriate preparation, pupils are invited to confess their faith in Christ. Through such direct appeals and through the indirect influence of the whole program of teaching and fellowship, the work of Christian education makes a major contribution to evangelism. It is the experience of most ministers that the majority of persons added to the church have had an active relationship with the church school.

"Visitation evangelism" is a technique which relies on the witness of laymen. Employed with considerable success in the nineteenth century, it has come to the fore again within the past decade. A carefully organized procedure, it has proved highly effective and has revived evangelism in many congregations. Various reasons may be given for its emergence: the fact that the results of educational evangelism were limited largely to young people as over against adults, the general ineffectiveness of pleas from the pulpit to accept church membership (because of their constant bombardment by the extravagant claims of advertisers on radio and television, the American public tends to discount an impersonal public appeal), the inability of a minister to seek out and interview all the people who are the evangelistic responsibility of his congregation. The method of visitation evangelism sends Christians out, usually in pairs, to call in the homes of persons who have shown interest in the church. Most of the "teams" are made up of men, who contribute evenings to the work, though sometimes of husband and wife. While some plans call for one or more visits to cultivate a sense of friendly involvement in the life of the congregation, the crux of visitation evangelism is the appeal in the home, usually in the presence of the whole family, for a Christian decision. Customarily the new converts are asked to sign cards promising to make their public profession of faith during the hour of worship on a subsequent Sunday. The callers find their own spiritual life strengthened by this kind of witness. In many churches they receive careful training from the minister and are given manuals which outline the best way of opening an interview, set forth answers to objections they are likely to meet, and warn against common pitfalls.

Amazing numerical results have come from visitation evangelism. After a period of careful preparation, prayer, and intensive calling a church at Eugene, Oregon, had 174 additions on one Sunday; another at Maysville, Kentucky, had 307; a third at Seattle, Washington, had 418. Even small congregations have had an increase of 40 or 50 per cent after a sustained effort. The Lutheran churches in the Chicago area received nearly 10,000 new members through a week-long mission carried on by their laymen.

In the minds of some the method seems almost too casual; it lacks the atmosphere of impending crisis created by the music, the prayers, and the earnest invitation from the pulpit in the old revival meeting; it seems a little like selling an insurance policy or a set of aluminum ware. But through visitation many are truly brought to Christ. The fact of being sought out, the simple integrity of the personal witness by laymen, the confrontation by earnest Christians with the necessity of making a decision—these are some of the human factors which have moved men to respond, although evangelism can never be fully understood except in terms of divine grace. Many converts become "soul-winners" themselves. A former All-American basketball star, after a period of playing professionally, came to a town in Kansas to coach high school boys in the sport. There he was led to Christ and the church by a team doing evangelistic visitation. He became a devoted layman and evangelist himself. Later he was called to be athletic coach in a church-related college where he bore his Christian witness among youth.

Any human achievement involves its spiritual dangers, and American evangelism is no exception. We stand constantly in peril with respect to our motives. Does our "evangelistic" concern arise from a burning constraint to proclaim the evangel, the good news of God? Or are we driven by the secular necessity of keeping our institution alive? We must confess that often we fall before the temptation of this latter alternative. We become concerned to *get new members,* and sometimes calculate far too quickly just which persons among our "prospects" appear most likely to strengthen our congregation in leadership and financial resources. Yet, if we too often tend to think first of the church rather than of a gracious God and of persons who need him, we do nevertheless bring them into that fellowship where God is to be found. It would appear from the account in Acts that Barnabas was drawn to Saul of Tarsus through some perception of what this new convert might contribute to the Christian mission.

Our evangelistic efforts confront us with other dangers as well. In our zeal to "win men"—and we might well give some serious study to how adequately the image of "winning men" reflects the Christian conception of witness—we come perilously close at times to violating their integrity as persons. In our eagerness to overpower their objections, whether by emotional appeals from the pulpit or by the low-keyed but calculated maneuvers of the expert in visitation evangelism, we may find ourselves trying to make the decision rather than letting them do it. Yet what Christian can exercise the restraint of complete objectivity at such a time?

It is easy to place an undue emphasis on numbers in attempting to measure the "success" of a particular effort or of a pastor's ministry in a place. (Both the advocates and the opponents of mass evangelism fall into the statistical trap, as is seen in the occasional article "six months later" asserting that Billy Graham had quite a small number of permanent additions after all.) Or it is possible that our churches may become preoccupied with techniques. As soon as a minister or congregation is successful, the universal question arises: "*How* is it done?" Yet, if there is some tendency in both mass and visitation evangelism to follow mechanically the steps set forth in a guidebook, it must be added that the abiding results are attained only where there is also a pervading atmosphere of faith and prayer and commitment to the divine mission. Some ministers or even denominations that experience marked evangelistic success tend to assume that the special favor of God rests upon them and upon all their works. The attitude may be offensive to others with less evangelistic zeal, but perhaps there is enough truth in it to serve as a judgment on the coldness of many.

It is frequently charged that the evangelist disregards the church's witness to society. In a sense this is almost inevitable. He must win individual commitments; he cannot call on the city of Chicago or the United States Steel Corporation to repent. If he makes it clear that a personal decision is not the end but the beginning of the Christian life, he may rightfully expect the church in its task of Christian nurture to guide the new convert into a fuller understanding of the implications of his faith. Yet it must be admitted that few contemporary evangelists summon individuals to repent of the social sins. Reinhold Niebuhr has proposed that our best-known revivalist call on his converts to renounce race prejudice as well as such a conventional iniquity as adultery or intemperance.

Public evangelism tends to appeal to the emotions at the expense of reason, and the tendency is pronounced in the case of certain American denominations and many of the evangelists heard on the radio. Yet again there have always been exceptions. Jonathan Edwards, Walter Scott, Dwight L. Moody, E. Stanley Jones, Charles Templeton—all appealed to the thinking of their hearers; the emotion which pervaded their efforts either was incidental and inescapable or was sought as a restrained corrective against cold rationalism in religion. The communion known as Disciples of Christ protested against hyperemotionalism and popularized "a sane, reasonable, scriptural plan of salvation." The University Christian Missions, sponsored by the National Council of Churches, have sought to win the intellectuals.

A serious danger, now being overcome, was the failure to conserve gains. The concern of many a nineteenth-century evangelist was to "save souls" by inducing a cataclysmic experience of conversion. Often he "went everywhere preaching the gospel," but left no pastor to follow up his labors; a pattern emerged of a glamorous and sensational revivalism carried on almost independently of the churches. Yet where the evangelist has worked in careful co-operation with the local ministry there has been a different story. A wise and devoted pastor of a small congregation has been known to shepherd more than a thousand additions from a single meeting and to guide his suddenly augmented flock into becoming a church great for spiritual maturity as well as for size. As more congregations have been able to secure full-time ministers, the danger has receded, and our best evangelists today are certainly alert to it. But no one can really understand the American churches unless he ponders the tremendous task of spiritual nurture which confronts a congregation as it is constantly receiving new members into its life.

The necessity for evangelism imposed upon the church by its separation from the state has had profound effects on the character of American Christianity.

A sense of mission runs through the life of our churches, an awareness not merely of a general responsibility but of a specific obligation to neighbors in the community. A congregation normally maintains a "prospect list" of persons considered ready for Christian decision, of those who attend services on occasion, of those who have no relationship to the church and who ought to receive friendly attention. In many communions, every sermon ends with a call to discipleship, followed by a "hymn of invitation," during which persons wishing to make a profession of faith come to the foot of the chancel and those who are already Christians prayerfully renew their dedication. So a sermon is no mere academic exercise in exegesis; it comes to its climax in that moment when every soul present says "Yes" or "No" to Jesus Christ. An urgency enters into preaching with the knowledge that someone in the congregation may be converted by what is said on a given occasion. A minister at a university church in Iowa, with the aid of a carefully planned program of evangelistic calling, had responses to the invitation every Sunday for fifteen years and nine months; many an ordinary congregation, if a a few weeks pass without conversions, begins to feel that something is wrong.

There are, of course, exceptions. Many of the foreign-language churches, retaining the cultural outlook as well as the speech of the Old World, thought of themselves as limited to a particular constituency and have not gone beyond their own group to "win souls" in the neighborhood. I once preached for a Danish Lutheran Church whose self-contained membership was smaller than it had been a generation ago. However, as the process of assimilation takes place, such churches do more than introduce the English language in order to hold their children and grandchildren; from their contacts with other churches in America and from the necessity of the situation they become concerned about evangelism. Many Lutheran groups have broken out of their shell and are evangelizing quite effectively. The Roman Catholic Church has passed through the same process. Once it was a church of the foreign-born, relying on immigration for its members; now it is aggressively evangelistic. There are signs that the Orthodox churches are beginning to overcome their static condition at this point and to seek members beyond their own flock.

It is important not to convey false impressions. The whole church in America can hardly be described as charged and tingling with apostolic zeal. Many congregations are cold to their evangelistic responsibility, and even in the best churches many members are not vitally concerned. Yet throughout our history the Great Commission has confronted us as a living reality. Decade by decade since we became a nation the proportion of our people affiliated with some church has increased until in 1955 it had reached 60.9 per cent; since 1920 church membership has grown four times as fast as the gain in the population. Yet the task is not done. As long as two persons out of every five in our own land remain "outside of Christ" we stand under the obligation of the Great Commission. And we dare not forget the rest of the world.

A strong subjective element characterizes American worship, in that the service is oriented toward "reaching the unreached" as well as toward the praise of God. (It must be remembered that all the "liturgical churches" added together —Roman Catholic, Eastern Orthodox, Lutheran, Episcopal, Old Catholic—comprehend not quite half of the church members in our country; Lutheran and Episcopal strength constitutes only about 20 per cent of American Protestantism.) A dominant mood in our services is the joy of salvation. Unsophisticated congregations make almost exclusive use of revivalistic music; churches whose members are more conscious of newer cultural standards and interpret more strictly the admonition that worship be conducted "decently and in order" have gradually banished those gospel songs which they regard as banal in sentiment and primitive in beat. Yet even in such churches many of the hymns relate to conversion and are sung to appealing melodies marked by strong and simple rhythms:

"We have heard the joyful sound: Jesus saves! Jesus saves!"

"I love to tell the story of unseen things above."

"Just as I am, without one plea, but that Thy blood was shed for me."

"Out of my darkness, sorrow, and night, Jesus, I come."

"O Jesus, I have promised to serve Thee to the end."

When one recalls that our nation was converted by the appeal of the evangelist and the response of the believer, one must grant a continuing place in our worship for those hymns which celebrate redemption, singing out of the dignity of a transformed heart. They express the mood of gladness which is a part of our heritage from generations of evangelism. On coming to Europe, many Americans find much of the congregational music doleful and sad.

Church architecture was affected by the requirements of mass evangelism. The "Akron Plan," which predominated among buildings erected for two generations after its introduction in 1867, was designed especially for the revival meeting and the Sunday-school rally. It set a platform with a central pulpit in one corner of the "auditorium," with the pews ranging about it in concentric semicircles. No one was very far from the preacher, and one could see most of the other people in the church without difficulty. Many aisles, provided so that no one would have trouble getting out from his place to answer the invitation, converged down a sloping floor toward the pulpit. One wall was usually a movable partition opening on additional seating space for big crowds, and in case of an overflow attendance the classrooms which ranged along the back and sides of the auditorium could be brought into use. The few stained-glass windows were pictorial rather than symbolic, and one of the scenes was certain to be the Good Shepherd returning to the fold with the lost sheep. Happily, this vogue in ecclesiastical architecture is now passing. Yet our newer churches—with their nave and center aisle, more formal windows, elevated pulpit and lectern, vested choir and gowned minister—while much more conducive to worship, present some difficulty in creating the atmosphere of intimacy and of joyful expectancy which characterized the revival meeting. Such churches, especially if they have been affected by the trend toward a liturgical type of service, seem foreign to many of our people, in particular to those who come from rural areas and whose only experience of praising God has been in the revivalistic mood.

So we have had to make haste slowly in leading our people from the exuberance of the sawdust trail to the beauty of the sanctuary, seeking at the same time to retain those values of individual encounter with God, of decisive personal commitment to Christ, of the joy of salvation, of the church as a redeeming fellowship, of the urgent sense of mission, all of which constitute so precious a part of our religious heritage.

The ethos of American Christianity has been profoundly affected by the place of evangelism in our religious life: at this point a contrast may be made with religion in Europe. The typical believer within the Protestant fellowship in the United States carries in his heart the memory of a personal decision, a personal commitment to Christ, at the time he became a member of the church. Europe was converted, to a large degree, by missionaries preaching in royal courts centuries ago. Whole nations or tribes were brought into Christendom by royal decree and were baptized en masse. Then the disciplinary machinery of the church went into operation: the baptism of every infant born into the community, the confirmation of all baptized children, obligatory confession and penance. At the Reformation, the decision to become Protestant or remain Roman was made by the prince or the civil government. Broadly speaking, Europe was Christianized by the sacramental life of the church in a general and somewhat impersonal way (though, of course, there were many acts of individual commitment); America was converted by preaching, as men came to Christ one by one. In Europe there is a great tradition, a national or racial memory of the conversion of the people by St. Augustine or St. Columba or St. Boniface. In America there is no such inheritance, but rather a personal memory of when *I* was converted by the preaching of Brother So-and-so or the personal interest of some Sunday-school teacher or other earnest layman.

Few experiences in the life of a devout American Christian match in spiritual intensity the moment when he sees new converts pressing forward for decision, especially if by intercessory prayer and personal witness he has had a part in bringing about the event. The closing stanza in Sankey's paraphrase on the parable of "The Ninety and Nine" still has power to describe the mood of such an occasion:

> But all thro' the mountains, thunder-riv'n,
>   And up from the rocky steep,
> There arose a glad cry to the gate of heav'n,
>   "Rejoice! I have found my sheep!"
> And the angels echoed around the throne,
>   "Rejoice, for the Lord brings back His own."
>   "Rejoice, for the Lord brings back His own."

Here is the root of the individualism in American Christianity and the secret of much of its dynamism: that at a given moment in his experience, when confronted by a decision for or against the Son of God, the believer, overwhelmed by an awareness of the divine love, has said "Yes" and has yielded his life to Jesus Christ as his Savior and Lord.

The ecumenical significance of American evangelism is difficult to assess. Even when it has been explained it sometimes seems blatant to churchmen in the Old World, conditioned to such a different spiritual tradition. To the clergymen of established liturgical churches the enthusiasm of Pentecostal or Southern Baptist "missionaries" to Europe is annoying and regrettable. Yet Dwight L. Moody in an earlier generation and Billy Graham in our own have succeeded in challenging the attention of a nation and winning decisions on the other side of the Atlantic as well as on our own. Obviously, the Christians of Europe themselves, in their growing concern to evangelize a "post-Christian" continent, will determine whether to adopt methods which have proved successful in the United States or to develop others more indigenous to their own spiritual culture.

Here I affirm my own conviction that there is more ecumenical significance for evangelism in the separation of church and state and in the implied corollary of a responsible church membership than in the particular revivalistic techniques worked out on the American scene. If European churches could effectively rid themselves and their nations of the ancient delusion that every person born within the national boundaries is a member of the body of Christ, they would be well on the way toward that renewal of the church for which we all pray. Our experience in the United States has emphasized the spiritual value to the church of that freedom which she knew in the first three centuries of her life and of that vigor which comes from admitting that she is only a minority in an indifferent or a hostile world, yet a commissioned minority, under obligation to lead that world, by the foolishness of preaching, to an acknowledgment of Christ as Lord.

IDENTIFICATION OF PASTOR WITH PEOPLE

The clergy has not been a privileged class since the United States became a nation. It has no prerogatives deriving from establishment. No minister by virtue of his office holds any governmental position. Two of the rare exceptions before the law are exemption from jury service (in some states) and from military conscription, but questions are being raised about the former and there is less and less of the latter as younger men are drafted and many pretheological students waive their exemption. There are no financial sinecures for religious leaders. Almost universally, a pastor must "raise his salary," that is, he must lead his congregation in underwriting the budget of which it is a part. He is responsible for maintaining an institution and must constantly bring in new members. The tradition of quiet scholarship and of writing of books on the part of the parish clergy, which has been such an ornament to the intellectual and spiritual life of Britain and the Continent, is almost nonexistent among us. The whole spirit of our churches has been so closely dependent on the current responsibility of the membership, which the minister must ever hold before his people, that the rare congregation among us which has received a large endowment tends to lose its vitality.

Generally speaking, an American minister remains close to the common people. In the frontier era, more often than not, he was a layman who preached, and also taught school or farmed. We have had no nobility, as in Old England, to give their younger sons to the clergy and to impart to it a blue-blooded tradition. A recent survey of theological students among Disciples of Christ revealed that they come largely from homes of farmers, skilled laborers, and ministers; very few are the sons of bankers, lawyers, and physicians.

The ministry is much less a separate class than the Roman priesthood or even the Protestant clergy of Europe. Among American Protestants, outside the Episcopal and Lutheran churches, the clerical collar is rarely seen. Although some pastors resort to it to combat urban anonymity, it is safe to say that west of the Atlantic seaboard the majority of ministers have never worn one. In the nonliturgical churches, most pastors conduct worship in street dress, although an increase in the use of a simple pulpit gown has been under way for a generation, and the advent of television has emphasized the dramatic value of clerical vestments.

Our preachers generally have known the meaning of sacrifice. In early days pioneer ministers were always close to poverty if not in actual hunger. Many of the men in pulpits today faced a hard struggle for an education at the time of the depression, and worked at menial tasks to earn their way through college. The average ministerial income at present approximates the prevaling union wage for production workers in industry. The situation is altered in individual cases by the fact that pastors of prosperous suburban churches are now receiving salaries that would have seemed fabulous a few years ago. One of the spiritual problems of such a clergyman is the realization that he is not serving at a sacrifice, as in former days. Yet, he tells himself, he is earning far less than if he had taken his abilities and a comparable education into some other line of work, and this is unquestionably true.

For these reasons, and because the church has no political advantages, there is very little anticlerical sentiment in America. Some nonchurch people feel ill at ease at the thought of having to meet a minister socially. But there is almost no agitation against the church or against the clergy as an exploiting or useless class.

The minister's role in community affairs is essentially one that he must create for himself. There is, especially in the South and the Midwest, considerable respect for his office. Yet, because of denominational multiplicity and the tendency of Americans to concede less to position than Europeans traditionally have done, no pastor is assured of leadership in the life of his locality simply because he preaches for a certain church, however important. He must win such leadership. Since the success of his church as an institution in its neighborhood and as an agency of evangelism, in which its own self-perpetuation is involved, depends on his standing in the community, the minister is under compulsion to achieve a place of recognition. Generally he joins a "service club" (Rotary, Kiwanis, Lions), certain agencies for civic improvement, and perhaps the Country Club, where he plays golf with men of influence. Usually he holds posts of service, working on committees of the Red Cross, welfare agencies, the symphony orchestra, and similar organizations. He faces a delicate problem in dividing his time between his community and his congregation. Yet in due course he becomes well acquainted in his locality, calls its leaders by their first names, and is in a position to exert a wider influence for good.

The American minister is intimately involved in the lives of his people. Because his congregation is a gathered church, he comes into a genuine covenant relationship with its members. He is not a fixture in the community, like a Roman Catholic priest in Italy, who has an official, but frequently quite impersonal, tie with every one in the village. The covenant relationship is heightened by the fact that in most Protestant churches he is "called" by the congregation. He must win and retain their support in order to maintain his job. Although most American pastorates are relatively short by European standards, ties of peculiar intimacy are woven by a man's ministry.

In the work of evangelism the minister comes into a special relationship, not with everyone born in a certain area but with the persons whom he has sought out and led to Christ. Many church members cherish a lifelong affection for the pastor who converted and baptized them. A particular minister is called upon for weddings and funerals, not because he is the clergyman in a locality—there are many—but because of some personal contact in the past; in the ministry that follows such an event the personal ties are more closely knit.

Pastoral calling among us has a different emotional quality than under establishment, where, theoretically, the priest visits everyone in his parish who is in great need—only to find his concern often discounted with a shrug: "After all, it's his job." Such cynicism is not limited to Europe. But when I belong to a gathered church, my minister calls on me because he is *my* pastor; there is a peculiar personal relationship between us. American church people generally place a high premium on pastoral calling. They want their minister to come frequently to see them, as a friend, and not to wait for emergencies. The current emphasis on counseling creates additional ties between a pastor and his people. Also in his relationship to the many groups in his church—Boy Scouts, the youth fellowship, the women's society, the men's brotherhood—the minister comes to be known as adviser and friend. His people see him frequently; he is no mere distant figure in a pulpit.

In most Protestant churches the minister's wife likewise plays an important role; her talents complement his own in the service and leadership of the congregation; she too becomes a confidante and spiritual counselor; she frequently accompanies her husband on pastoral calls; she acts as both inspiration and unofficial moderator in the women's work; she serves as hostess for the many activities which take place at the parsonage and which, incidentally, bring many young people and adults into intimate association with the minister's family. She is a major factor in the success of her husband.

The widespread custom of entertaining the pastor and his family in the homes of the congregation helps to keep him close to his people. In the days of the frontier and of rural life, when the circuit rider or itinerant evangelist was dependent on others for meals and lodging, the scriptural admonition to hospitality was quite literally interpreted to include setting a good dinner before the preacher. But more than a matter of physical necessity was involved; as a family of believers broke bread with a minister they came to know him as their Christian brother. Formality gave way to good humor: many stories circulate among churchfolk celebrating the heroic appetites of preachers—especially Methodist preachers —for fried chicken. Pastor and people met where life was lived, and friendships were established at a basic human level which made possible a more effective ministry. The blessed tradition continues, somewhat attenuated by the rush and confinement of urban life, but not forgotten. When a revival meeting is held in a church, it is not uncommon for visiting evangelist and host pastor to be dinner guests in a different home every day for two weeks, so that they may know the people better. In many congregations, especially in rural areas, the minister and his family are invited to some home for Sunday dinner every week of the year. In the year past I have been a Sunday-dinner guest, often with my family, in at least forty homes. Some of the persons by whom I have been entertained in recent months include farmers, factory workers, loggers, a labor union organizer, the principal of a public school, an electrician, an automobile dealer, two spinster sisters, the manager of a store, the mayor of a small city, a railroader, a plumber, a soil conservation worker, the owner of a small business.

The affection which develops between a good pastor and his people during a long association may create problems for his successor. A congregation sometimes finds it hard to transfer to a new minister the devotion which it has cherished toward his predecessor, and the difficulty may be intensified if the older man retires in the scene of his former labors. Another problem arises from our tendency to honor a clergyman personally rather than officially. In the case of nearly every minister there are some individuals who do not respond to him, even some who actively dislike him. When such persons exercise influence in the congregation, the pastor may find himself engaged in a conflict, essentially political in nature, for mastery of the situation. Oppressive as such difficulties often are, American churches accept them as limitations of our system, in which the minister is a man of the people.

The involvement of the minister in the lives of his people has left its mark on American preaching. There is a quality of earthiness about our sermons, a tendency to move more on the level of daily experience than in the theological stratosphere, a "human touch," with both the possibilities for good and the dangers which characterized the popular preaching of the medieval friars. In a searching discussion of the ministry, Clarence E. Lemmon once spoke of the difficulty in being both a friend to one's people, bound to them by intimate ties of personal affection, and at the same time a plain-spoken prophet of the living God. Yet American preachers have set themselves no less a goal, and the best of them have attained it.

It is well known that through the centuries the life of the established churches has been blessed by the ministry of countless faithful and beloved pastors. For the fundamental motivation to be a true shepherd of the flock arises not from any circumstance in the social environment, but from the nature of the ministry itself as it is revealed in the public work of our Lord and in the teaching of the Scriptures. Nevertheless, the absolute dissociation of the American minister from the civil and political structure and his sole responsibility, under God, to the company of believers who have called him to preach and serve among them have produced among us an identification of the pastor with his people which to us is one of the most precious benefits of the separation of church and state.

A RELIGIOUS VALUE

Many European churchmen cherish values in ecclesiastical establishment which they fear would be lost without it. American Christians know this, yet believe that the spiritual gains to the churches under our system have far outweighed anything that may have been surrendered. Indeed, as we consider the criticism which may be leveled, with justice, against Christianity in our land, we are convinced that the weaknesses pointed to are, for the most part, defects in the churches themselves and not in the principle of liberty. Because our churches are free the believers themselves have undertaken the burden of support as a personal responsibility, a stewardship toward God. The Great Commission has been heard by us with constant and immediate urgency. And our ministers have kept the common touch.

If you should enter an American church when laymen were offering public prayer, you would more than likely hear something like this in the course of their thanksgiving: "O God, we thank thee for a land of freedom where we may worship Thee according to the dictates of our own conscience. Be with those in other lands who do not enjoy this liberty." I have heard such a prayer on the lips of lay elders even at the communion table. Who will say that it was inappropriate? If the chief end of man is indeed the knowledge and service of God in sincerity of heart, the freedom to pursue it without penalty or interference may well take on the quality of a religious value, and it has done so for many of us. We are constrained, as a part of our ecumenical witness, to bear testimony to the blessings which have come to us as fruits of the separation of church and state.

IV.

Expressions of Our Faith

For three and a half centuries Christianity has flourished in the English-speaking area of the New World. Imbued with the American spirit, conditioned both by the freedom it has enjoyed and by the needs to which it has responded, it has emerged in the United States as an indigenous faith. It recognizes its indebtedness to centuries of Christian history, just as do the so-called "younger churches" of Asia and Africa, and it gratefully acknowledges the spiritual bonds by which it is united in an ecumenical fellowship encompassing the earth. But our churches did not long remain in tutelage to their spiritual fathers in Europe. Even in the early days they considered themselves mature in the faith and, since they were not dependent financially upon churches in the "old country," they soon asserted their spiritual independence also. Almost immediately the pioneers began to think as Americans, and in typical dissenting spirit to deny normative authority to the religion of the Old World. Our Christianity is the product of obedience to God and searching of the Scriptures on the part of earnest men and women living in the peculiar American environment. What are the characteristic expressions of this faith?

ACTIVISM

American Christianity cannot be understood except in terms of earnest response to a missionary situation. When the advancing tide of settlement broke over the Appalachian Mountains at the beginning of our national life, there were no churches in the West. A century later, when the frontier disappeared, not only was the continental vastness inhabited but its people had been evangelized and gathered into congregations. Still the process goes on, the effort to win to Christian allegiance that 40 per cent of our population still uncommitted to the faith. Europe too had its period of missionary activism, the era of the evangelizing monks (especially the Irish, and then the English) and of Christianizing conquests by Charlemagne and the Ottonian emperors; it was followed by the age of cathedral-building, a time of incredible activism as it is described in the accounts of the chroniclers. But that was long ago, and subsequent influences have altered the character that then emerged. The churches in America had lived under the missionary imperative from the beginning, and the task is not yet finished.

A tremendous urgency actuated our fathers. Scarcely more than a century ago Lyman Beecher proclaimed:

Whatever we do, it must be done quickly; for there is a tide in human things which waits not—moments on which the destiny of a nation balances, when the light dust may turn the right way or the wrong. And such is the condition of our nation now. Mighty influences are bearing on us and a slight effort now may secure what ages of repentance cannot remove away. We must educate the whole nation while we may. All—all who would vote must be enlightened, and reached by the restraining and preserving energies of heaven.[1]

The concern was not merely oratorical. It expressed itself in the devotion of frontier preachers who faced every kind of hardship to carry the gospel to the people of the West. There is an eloquent tribute in a complaint which a Presbyterian missionary voiced in his report to his home board: his ambition was to find a settler's cabin so isolated that it had not already been visited by a Methodist circuit rider. A magnificent bronze on the grounds of the state capitol of Oregon com-

[1] Quoted by Brauer, *Protestantism in America* (Philadelphia: Westminster, 1953), p. 143.

memorates these heroic horsemen of the Lord who braved the rigors of the wilderness, who struggled through the swollen waters of unknown streams, who bore penury and loneliness and a solitary old age in order to preach to wild and friendless pioneers the unsearchable riches of Christ.

It was not enough to evangelize; believers must be gathered together into congregations. The work of "church extension" challenged the missionary conscience of the denominations and made dramatic progress in the West. Sheldon Jackson, tireless Presbyterian apostle to the Rocky Mountains from 1870 to 1882, once formed seven new churches in sixteen days. For arid regions where there was no timber he had church buildings assembled in sections and shipped out by rail from Chicago. One of his contemporaries, C. C. McCabe, engaged in similar work for the Methodist Church Extension Society. Traveling one day on the train, he picked up a newspaper and read a report concerning the celebrated infidel, Robert G. Ingersoll, who had just told a "freethinkers' convention" that "the churches were dying out all over the land." McCabe got off the train at the next station to dispatch a telegram: "Dear Robert: 'All hail the power of Jesus' name—we are building more than one Methodist Church for every day in the year, and propose to make it two a day! C. C. McCabe." Methodists rejoiced in the incident and soon found themselves singing:

> The infidels a motley band,
>   In council met and said:
> "The churches die all through the land,
>   The last will soon be dead."
> When suddenly a message came,
>   It filled them with dismay:
> "All hail the power of Jesus' name!"
>   We're building two a day.[2]

One of the most colorful events in the settlement of the West was the opening of the Cherokee Strip, a tract of land stretching across northern Oklahoma. Acquired by treaty from

[2] Sweet, *The Story of Religion in America* (New York: Harper, 1950), p. 337.

the Cherokee Indians, it was thrown open to settlement at high noon on September 16, 1893. For miles along the border, in Kansas and "old Oklahoma," an impatient multitude waited behind a restraining line of United States troops until the gun was fired and "the Run" began. It was a race for 160 acres of free land or for lots on the projected townsites. Traveling on horseback, by sulky, by buckboard, by bicycle, by train (restricted to a speed of 15 miles an hour), even on foot, the eager host surged across the prairie, into the land of promise. Long before sundown they had staked out their claims, hurried to the federal land offices which were set up in tents, and filed the papers required for a legal title. The last great tract of arable public land was gone, and still many had no farms.

Riding a Missouri race horse on that storied day was S. F. Boggess, minister of the First Christian Church in Guthrie, Oklahoma. He had been commissioned by the Board of Church Extension (Disciples of Christ) to make the Run in order to secure desirable locations for new church buildings. At the townsite of Perry he staked a claim. Like hundreds of others, it was "contested," but he secured a lot for a church. In the next few days he rode to other new "towns" in the Strip—already inhabited, with tents and makeshift cabins lining their streets—and acquired ground for church buildings. "Boggess's Ride" became a colorful incident in the lore of the Disciples of Christ, another vivid example of the missionary activism by which the vast reaches of a continent became a possession for the people of God.

The maturing of a frontier community sometimes occurred in an incredibly brief period of time. I mention the Cherokee Strip, for there I spent some years of my boyhood, and there I began my ministry. The settlers endured considerable hardship at first, for most of them had few assets except hope and a willingness to work. But soon wheat was sprouting where nothing but buffalo grass had ever grown, and farmers moved out of their sod houses into permanent structures of wood. In town frame buildings rose—homes, stores, churches, schools, banks. Before long imposing edifices of brick or stone, some even boasting classic lines and Corinthian columns, faced the courthouse square. The Strip opened in 1893. Phillips University, my alma mater, was chartered in 1906 and began instruction the following year. Oklahoma entered the Union as a state in 1907. (When I was a boy we celebrated Oklahoma's "coming of age," the twenty-first anniversary of statehood; then we went to Scotland and the following year helped keep the six hundredth anniversary of the granting of the charter to the city of Edinburgh!)

When I returned to Oklahoma as a student in the thirties, our city of Enid had a symphony orchestra and enjoyed summer opera. Yet we could still reach back to the beginnings. On our campus, undisturbed in those days by the designs of a modern landscape gardener, was an old buffalo wallow. Every year, on the anniversary of the opening of the Strip, we had a parade; at the head of the procession, still riding on horseback, came the men and women who had made the Run. When I began to preach, the leaders of the congregation at Lahoma were the original pioneers and their children, living on farms they had won in '93. I buried some of them in the ground they had claimed under that far September sun. Yet our university had already worn out its first set of buildings and was putting up new ones to accommodate a thousand students. Since I enrolled there in 1936 it has erected seven major structures, including a seminary building of cathedral proportions, and has almost entirely replaced the buildings which were in use twenty years ago. The funds have been contributed, for the most part, by the churches of one communion, to provide the means of Christian education. Though Enid is not a large or unduly prosperous city it has fine churches and schools and stores and a flourishing cultural life. All this within a generation or two, while a few snowy-haired pioneers still walk the streets and behold what their hands have wrought!

Such achievements required tremendous activity. In farming and business and education they came about only through the most daring dreams and unremitting toil. In religion, too, men and women gave themselves to the point of exhaustion that the work of the Lord might be done, and no one can convince us who have entered into their labors that God had any other way of accomplishing these things except by their dedicated activity. The hymns I learned as a boy in Sunday school expressed their spirit:

"Work for the Night Is Coming"
"To the Work! to the Work! We Are Servants of God"
"True-hearted, Whole-Hearted, Faithful and Loyal"
"Bringing in the Sheaves."

Many of the "work songs" were phrased in agricultural metaphors. A note in our hymnal told us that the following was President James A. Garfield's favorite hymn:

> Ho! reapers of life's harvest,
>   Why stand with rusted blade
> Until the night draws round thee
>   And day begins to fade?
> Why stand ye idle, waiting
>   For reapers more to come?
> The golden morn is passing,
>   Why sit ye idle, dumb? [3]

Today we sing more worshipful hymns, but the spirit of activism still continues.

It is still needed. In our three states on the Pacific coast, the population increased by more than 50 per cent in the decade between the two most recent censuses (1940–1950) and the growth still goes on. Every Monday morning, we are told, in the county of Los Angeles a thousand new children turn up for school; people are moving in that fast. Unless the newcomers and the children in such areas are to grow up as pagans, new churches must be planted, ministers recruited, men and women evangelized; in short, the missionary task in which we have been engaged on our own home ground ever since the nation began must still go on. Without Christian activism the expanding population of the United States would soon be engulfed by paganism.

The activism of American Christians is more than a reli-

[3] I. B. Woodbury, "Ho! Reapers of Life's Harvest," *Wonder Hymns of Faith* (Cincinnati: Standard Publishing Co., n.d.), No. 93.

gious reflection of the national character. It is a matter of faith. It is not a repudiation of theology; it is the fruit of our theology. Christian thinkers around the world are affirming that the gospel is the message of "the mighty *acts* of God." Our Lord asserted, "My Father is working, and I work," and again, "I must work the works of him that sent me." St. Luke has written for us of "all that Jesus began *to do* and to teach." Indeed, we hold it significant that in our New Testament the book that follows the Gospels is the *Acts* of the Apostles. Disciples of Christ speak of their early American leaders as having rediscovered the Book of Acts, and we are frequently reminded that it is an unfinished book. The church in the United States finds itself in this respect in the position of the apostolic church; it is an expanding, not a static community, primarily missionary rather than primarily liturgical.

Our activism has not betrayed us into distorting the faith. We know that only God can save us. Only as his power works within us does our activity take on religious significance. We have heard the word of the Lord, "Without me you can do nothing." A Bible study group at the Ecumenical Institute discovered with interest that the American translators who produced the Revised Standard Version of the New Testament rendered the key verb in 1 Peter 2:5 as passive rather than middle: "Like living stones *be yourselves built* into a spiritual house." The King James version says *"Build your-selves up,"* the French rendition by Louis Segond reads *"Edifiez-vous,"* and the German also is active. We in America stand ever ready to confess that the transcendent power belongs to God and not to us.

But because he is our Savior we find ourselves under obligation to do what he has given us to do. Our activism, then, is not a substitute for our religious faith; it is an expression of that faith. The Epistle of James is more acceptable to us than it was to Luther. Our Christianity expresses itself not so much in liturgy or in dogma but in a program of dedicated activity and service to Christ. Professor Homrighausen of Princeton has written:

We are not willing to be *theologians* of the gospel merely; we believe that the Holy Spirit is actively at work now in history, in the church, in the believer, and that there is an integral relation between faith and obedience, between the gospel and life. While this spirit may have its dangers, it is something which Christians of Europe should seek to understand.[4]

With the European churches confronting a continent now grown cold to the faith and a culture widely described as post-Christian, it may well be that they will experience a renewal of that missionary activity which surged through the apostolic church, which drove the evangelizing monks through the islands and across the English Channel to hostile and heathen shores, which in the nineteenth century sent evangelists from Germany and Scandinavia and Britain and Holland around the world, and which has imparted an epic quality to the story of the faith in America. There are signs that such a spirit is already stirring. If it does bring a revivification of the religious life of Europe, we do not suppose that it will manifest itself in the same forms we have known. But perhaps after such an event European and American Christians will understand each other better.

THE PROMINENCE OF PREACHING

The religious groups that occupied our West were those of the Reformed and the evangelical tradition—chiefly Baptists, Methodists, Presbyterians, Disciples—among whom preaching played a prominent role.

Of all the functions of the church, preaching was best adapted to the conditions of the frontier. To begin with, there were no temples in the new land; meetings must be held in groves, barns, or schoolhouses. The famous Methodist pioneer of the Midwest, Peter Cartwright, looked with scorn upon the "educated preachers" who came out from the East, with their manners unsuited to the unsophisticated frontiersmen.

The great mass of our western people wanted a preacher that could mount a stump, a block, or old log, or stand in the bed of

[4] E. G. Homrighausen, "When Europeans Come to Evanston," *Christian Century*, Oct. 7, 1953, p. 1128.

a wagon, and without note or manuscript, quote, expound, and apply the Word of God to the hearts and consciences of the people.[5]

Even when the first churches were built they were crude log buildings—without stained glass, without precious furnishings, without artistry or symbolism, often with no altar but a table of the plainest sort. From a confessional standpoint, the congregations were hopelessly conglomerate, and many who came to service had no background of religious instruction. Such a crowd could not corporately follow any of the historic liturgies. If communion should be served, a majority of those present would be disqualified from partaking. But the Word of God could be preached, and men were brought to Christ.

Preaching remained the chief means of evangelism until well into the twentieth century. Because of the earnestness of the appeal to sinners to accept the redeeming grace of God, it took on an emotional quality which sometimes descended to the exploitation of sentiment, but which at its best rose to the dignity of a great heart swept by a realization of the divine love. And there was more than fervor. The sermon, along with the closely related debate, was the most effective vehicle of denominational apologetic. There was much dogmatic preaching, with a careful regard for the rules of logic, a constant appeal to "chapter and verse," and the authority of the conviction that the preacher was engaged in battle for the truth of God. Even in the raw and untutored West, pulpit eloquence was highly prized, and there was much of it. The democratic citizens of the young republic loved to listen to oratory from the lips of both politicians and preachers. The prose style of Abraham Lincoln reveals the nobility of utterance that might be attained by a speaker who shaped his manner of speaking largely through familiarity with the Bible, Bunyan, and Gibbon.

The church service that developed in the conditions just described tended to center in the personality of the preacher. Worship was free, direct, usually not disorderly, but spon-

[5] Brauer, *op. cit.*, p. 144.

taneous, coming "from the heart." If there was anything more reprehensible than a sermon read from notes it was a prayer read from a book. Congregations wanted their preaching "straight from the shoulder" and took pride in preachers who could recite long passages of Scripture from memory. Even today we have ministers who make a point of memorizing their lesson for the day so that they may convey the message more directly. Teachers of elocution emphasized the importance of "eye contact" with the hearers. On first conducting worship in Europe, I found members of the congregation disturbed by my habit of looking up from the Book to the faces of the worshipers during the reading of the Scripture. Americans do not object to the individuality, even the mild idiosyncrasies, of the man in the pulpit. In his famous lectures at Yale, Phillips Brooks defined preaching as the art of conveying "truth through personality." The conventional invitation given by a Christian to a new acquaintance came to be worded, "Come to our church; you'll like our preacher." And in smaller communities yet today a common greating to a minister as men meet him on the street is "Hello, preacher."

The men who have left their stamp on American Christianity have been the preachers rather than the theologians. This is not to say that they had no theology; some of them were masters of the discipline. But their influence was exerted primarily through the preached word, only secondarily through books on systematics. Such names as Cotton Mather, Jonathan Edwards, George Whitefield, Francis Asbury, the Tennents, Charles G. Finney, William Ellery Channing, Lyman Beecher, Horace Bushnell, Alexander Campbell, Walter Scott, Peter Cartwright, Matthew Simpson, Henry Ward Beecher, Phillips Brooks, Dwight L. Moody, Washington Gladden, Charles Edward Jefferson, George W. Truett, Harry Emerson Fosdick, Peter Marshall, emphasize the point. Even today, when men of such theological brilliance as Reinhold Niebuhr, Paul Tillich, and Nels Ferré have found an eager hearing among seminarians, the "headliners" on the program for a ministers' conference turn out to be preachers— George A. Buttrick, Harold A. Bosley, Robert J. McCracken,

Ralph W. Sockman, Bishop Gerald Kennedy, Dean James Pike.

The pattern of our church life has changed from the rugged simplicities of the frontier. The communions of the historic liturgies are much stronger among us in proportion than they were a century ago. But even they have produced eloquent preachers whose homiletical manner is strikingly American. In all the churches worship is more orderly, music more stately, architecture richer in symbolism. In deference to the modern demand for brevity, the sermon has been cut to twenty minutes. Judging from the amount of time and energy he spends on the various phases of his work the minister is no longer primarily a pulpiteer, but rather a pastor or counselor or administrator. Yet the sermon still holds a unique place. In a world that has become largely depersonalized and mechanized, here is the sound of a living voice, from a visible man of flesh and blood, bearing witness to the grace of God. Even in our time, when a sermon strikes home to the heart of the hearer an American will say, "Today I've really been to church!"

THE MINISTRY OF FRIENDSHIP

The frontier was a place of desperate loneliness. The pioneer found himself isolated by distance from the scenes of his youth, from loved ones, often from anyone. Day after day he looked out on the bleakness of the prairie—hopeful enough in spring and summer, but depressing in autumn rains, and only a white blank through the long winter months. A friend of mine talked with an old settler in the Dakotas who had been there "in the early day." After a trying winter he took his wagon and drove for miles, returning with young trees to set around the house; he feared that his wife would lose her mind if she should pass another winter with nothing to be seen in any direction but the drifting snows swirling across the flat and barren plains until all was blurred in the distant gray horizon.

The drabness of poverty was the frontiersman's lot. There was little money in circulation and little that money could buy. He had his land, he struggled to improve it, but his life was hard and his fare was meager. The cultural barrenness was even more depressing; it is difficult to imagine the intellectual and spiritual hunger of cultivated and sensitive spirits. That hunger still prevails in small communities where distance from larger centers is a factor. The novelist Sinclair Lewis analyzed it a generation ago in *Main Street*, his depressing picture of life in Gopher Prairie, Minnesota.

The spiritual desolation of the pioneers was hardest of all to bear. What loneliness can be compared to that of the sinner who clung to his sin, of the sinner under conviction and seeking assurance of forgiveness, of the Christian who longed for spiritual fellowship with others of like mind? One wonders at the pathetic isolation and the bravery of a single family that regularly kept the Lord's Supper about their own table on the Lord's day, because there were no others with whom they could join.

The work of the frontier churches was a gracious ministry to this loneliness. Here along the trail comes the circuit rider or evangelist. He stops at an isolated cabin and takes a meal or even stays overnight. There is talk by the fireside—and news. Week before last he saw someone you know. Three months ago he was in Cincinnati for a convention. He is here because he is interested *in you*.

Today there is preaching at Oak Grove. From the whole neighborhood people are coming together, lots of folks. Much friendly visiting ensues, and between the morning and afternoon services the ladies spread out a basket dinner. In such a setting of reunion after loneliness the handshake becomes a sacramental act, truly the "right hand of fellowship." It is even celebrated in an old frontier hymn, now long forgotten, to be accompanied by the appropriate action:

> Take your companion by the hand,
> And all your children in the band.[6]

Singing, too, becomes an act of fellowship. It is easy for a later generation to criticize their hymns from an aesthetic or

[6] *Ibid.*, p. 111.

even a theological standpoint. But in a lilting song that made people pat their feet to the rhythm they were caught up in the spirit of the group. If there was a bouncy refrain and the men could come out with extra words in the bass, it met an elemental hunger—to belong, to be needed.

Later on, in better established rural communities, the same ministry continued. The Sunday services, the revival meeting, the prayer meeting, the annual reunion brought human beings together in the name of Christ. All this was not mere gregariousness. (But why are Americans gregarious? Why do they want to be liked? May it not be because the corporate memory is still haunted by a recollection of loneliness, of an isolation which perhaps the Englishman seeks by his reserve?) This was friendship given a spiritual quality. It expressed itself in the "circle of prayer," an intimate act of worship in which each believer in turn offered up his thanksgiving and supplications to God. It took on moral sternness. Neighbors who became estranged knew that they could not approach the sacred things of God until they were right with each other; in many a simple rural church penitent farmers confessed their sin in the presence of the congregation and standing before the Table of the Lord extended to one another the right hand of reconciliation. A stanza written by an English clergyman, but sung often in America, speaks clearly of the friendship prevailing among the people of God:

> Blest be the tie that binds
> Our hearts in Christian love;
> The fellowship of kindred minds
> Is like to that above.

The ministry of friendship remains an important part of the church's service to modern America. For there is loneliness still—in the crowded city, where so often men and women cease to be regarded as persons; in factories and offices, where one confronts machines rather than people; in the overgrown smooth-running institutions which many of our schools and hospitals have become. The most common advertisement of a congregation is that it is "a friendly church." Newcomers seldom return to a church if it seems "cold," if no one speaks to them. More often than not there are ushers at the door to greet worshipers as they arrive, and the minister is there to shake hands as they leave. Even city-dwellers are slow to outgrow the custom of visiting in the pews right up to the moment when the organ prelude begins; after the benediction there is even more extended chatting with friends, and some linger for a long while. Many of our groups in the church—for men, for women, for young people, even many of our church-school classes—center their work largely in Christian friendship and its transforming power.

The concept of *fellowship*, which bulks so large in American Christianity, means to us a human togetherness, a belonging to one another, which is created by God's grace. But it is not just to one another that we belong. It is to him. That is why we can be together. The contagion of such a fellowship is a major element in our evangelism. Men and women searching for companions, groping dimly after a better life, are drawn into the circle of some group within the church, doubtless on a purely human level first of all. But as they enter more intimately into the life of the group they are brought into encounter with him who is the source of this togetherness, they are confronted by the Friend of publicans and sinners, and they yield their lives to him. Another old song celebrates this transformation:

> I've found a Friend, oh such a Friend!
> He loved me ere I knew Him;
> He drew me with the cords of love,
> And thus He bound me to Him.

All this can be criticized, and sometimes is, by the spiritually elite, who imagine that they do not need the love of a brother. Certainly the New Testament concept of *koinonia* is not exhausted by such an interpretation. Yet the apostolic church was a fellowship which could draw men to Christ, which upheld them in the rigorous ethical demands of discipleship, and in which the Christian life could actually be realized.

On a recent Sunday I attended morning worship at the First

Methodist Church in Chicago—the "Chicago Temple" housed in a modern skyscraper at the heart of the Loop. Perhaps 2,500 persons were present, and as we sat in a lofty rear gallery the minister seemed a great distance away. The worship was stately, in keeping with the dignity of the Gothic interior. But before the sermon the minister took ten minutes for a sort of ritual of friendship. In a winsome human way he talked to that vast assembly of summer visitors and seekers-after-God. A "Twins' Convention" was going on in Chicago; he had all the twins stand up. The national meeting of a labor union had just ended, and he took note of the members of that brotherhood. Similarly, he recognized others: visitors from Rhode Island, "the smallest state"; visitors from Texas, "the largest state"; visitors from anywhere outside Chicago; all those living in Chicago. The procedure could have descended to the level of a circus, but it did not. It was a skillful manifestation of friendliness, in quiet good taste, a ministry to individuals caught in a lonely, impersonal city. Afterwards a visitor said of the sermon, "I felt he was talking to me."

LAY LEADERSHIP

A striking characteristic of congregational life in America is the large number of men, women, and young people who are actively engaged in carrying on the work of the church. In many of our communions laymen assume responsibilities which in other parts of the world are reserved to the ministry or the priesthood.

Our peculiar history has affected the situation. Our churches came into being in an atmosphere of fierce democracy; there was no feudal tradition to elevate either the clergy or a noble class as the ruling element in congregational life. The egalitarianism of the frontier, the suspicion of the expert, made for prejudice against a "hireling clergy." The idea of the covenant, implicit in the polity of the various congregational bodies, but not limited to them, conceived of the believers in a certain place as solemnly banding together under God to constitute a church; such a concept inevitably made for the assumption of lay responsibility.

A fact against which there was no good theoretical answer was the sheer lack of ministers on the frontier. Those communions whose life centers in the sacraments as administered by an episcopally ordained priesthood just could not keep up with the westward-moving population, because they lacked priests. Heroic missionaries carried Roman Catholicism into the West, but their numbers were too few to provide their scattered people with a continuing sacramental life. For a while they experimented with lay preachers, but these men could not say Mass, and without it Roman spirituality cannot live. The Protestant Episcopal Church required a generation or more after our national independence to recover from the separation from England, to establish its own episcopal institutions, and to recruit a ministry; it was destined to play a much larger role later in our history than it did in the days of the western migrations. If the sacraments were administered with any frequency, it was at the hands of laymen. In early Pennsylvania in the 1720's John Philip Boehm was prevailed upon to preach and to baptize among the German Reformed people, though he had not received ordination. The situation was reported to the Classis of Amsterdam, which recognized the validity of what he had done, but insisted that he now be ordained. The doctrine of the sacraments held by most churches recognizes a situation of emergency in which a layman may lawfully administer them. On the frontier that emergency was a continuing condition.

The priesthood of believers was bound to be emphasized in such circumstances, sometimes in radical fashion. The farmer-preacher of the Baptists and the Disciples, or the lay exhorter of the Methodists, usually lacked the rudiments of divinity. But he had the respect of his neighbors who knew that he earned his living with his hands, as they did. He had sufficient zeal to leave his own work and to forget his own comfort for the sake of others. He had a working knowledge of the English Bible and a devotion to the Christ whom he served. So he gathered the congregations and instructed them in the nurture and admonition of the Lord. Vachel Lindsay's tribute to his Grandfather Frazee catches the spirit of these men:

Into the acres of the newborn state
He poured his strength, and plowed his ancient name,
And, when the traders followed him, he stood
Towering above their furtive souls and tame.

That brow without a stain, that fearless eye
Oft left the passing stranger wondering
To find such knighthood in the sprawling land,
To see a democrat well-nigh a king.

He lived with liberal hand, with guests from far,
With talk and joke and fellowship to spare,—
Watching the wide world's life from sun to sun,
Lining his walls with books from everywhere.

He read by night, he built his world by day.
The farm and house of God to him were one.
For forty years he preached and plowed and wrought—
A statesman in the fields who bent to none.

His plowmen-neighbors were as lords to him.
His was an ironside, democratic pride.
He served a rigid Christ, but served Him well—
And, for a lifetime, saved the countryside.[7]

James A. Garfield, before he entered politics, eventually to become president of the United States, was a teacher-preacher who served Disciples of Christ in rural Ohio in such a spirit.

Lay leadership today does not center primarily in the work of the ministry. The farmer-preacher emerged in a particular environment and served the needs of his time, but no sizable American denomination today takes a dogmatic stand against a paid ministry; it long ago became apparent that if a congregation was to survive it must have a well-qualified, full time leader. But the layman still renders large and significant service in the church school, the board of officers, various committees, men and women's work, evangelistic calling, and the like. In the work of the denominations he also has an im-

[7] "The Proud Farmer," in Vachel Lindsay, *Collected Poems* (New York: Macmillan, 1946), pp. 71, 72. Used by permission.

portant place. The Methodist Church, for example, has in its national conference a house of lay delegates corresponding to the house of clergy. The outstanding American layman probably spends much more time in the work of the church as an institution, less in exploring deeply the Christian implications of his vocation in the world, than his European counterpart. Yet our tradition of lay leadership has given to the Christian world such men of influence as Dwight L. Moody, Robert E. Speer, and John R. Mott. It has saved us from that abysmal gulf which yawned between priest and people in the Middle Ages and has helped us, at least in our congregation, to realize that wholeness of the church which the Reformation arose to proclaim.

THE CONTINUITY OF A LIVING FAITH

In recent discussions on Faith and Order, the question of continuity has been much to the fore: how may we assure ourselves that the congregation to which we belong is in unbroken historic relationship with the one, holy, catholic, and apostolic church? Several theories of "succession" have been advanced from various quarters. This is not the place to explore the theories systematically; it may only be remarked that some of them have arisen out of a corporate experience which differs markedly from that of the churches in the United States. A greater degree of realism may be injected into the discussions of continuity by setting forth some pertinent facts out of our religious history.

Continuity in early America was not a matter of theological speculation, but a question of the survival of the faith. Where there was a living faith in the hearts of believers, a faith that reached out to share the gospel and to bring into being a new community of Christians, there was continuity. A good example is a congregation at Kremlin, Oklahoma. On the first Sunday after the Run into the Cherokee Strip in September, 1893, a devout woman gathered a few Christians together to read the Scriptures and to keep the Lord's Supper. They continued to meet week by week, in her three-room tent. Soon an evangelist came, the little company of believers was strengthened by new accessions, they were "set in order" as a church, and a building was erected. The life of that congregation has continued through the years without a settled pastor. Annual revival meetings brought a preacher to the community for a brief period of time. After Phillips University was established at Enid, only a few miles away, a succession of immature undergraduates began coming to Kremlin on weekends to serve as best they could and to gain their first taste of the work of the ministry. Amid all the changes and uncertainties of such a situation, without ever having seen a bishop, without ever having had a mature permanent pastor of its own, that little church has continued for more than sixty years. Week by week, each Lord's day, its members have "continued stead-fastly in the apostles' teaching and fellowship, in the breaking of bread and in prayers." It has sent some of its own young people into the ministry; at least one statesman of the world Christian mission looks back to that congregation of believers as his spiritual home.

When the settlement of the Oregon country began on a large scale in the 1840's, most of the Great Plains area, sweeping up from the Mississippi River to the Rocky Mountains, was considered uninhabitable. To reach the fertile valleys of the Pacific slope required an overland journey of nearly two thousand miles, across the open range, over mountain passes, and through burning desert; the trek took six months, from the "jumping-off place" at the edge of civilization until the pioneers came again to white settlements. For the long and dangerous march they banded together in companies of several hundred. At night they drew their train of wagons into a circle to make an enclosed stockade and sang or talked by their campfires. And on Sundays they worshiped their God. Then was fulfilled the promise of the hymn:

> Jesus, where'er Thy people meet,
> There they behold Thy Mercy-seat,
> Where'er they seek Thee, Thou art found,
> And every place is hallowed ground.

After their arrival in the Oregon country, one of the earliest reports to appear in a church magazine came from a certain Disciple, apparently a layman, who had baptized his son-in-law and was gathering a congregation of believers.

Instances like these recurred thousands of times in as many different places during the first century of our national life. It was not the clergy that kept the church alive, but the "lay" believers. Through their faithfulness the faith continued. They waited hungrily for the coming of ministers, in order that they might hear the proclamation of the Word, and the work of pioneer preachers built up the churches through evangelism and edification. But often it took a circuit rider two or three months to make his appointed rounds. The Christians held fast without a pastor because they looked to the great Shepherd and Bishop of their souls. The church endured through the continuity of a living faith.

Here is a fact of which we would remind our brethren who discuss the continuity of the church in an ecumenical setting. When we hear an archbishop of an ancient church say, "The One Holy Catholic and Apostolic Church . . . is the Greek Orthodox Church," [8] we can respond only by bearing witness to the way in which the Lord has called us. When the arguments for a certain type of succession are pressed, we cannot help crying out: "Where was this one true church when we were baptized into Christ? What were its apostolic bishops doing when the gospel was preached to us? We have never consciously rebelled against the one true church. But this we know: we were called by the gospel out of darkness into his marvelous light." We must bear witness to the actions of the Lord of history as he has made himself known to us. Not through particular forms and traditions, but through the continuity of a living faith, has he graciously maintained the church in our midst.

One American churchman has gone so far as to write that if a copy of the New Testament were to be washed up on the shores of an island where Christ was not known, if it were

---

[8] See "Address by Archbishop Athenagoras" in Oliver S. Tomkins (ed.), *The Third World Conference on Faith and Order* (New York: Harper, 1953), p. 126.

read, if the gospel were believed and obeyed, if the believers baptized one another and met on the first day of the week for the Lord's Supper—here would be a true church, constituted by faith in the living Word, continuous through the present action of the Holy Spirit with the church of the apostles.[9] Whatever we may think of this hypothesis, the living faith which maintained the life of our churches has come down to us as a most precious heritage. Reports from churches under persecution indicate that in troubled lands, again in our own time, religion has become a matter of personal faithfulness and family worship, without the liturgy or clerical ministration. Thus the experience of others confirms our own and the Lord of history reveals to our eyes once more the power of his Spirit to maintain the continuity of a living faith.

THE SPIRIT OF INDEPENDENCE

Since individualism and localism were two traits of the frontiersman's character, and since most of the western churches came into being largely through the initiative of the pioneers themselves, it is not surprising that many of these churches subscribed to theories of congregational government and self-sufficiency. The mood of self-sufficiency which characterized the pioneer had been given special sanction by the Declaration of Independence; that was to him not merely a document associated with a particular historical event, but rather a principle of living.

The spirit asserted itself quite early in our history. During the colonial period violent objections were expressed against the appointment of a bishop, whether Anglican or Roman Catholic, in our part of the world. The opposition came largely from persons of other communions who feared political overlordship and was so vehement that some Anglicans also shared in it on grounds of expediency. Because the ecclesiastical authorities in the Old World were reluctant to appoint bishops for the colonies, we had no episcopal figure of our own until we had become a nation.

[9] Dean E. Walker, *The Authority of the Word* (Milligan, Tenn.: Milligan College Press, 1950), p. 21.

In 1784 Francis Asbury refused to accept appointment by John Wesley as superintendent of the Methodist churches in America until he had been elected by the ministers themselves in the Christmas Conference at Baltimore. Even more striking was the special concession by the Pope in 1789 permitting the priests of the United States to elect their first bishop, John Carroll, and to select the location of his see, Baltimore. One of the stormy periods in the history of Roman Catholicism on our shores came when laymen attempted to assert the right of choosing their own priest and rejecting him at will, as the members of neighboring churches could do; only after battles in the courts did the bishops succeed in establishing absolute control over the church buildings in their dioceses, to which the local trustees had laid claim. The Roman Church succeeded in overruling independency, at least in its more violent expressions: in some other communions it was elevated into a principle.

In 1803 when an attempt was made to gather the Congregational churches of Massachusetts into an association, Nathaniel Emmons opposed the move, and won the fight, with his famous statement: "Association leads to Consociation; Consociation leads to Presbyterianism; Presbyterianism leads to Episcopacy; Episcopacy leads to Roman Catholicism; and Roman Catholicism is an ultimate fact." On the frontier, local preachers often objected to the missionaries sent out from the East and to the boards who sponsored them, fearing control over their churches. The idea of independence, sometimes carried to extremes, has been enshrined in much American religion. An English bishop used to say that, compared with England, "all churches in America, whatever their polity, are congregational." [10] Figures published in 1943 indicate that ninety-nine denominations in the United States, with 35 per cent of the total church membership, hold to a congregational polity.[11] Our most rapidly growing churches at the present

[10] Willard L. Sperry, *Religion in America* (Cambridge, Mass.: University Press, 1945), p. 9.
[11] *Ibid.*, pp. 283, 284.

time are the Southern Baptists, the Churches of Christ,[12] and the Church of God, and they all adhere to this form of government.

The spirit of independence has made for great vigor in American Christianity on the local scene. It has encouraged a sense of responsibility for doing the Lord's work in one's own situation and has animated a healthy if occasionally obstreperous democracy in our congregational life. The excesses of freedom are often annoying, but our people have learned to exercise responsibility along with liberty and to fear autocracy in religion more than their own mistakes. After the pope issued his heartfelt Christmas appeal in 1949, entreating non-Roman Christians to "come back home" in the interest of unity, one of our well-known authors on religious subjects wondered "what the pope would do with the Protestant nature were Protestants to respond to his invitation." [13] Whimsically she expounded some of the problems which had exercised members of her own communion during the past fifty years and the way in which time, common sense, and democracy had brought a solution to them. Her implication was clear: Rome was never like this.

It must be admitted that some of our most vexing problems arise from an exaggerated independency which expresses itself in a spirit of separatism. Many local congregations have little sense of really belonging to their own denomination as a general spiritual fellowship, to say nothing of participating in the universal church. The process of denominational merger becomes cumbersome when every congregation must vote on a proposal for union, and the independency enshrined in this polity is easily aroused into antiunion sentiment.

Within the various denominations practicing congregational government some searching questions have recently been raised about the assumptions underlying the attitude of ex-

[12] Churches of Christ in the United States are not to be confused with Churches of Christ in Great Britain. The latter are related to Disciples of Christ in America.

[13] Margueritte Harmon Bro, "Problem for the Pope," *Christian Century*, Feb. 8, 1950, pp. 170–172.

treme independency. The narrowness of vision which marks this attitude at its worst is certainly being redeemed by the awakening ecumenical spirit. But when the vigor of these communions is taken into account it is apparent that their polity will remain within American Christianity for a long time to come.

THE CONCERN FOR HUMAN WELFARE

The refugees who fled to the New World "for conscience' sake" cherished deep religious convictions concerning the rights of which they had been deprived in their homeland. Although the Puritan lawgivers of the "New Canaan" in early Massachusetts prescribed religious freedom only for themselves, the trend in America was toward liberty and justice for all, in the name of God. We think of our democracy as inspired by Christian principles, of our common life as standing under the judgment of the Kingdom, of our churches as being legitimately concerned with everyday life and common problems. In the mind of our people, the democratic spirit and the Christian faith belong together. One does not seem to be the foe of the other, as has often been the case in France and Italy. There the social encyclicals of the popes and the self-sacrifice of those present-day priests who have identified themselves with the poor still have not effaced from memory the tenacity with which the feudal church clung to its privileges and opposed the rising movements for popular welfare. On Montmartre I was shown an ancient church with the watchword of the French Revolution—"Liberté, Egalité, Fraternité"—carved over the doorway, and our guide said, "This is the only church in Paris bearing that inscription." (She was wrong, for I saw another.) When the building was taken over by the Revolutionists for use as a warehouse, the motto was placed upon it as a bitter jest. Here is a tragic situation: that democratic and social movements in Europe have often been secular and even anticlerical in motivation. In the providence of God our country was settled by multitudes of the oppressed who combined religion with political theory as a rampart against oppression, and a different mood prevails.

The affirmation cannot be made absolutely. In the early period of American industrialization even the denominations which in frontier days had prided themselves as being "people's churches" too often served as bulwarks of privilege; some champions of the emerging labor movement bitterly resented the unconcern, even opposition, of religious leaders. A determined rearguard of conservative capitalists still seeks to invoke "Christian" sanctions against such policies as government-financed housing, federal aid to education, socialized medicine, or even the graduated income tax. Many of our laymen continue to cling to the practice of racial segregation, refusing to admit its incongruity with their professions of Christianity and democracy. And it must be admitted that most of our church members are involved uncritically in our current prosperity, insensitive to the plight of our own less privileged and to the crying needs of vast parts of the world. Such examples as these, however, represent not so much an ideological conflict between democracy and religion as a failure to apply the faith that is professed.

Some months ago at Gaggio di Piano, in the Communist-dominated province of Bologna, Italy, Don Giuseppe Boninsegna climaxed his efforts to present Christ as a Friend of the laborer. Before the "House of the Worker," a large recreation center erected for the parish, the cardinal archbishop of Bologna dedicated a new bas-relief representing our Lord as a carpenter. It was characterized in news accounts as "the first monument in Italy to depict Christ as a worker." [14] There is nothing new about the idea in the United States. Many of our preachers have also labored. Our churches customarily observe Labor Sunday, for which our National Council of Churches issues an annual message on the Christian implications of work and of current economic issues. We sing a hymn celebrating the Carpenter in whom God was incarnate and who sanctified our daily toil:

> My Master was a Worker with daily work to do,
> And he who would be like Him must be a worker too.

[14] *Time*, Oct. 19, 1953, "Religion."

So welcome honest labor and honest labor's fare,
For where there is a worker, the Master's man is there.

Some of our seminarians spend a period of time in industry; in various ways our churches have been concerned to identify themselves with the life of the people and, in the name of Christ, to strive for human welfare.

The discussion in Chapter II has already given an account of the spiritual base of our democracy and has indicated the spirit out of which Abraham Lincoln could say at Gettysburg, "This nation, under God." Throughout the nineteenth century Christian concern for human welfare largely motivated the popular sentiment against slavery and efforts to prohibit the liquor traffic. The churches sponsored numerous enterprises to aid the "freedmen" after their emancipation in 1863, rendered service on a large scale to immigrant groups who did not speak English, and undertook a ministry in needy areas of the growing industrial cities. The climax of this concern was the emergence of the social gospel movement, which found its ablest spokesman in Walter Rauschenbusch.

Rauschenbusch's concern for a Christian society arose out of his pastoral ministry to a German Baptist congregation in a depressed area of New York City known as "Hell's Kitchen." In 1889 he began to publish a Christian monthly for workingmen and three years later organized the Brotherhood of the Kingdom, a fellowship of ministers sharing his concern. A professor in Rochester Theological Seminary after 1897, he wrote books on various phases of his consuming interest. *Christianizing the Social Order* stated the goal. *Prayers of the Social Awakening* revealed new dimensions in the Lord's Prayer, gave liturgical utterance to the longing for justice, and provided gracious intercessions on behalf of all sorts and conditions of men. *A Theology for the Social Gospel* laid a platform of robust Christian orthodoxy for the movement, discussing the implications for society of the historic doctrines of God, man, sin, redemption, the church; it is a book which still deserves to be read.

Other notable leaders arose, most of them pastors of

churches. Washington Gladden composed the hymn which begins

> O Master, let me walk with Thee
> In lowly paths of service free.

Frank Mason North caught the evangelical spirit of the social gospel at its best:

> Where cross the crowded ways of life,
> Where sound the cries of race and clan,
> Above the noise of selfish strife,
> We hear Thy voice, O Son of Man.
>
> In haunts of wretchedness and need,
> On shadowed threshold dark with fears,
> From paths where lie the lures of greed,
> We catch the vision of Thy tears.
>
> O Master, from the mountainside
> Make haste to heal these hearts of pain.
> Come, with these restless throngs abide,
> O tread the city's streets again.

Francis J. McConnell, Sherwood Eddy, Ernest Fremont Tittle, C. C. Morrison, Kirby Page, Harry Emerson Fosdick, E. Stanley Jones, and many others spoke to the conscience of the nation concerning the demands of the Kingdom of God.

The heart of the social gospel was the concept of the Kingdom as a potential, almost imminent, order in society, an era of peace and brotherhood toward which the processes of history were tending in the purpose of God. In the optimistic days at the beginning of our century, Christians hoped that the worst evils which had beset mankind were about to be banished forever. The abolition of slavery was an accomplished fact. The liquor traffic was being brought under control. It was hoped that war itself would soon be abolished. The *Social Creed*, adopted by the new Federal Council of Churches in 1908, set forth a few additional specifics: equal rights for all men, the principle of conciliation and arbitration in industrial dissensions, the protection of the worker, the abolition of child labor, the reduction of the hours of labor, a living wage, provisions for old age. The early advocates of the social gospel were not as naïve as they are sometimes considered. They believed the transforming grace of Christ to be operative in both individuals and society. The evangelists had long been directing the gospel to the heart of the sinner; they would apply it also to the social order. The complete transformation thus to be realized, they believed, was what Jesus meant by the Kingdom of God. "People will be living in heaven right here in the Scioto Valley," Washington Gladden told his congregation in Columbus, Ohio.

The tragedy of World War I shadowed the last days of Gladden and Rauschenbusch, but a younger generation who had caught their vision continued to proclaim the hope of a better tomorrow. The liberal movement in theology embraced the social gospel, but did not acquire a monopoly on its preaching. Especially during the Great Depression, beginning in 1929, when the minds of laymen were troubled by questions concerning our economic system, many sermons sounded from our pulpits dealing with international relations, unemployment, race relations, and other current problems. The tone was hopeful; if men would turn to the way of Jesus, a better day was at hand. But the rise of fascism and nazism in Europe and the ruthlessness of the Communist purges began to trouble our more thoughtful minds. These were systems that rejected the way of Christ; hope for the future gave way to fear before the demonic depths now revealed in man's nature. The leadership thrust upon the United States after World War II suddenly brought us to realize the complexity of the world's problems and the insufficiency of our idealism in achieving solutions. It was no longer possible to proclaim that "the Kingdom is at hand" with the earlier assurance. At the same time the impact of New Testament scholarship, with its emphasis on the eschatological element in the teaching of Jesus, led to a revision of the understanding of the Kingdom. A mood of "critical realism," symbolized by such men as Reinhold Niebuhr, John C. Bennett, and Walter G. Muelder, came over our Christian social thinking.

Today there is much less of a tendency for Christian leaders to identify the Kingdom, or even the "responsible society" for which Christians must strive, with any particular panacea or program. The spirit of crusade for a better social order has somewhat abated. Both in the seminaries and in the pulpits the zeal for social action has yielded "top priority" to other interests, such as pastoral counseling and the ecumenical concern. Yet the recognition of our social responsibility remains. The obligations of Christians in the matter of human welfare are constantly discussed in our religious journals and conventions, and frequently studied in Sunday-school classes, while most of the major denominations have boards of social education and social action. Some practical expressions of this concern have been the outpouring of material aid at the close of World War II, the increasingly clear line the churches have taken against enforced racial segregation, the efforts of Christian officials in our schools, as well as of young people and ministers, to help dispel mobs when disorder has broken out between whites and Negroes, the personal dedication with which thousands of sincere believers have entered on poorly paid vocations of service to their fellow men. If there has been less serious criticism of the capitalist system than was heard a generation ago, it is because many of its worst abuses have been corrected and because, internally at least, it now seems to be working reasonably well.

Cherishing no romantic hopes in inevitable progress or the imminent elimination of all evil, American Christians are yet determined to work and witness for the "responsible society," praying, "Thy will be done on earth as it is in heaven." If there is confusion in our present social thinking, it arises from the question: "Precisely what do we mean by the Kingdom of God?" We realize that the Kingdom transcends even our fondest, Christ-inspired hopes for the transformation of life, both public and private, on this earth, just as it is present to us by faith even when these hopes are frustrated. Yet we cling to the belief that it has meaning for our life here. We cannot consent to that trend in contemporary theology which excludes the Kingdom from history and leaves us working for human welfare only out of dread of the judgment and in order to gain a bit more time for the proclamation of the gospel. We are unwilling to give up the idea that the sovereignty of God, realized in "the Kingdom that now is," has implications for the bettering of man's life, spiritual and temporal, here and now. To that end we seek to serve our fellows, in obedience to the divine will. The spirit of our concern for human welfare is well expressed in a prayer by Reinhold Niebuhr:

For the Coming of Christ's Kingdom

O God who hast taught us to pray for the coming of thy kingdom on this earth, give us grace to build our communities after the fashion of thy kingdom, to set no boundaries about them which thou wouldst not set, to quiet the tumult and strife within them by brotherly love, and to work the more diligently for concord within them because our final hope is in the city which hath foundations whose builder and maker is God, through Jesus Christ, our Lord. *Amen.*

A "SIMPLE FAITH"

American Christianity tends to minimize the importance of that systematic theological discussion which has played so large a part in the tradition of the Reformation in the Old World. Sometimes the minimizing is so much a matter of course as to be unconscious; in other cases it is explicit. At any rate, it characterizes all American communions when they are compared with their European counterparts—Lutherans, Anglicans, and Roman Catholics quite as well as the so-called democratic churches of the frontier. There are historical reasons. The influence of pietism ran strongly in many of the religious groups which came to the New World; it emphasized experience rather than theology. The missionary situation in which they found themselves turned their minds toward plans for the Christian conquest of the continent and left them little time or energy for ordered speculation. The necessity incumbent upon the evangelist of presenting the gospel in simple and convincing terms to the man in the street discouraged technical theorizing.[15]

The very existence of 268 religious denominations within the nation renders ludicrous the insistence on sectarian peculiarities as a matter of life and death. Not a few of the old particularisms appear idiotic to men whose concern is a Christian witness to the urgent needs of the day; a theology that has fractionalized the Christian witness has lost its appeal. In our denominational schools until the present generation the departments of theology tended to concentrate on apologetics for their own sect, and broad-minded students rebelled not only against the narrowness but also against the discipline by which it was promulgated. Neighbors who attended different churches accepted their separation from one another before the altar of God, but not gladly, and they resented theological debate with its implication that persons holding views divergent from those of the speaker were less acceptable to Him.

To be a Christian meant to love the Lord and to do his will, not to argue interminably about fine points of dogma which seemed to have no practical bearing. The Puritanical moralism of much American preaching through all our history easily falls into legalism and self-righteousness; yet it was a major contribution of our churches to the civilizing of the rude frontier.[16] The "wild men on the Missouri" [17] had no need of an extensive *Dogmatik;* they knew what it meant to forswear drinking and swearing and brawling out of allegiance to Christ, and by his demands and his grace they were changed.

Preaching and instruction for church membership place the emphasis on "life situations," only a minority of our Protestant bodies making use of a catechism. Such a recent book

[15] Some of the insights suggested in this paragraph were set forth in a paper read at the School of Religion, Butler University, in 1952, by Professor Wilhelm Pauck, who knows both Germany and the United States with intimacy. See Wilhelm Pauck, "Theology in the Life of Contemporary American Protestantism," *Shane Quarterly,* XIII (April, 1952), 37–50.

[16] Sweet, *Religion in the Development of American Culture* (New York: Charles Scribner's Sons, 1952), chap. 5, "Barbarism vs. Revivalism."

[17] Quoting a remark of Congressman Josiah Quincy about 1811 in opposing the admission of western territories as states in the Union.

of sermons, for example, as Robert Luccock's *If God Be for Us,* while it reflects the deepening theological mood of recent years, is not a series of didactic essays. It deals in pastoral fashion with the practical outcome of our faith and it manifests a general concern of the American pulpit: to bring God redemptively into the experience of men by showing what his grace means in the specific problems which they face.

The growth of advanced theological education for our ministers during the past two generations has been phenomenal. In the nineteenth century Presbyterians, Lutherans, and Episcopalians maintained the most rigid standards of clerical training, and Congregationalists some of the finest seminaries, among Protestant bodies, but the vast majority of our ministry, especially in the West, had not studied "divinity." Within the past two generations, however, Methodists, Baptists, Disciples, and other communions have developed outstanding seminaries, and the proportion of pastors holding a Bachelor of Divinity degree is on the increase. Our seminarians and younger ministers are perhaps more interested in systematic theology than any generation of religious leaders since those of colonial New England. There is much reading of Kierkegaard, Barth, Brunner, Nygren, Dodd, Niebuhr, and Tillich. Yet the accent is different from that in Europe. Along with courses in exegesis and dogmatics our seminaries emphasize many practical subjects which do not appear, or which hold a minor place, in the Continental curriculum. It seems highly unlikely that in any foreseeable future the American churches will elevate theological interest to the dominant place it holds among German Lutherans, for example.

The simple faith that has risen and flourished in the United States is an important datum from Christian history and its significance for theology needs to be considered. What does it mean that, quite apart from elaborate systems of dogma, a belief in Jesus Christ as Son of God, Savior and Lord, has commanded the devotion of millions of faithful men and women, that it has resulted in strong, life-changing churches, that in spite of the multifarious separations imposed by historical circumstances it has produced a strong ecumenical con-

science and a growing sense of mutual responsibility among
Christians, that it has kept a large bloc of noncreedal churches
as free from heresy as those communions whose teaching is
protected by elaborate confessional symbols? Perhaps one of
the major needs of theology is an honest examination of its
own role in the life of the church. It is far from our purpose
to suggest that there is virtue in intellectual laziness, sloppi-
ness, or dishonesty; the Christian must abhor them all. But a
generation which has become as enamored of theology as ours
may well remind itself that the most imposing of dogmatic
systems is but a transient human artifact, bearing an altogether
inadequate witness to the good news which has been made
known in Jesus Christ. In his *Römerbrief*, Karl Barth elo-
quently described the struggle and demise of one theology
after another as a primeval battle of the jungle, each beast
yielding in turn to a younger with more powerful horns and
sharper teeth.[18] Christ, not theology, is the Lord of the
church.

The "simple gospel" proclaimed by the American churches
is not essentially a matter of rationalism or liberalism, but of
grace for all. Nearly all the factors mentioned earlier as con-
tributing to the nontheological spirit of our faith are much
older and run much deeper than the liberal tendency to discount the importance of dogma. The emphasis on simplicity is
in part a Christian application of democracy. Our preachers
have often quoted a saying attributed to Abraham Lincoln:
"God must have loved the common people, he made so many
of them." So the accent in our preaching has been not so much
propositional as personal—an effort to commend to all men the
Friend of Sinners. It has drawn inspiration especially from the
Gospels and from the mystical passages in St. Paul. Faith is
conceived in terms of a personal relationship to the living
Lord,[19] celebrated in sentimental gospel songs like "In the
Garden" and "He Is So Precious to Me," and well-loved

[18] Karl Barth, *The Epistle to the Romans*, translated by Edwyn C. Hos-
kyns (London: Oxford University Press, 1950), p. 372.
[19] George A. Buttrick, *Interpreter's Bible* (New York: Abingdon-Cokes-
bury, 1951), VII, pp. 276, 277 (Matt. 4:19).

hymns such as "Jesus, Lover of My Soul," "O Jesus, I Have Promised," and "O Master, Let Me Walk with Thee." Generation after generation hosts of believers have rejoiced in "the simplicity that is in Christ" (2 Cor. 11:3). For he is the center of our faith.

V.

The Search for Unity

Probably no aspect of the American religious scene is so bewildering to the European churchman as the number and variety of our sectarian divisions. Our freedom and individualism have produced a diversity of faiths that must be inconceivable to a Spaniard or a Swede. The Old World reads with dismay of 268 different churches in the United States and thanks God that Europe has been spared from such a fate: someone has even likened our complex array of churches to an "ecclesiastical zoo." Yet there are reasons for our religious diversity, and in that freedom within which it arose we are now seeking the oneness which God intends for his church. In our peculiar circumstances, compelling practical reasons add their force to the scriptural demand for Christian unity.

COMPETITION AMONG DENOMINATIONS

Of the 100 million Americans making a formal religious profession in 1955, 58.3 per cent are Protestants, 33.3 per cent are Roman Catholics, 2.4 per cent are Orthodox, and 5.6 per cent are members of non-Christian faiths (Judaism, Buddhism, Bahai, etc.). While the proportion of our people claiming a religious affiliation is on the increase, the strength of the major professions in relation to one another has remained virtually constant for a generation. (Of our 14 million Negroes, 8.3 million are church members; 8 million are Protestants, most of them being Baptists, and most of the rest Methodists.)

Sources of denominationalism. Americans are grateful for the liberty in which our more than two hundred denominations live and for the religious vitality which expresses itself in such diverse forms. We are not proud of our divisons. A generaton ago one of our ecumenical pioneers, Peter Ainslie of Baltimore, characterized our sectarianism as *The Scandal of Christianity*. But we cannot wish all these groups out of existence; they claim the religious freedom to which we all are entitled. No ruler bearing the sword by divine right will undertake to harry dissenters out of the land. Anyone in the country is entitled to gather a group of fellow believers about him, and many have availed themselves of the opportunity. It is instructive to inquire into the sources of the diversity which has ensued upon our practice of religious freedom.

The basic pattern of disunity was imported from Europe. At the time we became a nation we already had in our midst Episcopalians, Congregationalists, Presbyterians (regular and Seceder), Reformed (Dutch and German), Baptists, Friends, Roman Catholics, Swedish Lutherans, Mennonites, Dunkers, Moravians, Schwenkfelders, and Methodists. Many of these came to our shores because their faith was not tolerated in the Old World. Later immigration complicated the picture. We received all sorts of Lutherans, who organized separate denominations on the basis of language—German, Swedish, Norwegian, Danish, Finnish, Latvian, Slovak. We welcomed Orthodox—again separately organized—from Greece, Serbia, Romania, Russia, and Syria. This catalogue does not begin to exhaust the varieties of sects which came to us from Europe.

But the situation soon grew even more complex, with divisions over new issues. Speaking purely in terms of power politics (a subject about which, unhappily, neither the churches of Europe nor those of America are ignorant), it is easier to start a new group or to carry off a faction than to gain control of a whole denomination. Many schisms have occurred in our religious history, only a few of which can be mentioned. Baptists, Presbyterians, and Methodists all divided over slavery; only the last-named have been reunited. Baptists and Methodists suffered additional separations on grounds of race. Internal disputes caused other schisms producing Cumberland Presbyterians, Wesleyan Methodists, Free Methodists, Particular Baptists, and many more. A division occurred between Congregationalists and Unitarians over the rigid doctrines of orthodox Calvinism, between Disciples of Christ and Churches of Christ over "innovations," between the National Baptist Convention, U.S.A., Inc., and the National Baptist Convention of America over control of a publishing house.

New communions arose as the result of a particular religious experience or from the desire to meet a special need. The Evangelical Synod began essentially as a group of German-speaking Methodists. The Church of God (several varieties), the Church of the Nazarene, the Assemblies of God, the Pilgrim Holiness Church have been at the cutting edge of evangelism. The Church of Jesus Christ of Latter-day Saints (Mormons) and the Church of Christ, Scientist—both have known divisions—went beyond the limits of traditional Protestantism but have won many adherents. Other denominations, ironically, evolved out of movements intended to overcome division. The Christian Churches in Kentucky and the Disciples of Christ represented two such efforts on the frontier and succeeded in uniting with each other. The Churches of Christ in Christian Union hoped to realize a fellowship of brethren transcending the partisanship over slavery which led to our Civil War. The Community Churches sought to bring all followers of Christ in a given neighborhood into one nonsectarian congregation.

The denominational multiplicity in our land has resulted in the loss of a sense of the "Great Church." In contrast with the situation in Europe, there is among us no corporate memory of a time when all the Christians of our nation were one. We were divided from the start. So there is no feeling of incongruity in the heart of a zealous man if he gathers a new congregation related to no other. If converts continue to "come forward" in his Bible Tabernacle, he interprets the growth of his flock as the blessing of God upon his work. And if he is given grace to plant an additional congregation or two after the same pattern, a new denomination has been born. Against such a concept the ecumenical vision has had to make its way in America.

Yet among the 268 denominations, 82 bodies include 98.4 per cent of the total membership (that is to say that 186 of the bodies are almost infinitesimal) and 75 per cent of the non-Roman Christians are found in five major confessional families. For example, there are twenty-seven Baptist denominations (18.8 million members), twenty-two Methodist (11.7 million), eighteen Lutheran (7 million); these three families alone account for 67 denominations and 37 million Christians.

Eighteen American denominations claimed a membership of a million or more in 1955:

1.	Roman Catholic Church	33,396,647
2.	Methodist Church	9,292,046
3.	Southern Baptist Convention	8,467,439
4.	Jewish Congregations	5,500,000
5.	National Baptist Convention, U.S.A., Inc.	4,557,416
6.	Protestant Episcopal Church	2,757,944
7.	Presbyterian Church, U.S.A.	2,645,745
8.	National Baptist Convention of America	2,610,774
9.	United Lutheran Church	2,175,726
10.	Lutheran Church—Missouri Synod	2,004,110
11.	Disciples of Christ	1,897,736
12.	Churches of Christ	1,600,000
13.	Christ Unity Science Church	1,581,286
14.	American Baptist Convention	1,513,697
15.	Congregational-Christian Churches	1,342,045
16.	Church of Jesus Christ of Latter-day Saints	1,230,021
17.	African Methodist Episcopal	1,166,301
18.	Greek Archdiocese of North and South America	1,000,000

These eighteen bodies include the vast majority of American believers.

Sectarianism in action. One of the fruits of multiplicity has been competition among the denominations. Originally nearly every group cherished the conviction that it alone was right.

The old established churches of Europe thought of themselves in such a way, as did the "sects" that broke off from them; and in both instances their notion of being alone pleasing to God migrated to the New World. The evangelistic opportunities and rapid expansion in America led the adherents of more than one confession to believe that the "true faith" (their own) would ultimately "take the country." Today such an impression lingers only with a few—Roman Catholics, Southern Baptists, and Churches of Christ, for example (and a member of any of these three may find some reasons to justify his optimism). Yet in spite of the bigotry and unseemly competition which have at times been in evidence, it must be said that the sense of mission to extend one's own denomination has been a source of great vitality. It was a primary motive in the evangelism of the nineteenth century.

Until recently there has been little hesitancy about "proselyting" (although ministers who suffered the loss of members dubbed the practice "sheep-stealing"). One does not have to go too far back in denominational journals to find listed under the reports of evangelism such triumphant items as the following: "Twenty-five additions—fourteen by primary obedience, five from the Methodists, and six from the Baptists." Within some communions this frame of mind still prevails, and they energetically send missionaries to Germany, Italy, and Greece. The Greek Orthodox churchman in Europe is deeply wounded by attempts on the part of foreign evangelists to "convert" him to another church. A zealous American, reared in an atmosphere of religious liberty, sees the matter purely as an issue of his freedom to carry out the Great Commission; if he comes from the far left wing of Protestantism he may even regard the Orthodox as "almost as bad as the Catholics" and "in need of the gospel." One ecumenical problem is to help Christians of such diverse outlooks understand one another's position in the matter of proselytism. Meanwhile, the Southern Baptists remain aloof from the World Council of Churches, and one of their reasons is the Orthodox protest against proselytism; to the Baptists such an objection seems a denial of religious liberty.

Americans speak of the free competition of ideas in the market place of public opinion, and they are not shocked to see religious systems of thought and loyalty set in competition with one another. Yet from a Christian standpoint not all the results have been happy. Unrestricted denominational competition has resulted in a weakening of the Christian witness, a fracturing of community life, a *reductio ad absurdum* of sectarian peculiarities. The Babel of conflicting creeds is most discordant on the radio; every kind of preacher who can raise funds to pay for the time may be heard on the air, and the extreme sectarian varieties are heard most often. Still, the gospel is preached and the benefits of freedom are available to all.

THE NONEXISTENCE OF THE PARISH

The shattering effect of denominational competition is most painfully felt in local communities. Without an ecclesiastical establishment, we in America have no experience of the medieval concept of the parish in its true sense. In nearly every community there is a multiplicity of churches.

Competitive congregations. After we became a nation, the pattern of settlement was largely individualistic. A man or a family went west and took up land. Among their neighbors considerable religious diversity prevailed. Preachers of different denominations traveled through the back country, holding services and gathering groups of believers. The result was the founding of several congregations in the same community, whether rural or urban. Often the various church buildings still face each other—two, or three, or four of them at a given corner. Today there is usually a spirit of co-operation and fellowship among such religious neighbors; but it was not always so. Their noticeboards sometimes bear an ironic witness: on one street in Oklahoma City a Church of God stands on one corner and a competing Church of Christ on the next.

There are a few exceptions to the pattern of neighborhood multiplicity, for some rural areas were settled by a particular religious community. Numbers of Mennonites, Lutherans, Waldensians, or Roman Catholics from Southern Europe would go west in a group, take up adjoining tracts of farm-land, and erect a church at the center of their settlement. Usually such companies were non-English-speaking, although some Baptists followed this procedure and (most celebrated of all) so did the Mormons. Today these old self-contained rural "parishes" are losing their distinctive character. Public education and the passing of the old language, intermarriage with "Gentiles," more mobile methods of transportation, the removal of families to other places, a failure to hold the younger generation—all these factors have broken down the boundaries enclosing such communities. Some of them have already experienced the incursion of other denominations.

Particular communions, of course, maintain their own parish systems. But the lines of a Roman Catholic, Protestant Episcopal, or Lutheran parish apply only to the members of the communion involved, not to the community as a whole. In most instances a majority of the people living in the "parish" are members of other denominations. The minister's primary ties are with his flock; to the entire community living within his "parish" he is related only personally, not officially.

As to its status in the community, then, every church is a "free church." No one congregation automatically enjoys a favored standing because it is of a particular confession. Perhaps the size of its building, a historic connection with a local college, or some such factor gives a particular church some eminence in one town, but in the next another denomination will hold first place. And all are equal before the law.

As to its internal life, every church is a gathered church. Its members are only such persons as have been brought to-gether in a covenant of commitment (and perhaps their children). It can lay no claim to the people of its community except as it presses on them the claims of the gospel and they voluntarily respond.

The relation of a congregation to the surrounding com-munity is not so simple or direct as that of a European church to its parish. Membership is drawn from a wider area because in any one vicinity there are several churches. Not only do the "parishes" of the different denominations overlap; so do those of the same denomination, in many instances. In fact, many American denominations have no sense of "parish" at all. A given communion will have a First Church near the heart of a city and other congregations in various neighborhoods. When members of First Church move to the suburbs, a few transfer their membership to a congregation nearer their new home, but many continue to drive to First Church the rest of their lives, often going right by another church of their own persuasion to get there. Neighborhood churches belonging to the same denomination may not even have a "gentleman's agreement" among themselves as to the territorial lines of their responsibility. They do not always look upon themselves as being in overt competition with one another, though at times they may be; in the thinking of the typical religious worker his congregation has been planted in a likely place and should seek to reach all the people it can.

An artificial community. An American congregation, therefore, is coterminous with no other existing community; it must create its own "community." A family known to the author illustrates the problem. The father worked in St. Louis, Missouri, but they lived in the suburb of Kirkwood, fifteen miles distant, and the children went to school there. Because Kirkwood had no congregation of their persuasion, the family went to church in Webster Groves, another suburb about five miles away. Many other members of that church also lived in Kirkwood or Brentwood or Maplewood or University City. So it was a "spiritual" or a "doctrinal" community, and thus an "artificial community." (The term "artificial community" simply indicates that it is created, that it corresponds to no other existing community.) For the family concerned, a practical question arose out of this situation. On Sunday evening should the young people attend the Christian Youth Fellowship in Webster Groves, where they went to church, or the Westminster Fellowship in Kirkwood, where they went to school?

In its concern for its own institutional life, a congregation has to draw people in by conversion and hold them in loyalty, just to maintain its existence. Hence it finds itself in competition with other churches for the community's resources of men and money. Such competition sometimes extends even to other congregations of its own denomination. Since a church is related primarily to an artifical community, it may frequently change location, following its membership and the source of its financial support. The typical urban congregation in America, if it is of any age at all (say a hundred years), has moved several times in its history. Sometimes it may move fifteen miles. A church centers in the artificial community of its membership rather than in a geographical spot. When it moves, its abandoned building may be sold for use by another denomination, perhaps by a congregation of its own denomination but of another race, or even for business purposes.

Because we do not know the tradition of the parish system in its full sense, our churches are not marked by a sense of territorial responsibility. They tend to think in terms of building themselves up, a process which is considered good for all whose lives are thus brought within the sphere of Christian influence. But in a parish, a city, or a state no one denomination is in a position to assume responsibility for the total life of the community. Because of its long history in the Old World, its exclusive claims, and its magnitude as the largest single religious body among us the Roman Catholic Church does think of its ministry in regional terms, from the parish to the nation. Its local churches stay "nailed down" and continue to serve the changing stream of humanity that flows by a particular spot. But it would be out of the question for the Presbyterians in Pennsylvania, with their limited resources, to assume that they alone were responsible for the moral and spiritual welfare of the whole state; the Southern Baptists might more effectively make such an assumption in Texas, but even they could only partially discharge so great an obligation.

There is always the danger that a church will "feed on" its community rather than serve it. (The danger is not limited to the United States, nor does the concept of a territorial ministry eliminate it.) Instances come to mind of too many sectarian congregations shattering the unity of life in a small town and "cannibalizing" its resources. The flight of the churches from great areas of urban blight is a shame to American Protestantism. From the danger of seeking to be ministered unto and not to minister the church can be delivered only by its faithfulness to the gospel and by co-operative planning. Increasingly our councils of churches—local, state, and national—as they grow in strength and experience are making possible a united Christian witness and a more adequate ministry to the whole community.

Some of our deepest problems in American Christianity arise from the fact that the cohesion among the members of a congregation tends to derive from social homogeneity. We do not solve them simply by disparaging "class churches." The situation is almost inevitable in our circumstances. Ostensibly our churches are constituted on loyalty to a particular spiritual tradition. But actually a congregation and even a denomination tends to become the church of a particular social or economic group. H. Richard Niebuhr documented the problem twenty years ago in his *Social Sources of Denominationalism*. A church does not necessarily remain at the original level; in its history it "moves up the ladder" of respectability as its members do socially, and it is itself partially responsible for their rise. There are, of course, shining exceptions to the rule of class churches. During his ministry at Madison Avenue Presbyterian Church in New York, Henry Sloane Coffin helped achieve a true Christian fellowship that embraced the very wealthy and the very poor. Many other examples could be cited. Every congregation that allows itself to be touched at all by the gospel it proclaims attains some degree of inclusiveness. As long as a congregation remains an artificial community, however, the danger of exclusiveness is imminent, even if not always actualized. Many a parish church in Europe, it must quickly be added, fails to achieve true Christian fellowship among all its members; our peril in America may be only an exaggerated form of a constant threat to the church's wholeness.

The fact that nearly every Protestant congregation in America represents an artificial, gathered community rather than a geographical community throws light on the problem of integrating Negroes, or members of other minority groups, into the life of dominantly white churches (or vice versa). The pattern throughout our history has been to form separate congregations—even denominations—on the basis of ethnic, linguistic, cultural, and economic, as well as theological, peculiarities. Only as the "melting pot" of Americanization has removed the original distinctions have the religious institutions coalesced. So much of our church program—our evangelism, our Christian nurture, our service—centers in the *fellowship* of the artificial community that rarely have we succeeded in incorporating into congregational life persons with whom we do not normally experience social contact. Hence the paradox of our voting in our denominational conventions year after year to approve racial integration in industry, in the armed forces, and in the public schools while for the most part we retain our segregated congregations. It may be expected that as members of different races become acquainted with one another in the "secular" walks of life they will find themselves entering into increasing religious fellowship with one another. Thus American Protestantism stands in the unenviable position of following rather than leading the world in the practice of racial brotherhood, even though we have proclaimed the principle for a long time. At this point the ability of the Roman Catholic Church to receive Negroes and members of other minorities into its life finds at least a partial explanation. Precisely because participation in confession and the Mass is impersonal and involves a minimum of social contact, white Roman congregations can accept Negroes more readily than do Protestant churches.

Yet Protestant churches are making progress. In 1948 only 4.8 per cent of Protestant congregations in the United States were interracial. By 1954 the figure had risen to 10 per cent. First Christian Church in Yakima, Washington, provides a heartening example. Typical of the large county-seat congregation, it is basically middle class, aggressive in evangelism, well organized in its various departments, setting the pace for other churches in its communion in stewardship and in giving to missions and benevolence, not motivated by any doctrinaire tendencies toward social radicalism. But the seriousness with which it faces its evangelistic responsibility has led it beyond the closed circle that so often limits the fellowship of our congregations. This church has baptized Indians, Chinese, Negroes, and Filipinos, and members of the ethnic minorities share in the various responsibilities of congregational life. Christ Church, the Protestant Episcopal cathedral in the heart of metropolitan St. Louis, offers another instance of a fellowship unrestricted by racial barriers. The processional by the boys' choir at the beginning of the morning worship dramatically represents the varied congregation. Black faces and white and brown peer above the vestments, youthful voices blending in the harmonies of praise, all advancing toward the altar of God "with the cross of Jesus going on before."

There are great values in the fellowship of a gathered church, as was shown in Chapter IV. But our peculiar danger in America is that instead of really creating a new and holy community that cuts across other lines we merely sanctify a congeniality that already exists outside the church. We have much yet to learn from the Christian community in India, which in heroic divergence from the mores of the surrounding pagan society refuses in its own life to recognize caste distinctions. In so far as a Christian congregation is limited by lines circumscribing a group or class in the world it must miss the richness of that full fellowship in which there is neither Jew nor Greek, slave nor free, male nor female, but one man in Christ.

WAYS OF EXPRESSING OUR UNITY

Out of the practical problems created by our divisions our American concern for Christian unity has arisen. In thousands of instances we are confronted by pressing needs—to eliminate unseemly competition for the resources of our neighborhoods, to enable the church to serve a whole community rather than a fraction of it, to realize within our congregations the fullness of the Christian fellowship. Consequently, our ecumenical interest tends to be dominantly pragmatic rather than ideological in motivation. It is our common sense, even more than our theology, which has told us that the church ought to be united, or at any rate less divided. The National Council of Churches and the World Council have emerged for us as symbols of a common Christian responsibility, and we applaud their various affirmations of unity. On the other hand, many among us have been bewildered, if not frustrated, by theological disputations in ecumenical circles, especially by analyses of "our differences" emerging from Faith and Order. The typical American is not sure that he knows how to bring about Christian unity, but he expects ecumenical leaders to show him the way, not to confuse him by presenting subtle new difficulties.

Early demonstrations of unity. In the practical realm, American Christians have long been seeking to overcome the weaknesses imposed by our divisions and to manifest the unity which arises from our faith in one Lord. The earliest efforts were personal or unofficial. During the nineteenth century individual believers from various communions banded together in associations for specific Christian purposes. Some of these were the YMCA, the YWCA, the Woman's Christian Temperance Union, the Anti-Saloon League, the Student Volunteers for Foreign Missions. In many communities there arose ministerial associations open to all Protestant pastors, and sometimes including Jewish rabbis or Roman priests. On its more grandiose international scale, the Evangelical Alliance attracted the enthusiastic attention of outstanding American ecclesiastics, some of whom packed eagerly off to Europe to attend its rallies. With the organization of an American branch in 1867, and the subsequent formation of branch alliances in local communities, it began to touch people where they lived. As many as fifty thousand churches are said to have shared in its annual Week of Prayer.

A more organic type of co-operation among congregations also appeared. County Sunday-school associations brought together officers, teachers, and pupils from the Protestant churches in a given area for the purpose of inspiration and instruction; in most of our cities a united school for the training of teachers is still an annual event. Before the emergence of denominational youth programs, county and state Christian Endeavor unions promoted co-operation among the young people's organizations in the churches.

In villages and towns, as well as in the various neighborhoods of our larger cities, "union services" are a familiar feature of our religious life. On Sunday evenings during the summer, on Thanksgiving, at sunrise on Easter, on Reformation Sunday, during periods of common evangelistic effort, the members of the different congregations in a community come together on common ground, with their several ministers sharing in the leadership. The author's earliest "ecumenical experience" was in such meetings where Baptists, Methodists, Presbyterians, Disciples, Mennonites, and others worshiped together in the easy familiarity of small-town life and in common loyalty to our Lord. As a rule, both ministers and people have favored such combined undertakings and have derived spiritual profit from them. Yet there has been no marked increase in them during the past two generations. The reason is not so much theological as institutional: a minister must keep an active program "going" in his own congregation in order to maintain its *esprit de corps;* hence united activities are almost always marginal, when "there is everything to gain and nothing to lose."

Councils of churches. An effective witness to the increasing sense of solidarity among American Protestant and Orthodox Christians is the National Council of Churches, which has emerged from more than two generations of experience in denominational co-operation. The National Council was constituted at Cleveland, Ohio, in December, 1950, by the action of thirty member churches, incorporating into one body the activities of eight previous interdenominational associations. Oldest of these was the International Council of Religious Education, with a history going back to 1881; probably the best known was the Federal Council of Churches of Christ in America, founded in 1908. Other merging agencies had long experience of co-operation in home missions, foreign missions, missionary education, stewardship, higher education, and women's work. Their various activities have found a place in the life of the National Council with its four divisions—Life and Work, Christian Education, Home Missions, and Foreign Missions—and its general departments of United Church Men and United Church Women.

Thirty American communions (with a total membership of 36.7 million in 1955) constitute the National Council of Churches: African Methodist Episcopal Church, African Methodist Episcopal Zion Church, American Baptist Convention, American Evangelical Lutheran Church, Augustana Evangelical Lutheran Church, Christian Methodist Episcopal Church, Church of the Brethren, Congregational Christian Churches, Disciples of Christ, Evangelical and Reformed Church, Evangelical United Brethren Church, Evangelical Unity of the Czech-Moravian Brethren in North America, the Five Years Meeting of Friends, Religious Society of Friends of Philadelphia and Vicinity, Greek Orthodox Church in America, The Methodist Church, The Moravian Church (Unitas Fratrum), National Baptist Convention of America, National Baptist Convention U.S.A., Inc., Presbyterian Church in the U.S., Presbyterian Church in the U.S.A., Protestant Episcopal Church, Reformed Church in America, Romanian Orthodox Episcopate of America, Russian Orthodox Greek Catholic Church of America, Seventh-Day Baptists, Syrian Antiochian Orthodox Church, Ukrainian Orthodox Church of America, United Lutheran Church in America, United Presbyterian Church of North America. The adherents of these churches comprise more than 60 per cent of the Protestant and Orthodox membership in the United States.

What does this varied host of Christians manage to do together? In reporting the third biennial meeting, held at Boston in 1954, the *Christian Century* presented the following summary of achievements:

1. In four years the National Council has brought nearly all the forms of Protestant and Orthodox inter-church cooperation into relation with each other in one organization.

2. The organization has advanced a good way into putting its own house in order and in winning for itself as the instrument of the churches freedom to consider and to speak publicly on national issues of current importance.

3. The council has greatly advanced the study of the Bible by publishing the Revised Standard Version and by promoting its circulation and use.

4. The churches have aided each other in good works through the council, whose department of Church World Service has brought into this country 62,644 refugees and has sent out 55 million pounds of food, clothing and medicine. It is launching a $7.5 million program to "share our surplus," and another effort to bring more refugees to this country under the law.

5. The council has organized chaplaincies on seagoing vessels and in the national parks.

6. It has set up 393 religious radio and TV programs, some continuing through the year, has opened religious radio stations in Tokyo and Seoul, has completed the first citywide study of the effect of TV on children and family life.

7. Its publishing program has issued more than a million books, has coordinated Sunday school materials for 35 million children, has developed and published a Sunday school curriculum for Spanish-speaking America.

8. Its work includes a million children in weekday schools of religion and three million in daily vacation Bible schools.

9. Its program serves 300,000 agricultural migrants and an equal number of people in atomic defense communities.

10. It has united 471 church colleges in a study of religion on the campuses. It serves 250 colleges with interdenominational religious programs.

11. It aids 100 foreign students in colleges and theological seminaries and arranges interchanges of American and British preachers.

12. It supervises and helps 50 overseas union churches for Americans living abroad.[1]

The General Board of the council puts forth occasional statements expressing the common Christian conscience on questions of public concern, and at its General Assembly the council issues a "Letter to the Christian People of America."

[1] *Christian Century*, Dec. 15, 1954, pp. 1512, 1513.

On various questions before the churches and the nation, such utterances affirm the spirit of American Christianity.

State and local councils of churches are increasingly important expressions of our religious life; in 1954 there were 925 known councils of churches in the United States, 236 of which had an employed staff. In all honesty, it must be admitted that many of these councils have a difficult struggle to keep going. The intensive programs of our congregations are closely geared to the life of their denominations, first of all, and only in quite secondary fashion to their association with other types of churches in their own communities. A minister's professional standing and his "opportunities for advancement," career-wise, are within his denomination and depend on successful prosecution of its program. The layman's religious loyalties center in his local church: it is a tangible institution with a demanding round of activities and a meaningful fellowship; the council of churches is difficult for him to visualize and its activities are removed from the normal center of his religious life. Probably not until we place a much heavier theological emphasis on the obligation to unity which derives from the very nature of the church rather than relying on mere pragmatic arguments for co-operation will our local councils receive the measure of support they so desperately need. Especially in our Southern cities where the largest denomination—and in many localities the two largest denominations—make a virtue of aloofness from co-operation, do our councils of churches have a difficult time. When all the congregations which are willing to co-operate constitute a minority of the Christian forces in a community, the possibilities for significant witness and service are limited.

The activity of these agencies falls largely in the areas of Christian education and Life and Work. Neither the National Council (including its predecessors) nor the typical local council has given much attention to questions of Faith and Order. In preparation for the North American Study Conference on Faith and Order at Oberlin in September, 1957, however, many local councils for the first time set up programs of theological discussion. Wide use was made of Professor Paul Minear's pamphlet, *Ecumenical Conversations on the Nature of the Unity We Seek*. Still the average American pastor tends to think of the "ecumenical attitude" as one which minimizes denominational differences and works quietly to overcome them while emphasizing common Christian activities of worship, preaching, evangelism, religious education, social action, and community service.

Local experiments in unity. In many places such an ecumenical attitude has not been content with the creation of a council of churches; it has sought to achieve outright Christian union in the local community. It is in the neighborhood, as we have seen, that the damaging effects of sectarianism are most keenly felt. In such circumstances, however, the American traits of localism and independence have not always been anarchical. Some neighboring congregations of different confessions have proceeded to solve the problem of reunion right in their own bailiwicks, even though their parent denominations were not yet ready to unite. Sometimes the pinch of a declining local economy or the lack of sufficient lay leadership to keep two or more congregations going has been a factor in such unions. But, generally speaking, the positive conviction of a common Christian commitment has been as large an influence as the negative realization that separate congregations could no longer carry on effectively.

One scheme of local union produces a congregation known as a "federated church." It is a way of eating one's denominational cake and having it too. The members of two or more congregations unite as one local congregation, while still adhering formally to their respective denominations. The membership roll of the new church is subdivided into, let us say, Methodist and Presbyterian lists, depending on previous status or the choice of each new convert. Usually there is an agreement that a pastor will be selected in turn from each communion involved, in accordance with the procedures it normally follows, and a ratio is agreed upon for the distribution of missionary and benevolent offerings to the denominational boards. The minister attempts to take some part in the general activities of the two (or more) communions to which the congregation is related. While maintaining this sort of ambivalence in its broader relationships, the federated church acts as one congregation in its own interior life and, after a time, the members no longer give much thought to the subdivisions of the roll. By this plan many communities shattered by sectarianism have found wholeness; it is perhaps the most effective scheme of local union where several congregations already exist. Of course, successful federation is most likely between congregations of similar outlook: a combination of Presbyterians and Congregationalists or of Baptists and Disciples is frequent; one would hardly find a Lutheran-Nazarene union.

The "community church" plan made a great appeal to liberals a generation ago. Essentially it was a scheme for constituting a congregation on a geographical rather than a confessional basis. Any person holding membership in any Christian denomination was accepted on his own terms as a member of the community church in a certain place. Impatient with sectarian divisions, the community church cut off all denominational ties to form one local fellowship. The result, along with the release from pressure to attend denominational conventions and meet quotas in missionary and benevolent giving, was a loss of the sense of belonging to the church universal. Ministerial supply also has been a problem. Many a community church has had an outstanding record of local service and in some instances has become a true "parish church." But without a parent denomination it has tended to be an ecclesiastical orphan. At present few new unrelated community churches are being established.

The practice of "comity" is an effort to create true Protestant "parishes" in new areas of our cities. The local council of churches assigns a given territory to a particular denomination for development, and by agreement the other co-operating denominations refrain from establishing a church there. In such a way the denominations share the burden of evangelizing our growing population and avoid the fractionalizing effects of unrestricted sectarian competition. The new congregation founded in such an area, though called Evangelical and

Reformed, or Augustana Lutheran, is in effect a community church which has ties with a larger ecclesiastical fellowship. In such situations most of our major communions have abandoned sectarian imperialism. Yet here a problem emerges. Much of our evangelism in the past emphasized the superiority of the preacher's particular denomination. Now as we center on Christ and on the common elements of our faith we have a much richer gospel. But churches without the ecumenical vision go on in the old way. Fired by their provincial loyalties, proclaiming their peculiar superiority, they appeal with their dogmatism to a certain type of mind; and they are growing faster than the more abstemious communions. Their unrepentant denominational pride may not be the only reason for their growth, but it plays a big part in their apologetic. Refusing to respect the "gentleman's agreement" of comity, they continue to impose the pattern of division on many new communities.

The merger of denominations. The large number of federated congregations and community churches in the United States, as well as the wide extent to which comity is practiced, reveals a widespread longing for Christian unity and a willingness to assume local initiative for its realization. The continued existence of separate denominational structures, however, remains a powerful divisive factor, difficult for local groups to transcend. The twentieth-century movements toward merger therefore assume a greater significance than mere adjustments in ecclesiastical polities. For hundreds of communities, every such merger removes a scandal from the spiritual life of congregations formerly hindered from uniting.

A significant number of mergers has taken place in the United States as a result of various influences. Like our fellow believers throughout the world, American Christians are taking more seriously the question of the church's nature; we realize that when it is divided it is spiritually impaired as well as practically hampered. We are rejoicing in the discovery that factors which have separated some of us in the past are no longer very significant. If the religious freedom we enjoy in the United States has encouraged the rise of many denominations, it also facilitates negotiations for union. Our various denominations can meet on equal terms: no one communion carries the prestige as the "norm" from which the others are dissenters. To us reunion represents a genuine spiritual victory, a recovery of something apostolic which all have lost; it is not a return to a *status quo ante*, prevailing in the seventeenth century, or the sixteenth.

In 1931 the Congregational-Christian merger took place, in 1934 that which produced the Evangelical and Reformed Church; between these two composite bodies a further union was consummated in 1957, eventuating in the United Church of Christ. The Methodist Church, our largest Protestant body, emerged in 1939 from the reuniting of three denominations in the Wesleyan tradition. The Evangelical and United Brethren merger took place in 1946. Wesleyan Methodists and Free Methodists are making plans to come together. Some of our various Lutheran groups have coalesced and other such unions are being discussed. There have been some failures in negotiations for merger: between American Baptists and Disciples of Christ, between the Protestant Episcopal Church and the Presbyterian Church, among our three major bodies of Presbyterians (although two of the latter continue negotiations).

Proposals for larger union. But reunion by the merger of denominations two or three at a time is a slow process. And while there is a certain logic in bringing back together separated Methodists or Presbyterians or Lutherans, the desire is growing among many American Christians for union on a much broader scale. We are thinking of the church in terms of our common experience of redemption and our common mission rather than of inherited dogmatic peculiarities which mark us as Methodists or Presbyterians or Disciples. Increasingly we are realizing that in the essentials of our faith many American Protestants are substantially agreed, that our differences are both accidental and incidental. It cannot truly be said that American Christians seeking reunion do not take theology seriously, even though we do regard many of our inherited particularisms as insignificant. What we are beginning to realize is that God in his providence has permitted a common type of faith and life to emerge from the freedom and the denominational variegation of American Christianity. Out of separate historical traditions which find it increasingly difficult to maintain their relevance we find ourselves meeting one another with common convictions, a common sense of mission, and common methods of doing our work. Many of us would like to join in a large-scale union.

Two different proposals for multilateral merger may be briefly mentioned.

A Federal Union of the Churches of America has been proposed by E. Stanley Jones in a series of nation-wide "crusades." The plan calls for the various denominations to cease regarding themselves as churches and to declare themselves branches of the One Church. Essentially the National Council of Churches, or something like it, would be renamed the United Church and certain powers would be delegated to it, with others being reserved to the branches. Stanley Jones has done much to popularize the cause of unity through the mass meetings he has held to promote his plan. It has not been adopted by a major denomination, but the widespread interest in it indicates a growing desire for organic union.

The other proposal is the Plan for a United Church, frequently called the Greenwich Plan, in the preparation of which nine denominations have officially participated. Informally it began in a discussion among a group of leaders from various communions who observed that nearly every proposal for large-scale union had foundered on one of two rocks: insistence on the historic episcopate or insistence on immersion baptism. But, said these friends, most of us are not concerned with these issues. We are divided by our inherited institutions. And these can be adapted. Current New Testament scholarship finds no one scheme—congregationalism, presbyterianism, or episcopacy—authoritatively set forth as a rule. And, whatever the denominations call their polity, their actual processes of operation are very similar. So, said these friends, why not call a conference of those denominations who already accept each other's ministries and sacraments to discuss immediate organic union.

After the necessary preliminary work, a conference was called at Greenwich, Connecticut, in December, 1949. Nine denominations sent representatives: Methodist, Presbyterian U.S.A., Presbyterian U.S., Congregational-Christian, Disciples of Christ, Evangelical and Reformed, African Methodist Episcopal, Colored Methodist Episcopal, and the Association of Community Churches. Agreeing to seek a plan for organic union, these representatives organized a continuing Conference on Church Union, with Bishop Ivan Lee Holt as chairman. The effort was to find a way of bringing into one ecclesiastical fellowship the values of all the communions involved, to preserve the strength of each without overriding the freedom of the others. In May, 1953, there went out to the churches for their study and criticism, but not yet for official action, a "Plan for a United Church."

The proposed church finds its coherence not in a creed nor in a ministry nor in a liturgy but in a covenant relationship. This relationship is not exclusive. It is open to all who accept Jesus Christ and recognize one another as belonging to the United Church. A series of connectional bodies—presbyteries, conferences, and a general council—gives the church clear institutional structure, through which the fellowship finds responsible expression. Each conference has a bishop, yet every congregation is free to determine its own mode of worship and use of the sacraments. The proposed church is not conceived in ultimate terms, but as a fellowship in which all who are ready to unite may do so.

Considering the many difficulties encountered in the mergers already undertaken on a smaller scale, it would be rash to predict the fate of this Plan of Union. But whether this plan, or that of E. Stanley Jones, is adopted or not, one may reasonably look forward to a clarification of the religious picture, to the consolidation of many existing denominations, and to the overcoming of much sectarian rivalry. As American Christians we feel constrained by the will of God to press toward such a goal. Because we have inherited a complex system of sec-

tarian institutions which obscure the wholeness of the church
we are forced to consider Christian unity as a *practical* problem. We will continue seeking ways and methods for expressing our oneness in Christ.

Since the matter of unity is for us so urgent, and since we
have had such good results from working together in the area
of Life and Work, many American Christians tend to be impatient with the heavy emphasis on theology in the World
Council of Churches and the insistence of some within the
Faith and Order movements that theological agreement must
be reached "before rushing into union." Our experience leaves
little room for hope of reaching theological unanimity—ever—
if men are free. In Europe, where the Protestant problem is
primarily one of reconciling Lutheran and Reformed views,
new speculative ventures, such as examining our differences in
the light of eschatology or of Christology, may seem to hold
promise. In a country where there is an ecclesiastical establishment and the "free churches" are looked upon as regrettable
and misdirected minorities, to be regarded with charity but
not to be taken seriously, there may remain hope that the
dominant theology will prevail again, if given time. In the
United States, however, it is not these ancient churches, but
the Baptists and the Methodists, which on the basis of size and
achievement have to be taken most seriously; and many
others stand as equals. There appears little realistic hope of
reconciling the many divergent theological emphases which
have driven us into a sectarianism we deplore.

But in our experience God has given to many of us a conception of Christian faith as primarily personal and practical
rather than primarily propositional. In spite of all our divisions there has been a common heritage of biblical belief, a
common loyalty to one Lord more important than our
peculiarities of sectarian doctrine. On this basis we have been
able to unite in evangelism, worship, and service in our councils of churches. When we call a man a Christian the word has
a common meaning and implies much more than that he is a

Southern Baptist or a Missouri Synod Lutheran. So as we think of Christian unity we think in terms of personal allegiance to Christ and of practical expressions of that loyalty, with theology in a subsidiary role to criticize our faith and to discipline our thinking but not to constitute an elaborate creedal basis of union.

Our experience with denominational diversity, regrettable as it is in certain of its aspects, has taught us that any viable conception of Christian unity must allow for a large area of liberty. Any plan for a united church which has any prospect of achievement in the United States and to which we would want to belong must make room for a wide degree of theological freedom and for great variety in practice, especially in worship and the administration of the sacraments. Is such a degree of liberty possible in the church? The answer is that it already exists with many of our denominations. Violent as was the controversy between liberalism and fundamentalism, no major denomination in America suffered schism on a large scale. (The one possible exception is the American Baptists.) Some new sectarian groups were formed, but not by grand defections from the older churches. There is even less prospect of division over neo-orthodoxy. Wide varieties of liturgical practice also prevail within our existing communions. We believe that such freedom could and must obtain within a united church.

American Christians, then, desire to bear witness to others concerning the importance of freedom to the unity we seek. Responsible thinking in our churches has already repudiated the sectarianism of an earlier era in our history. We are convinced, however, that the guilt for our denominational multiplicity must be charged not to the principle of religious liberty but to defective thinking about the nature of the church. Winfred Ernest Garrison has made a constructive analysis of the problem.[2] After Constantine and Theodosius,

[2] Winfred Ernest Garrison, "The Church's Unity—Three Revolutions," *Encounter*, XVIII (Summer, 1957) 259–286. See also his *The Quest and Character of a United Church*. (Nashville and New York: Abingdon Press, 1957).

the Christian Church had *unity without freedom*. Even that unity was incomplete (as between East and West), and such unity as prevailed was *compelled*, not by the irresistible persuasiveness of theological truth but by the power of the state. There has never been theological unanimity in the church without governmental coercion. The denominational system brought *freedom without unity*. In the United States, where freedom has been greatest, disunity has been most evident. Now in the ecumenical movement we are seeking *unity with freedom* and *freedom with unity*. To this search, trusting in the guidance of the Holy Spirit, the churches of America are increasingly committing themselves.

VI.

The Sea of Faith—the Currents and the Depths[1]

If the faith of a people is thought of as an ocean, a useful analogy may be drawn to guide a discussion of theological trends. On the surface of the sea the waves roll, the shifting winds drive the spray now in one direction, now in another, and occasionally a storm blows out its fury. This superficial portion of the ocean presents itself to the eye of the casual observer, its constant movement and change of color fascinate the painter and photographer, its challenge lures the sailor and adventurer. In our analogy the waves may be taken to represent the theologians and professors, constantly in movement, frequently intriguing, sometimes dazzling; the winds and occasional storms are the contemporary schools and trends, the controversies of the day which now and then manifest their fury, but soon are spent.

Beneath the surface move the currents and crosscurrents, mighty rivers of cold or of warmth, like our Gulf Stream, sweeping imperiously across thousands of miles, changing the climate of continents, determining the course of the world's shipping and of history. The currents represent the major

[1] The title of this chapter implies no literary allusion. The phrase "The Sea of Faith" conveniently and briefly expresses the image of the ocean developed in the opening paragraphs. It is in no sense intended to suggest the pessimism of Matthew Arnold's "Dover Beach," where the phrase also appears.

movements of Christian theology which affect the life of the churches and the preaching of the gospel for generations or a century.

Below these moving streams which so readily alter conditions on the surface rests the great deep. Cold and dark it lies, heaving with the pulsations of its own movement, but untroubled by the waves or surface storms and relatively undisturbed by the currents, though in some ways affected by them. The oceanographer may correct our description of the unfathomed depths, but they may be taken to represent the faith of the people, the possession of the wise and of the foolish, expressing itself in life and work and worship, all but unaware of the thinking of the theologians, though it is the source from which that thinking arises.

The three "strata" of the ocean may be designated the surface, the currents, the deep—academic theology, major movements of Christian thought, the faith of the people.

It is at the two lower levels—and more especially on that of the popular faith—that the life of the churches is actually lived. The majority of American disciples know the sea of faith at its depths, not at the surface of contemporary theological discussion. Except for the intelligentsia (a minority in any society!), few of our laymen know anything of Barth, Brunner, Niebuhr, Tillich, or even—in a systematic way—of Wesley, Calvin, or Luther. To a large degree, as was pointed out in Chapter IV, our ministers also are relatively unconcerned with systematics. If the pastors in a certain state invite John Mackay, Nels Ferré, or Georgia Harkness to deliver a series of lectures at their annual convention, they are first of all seeking inspiration, the guidance of a disciplined Christian mind, stimulating ideas, or illustrations for next Sunday's sermon; their dominant interest is not in comparing dogmatic structures.

A severe limitation of our analogy is its danger of implying that the surface (academic theology) and even the currents (major movements of Christian thought) are relatively unimportant either in themselves or in comparison with the great deep of popular faith. Such a conclusion would be a most regrettable inference. Because man's nature is crowned by intellect and rational inquiry is one of his noblest functions, the theological venture involves the application of his highest faculties (the mind) in considering the object of supreme worth (God). The intellectual enterprise which seeks to relate the concepts of the received faith to contemporary categories of thought is absolutely essential. The discipline of theology deserves, therefore, the long overdue attention which it is now beginning to receive in American Christianity. The popular faith of our church members will doubtless be strengthened as it assumes a more self-conscious and coherent theological structure.

The point of the analogy is that the popular faith is *there*. It is a major factor in American Christianity. And, for reasons which have been indicated throughout this book, it is relatively uninfluenced by formal theology. This is not to say that it is better without such influence than with it. It is merely to point out that this popular faith, unsystematic though it be, does exist as a wholesome and vital force.

It is the two upper levels of our sea of faith which generally attract the attention of scholars and writers. European theological students know something about Niebuhr and Tillich but tend to think of American Christianity primarily in terms of liberalism. Most of the ecumenical contacts involving personal encounter take place on these upper levels; the actual discussions at Amsterdam, Lund, and Evanston were to a large degree professorial powwows, and the literature about these meetings circulated among the churches issues largely from the studies of learned men or of popularizers interpreting what the learned men said. Through other types of ecumenical programs ordinary Christians from various parts of the world are brought together—in work camps, in the exchange of students and fraternal workers, in the resettlement of refugees. Contacts of this sort are more intimate and longer-lasting; they build bridges of understanding and friendship between churches separated by distance of geography and confession. But such contacts are limited, too often they are reported merely as statistics, and people do not write books about them.

As a result, ecumenically minded Americans too often think of Europe in terms of Barth and Schlink, Europeans of America in terms of Van Dusen aud Calhoun. Now, all these men are estimable representatives and are not to be dismissed because they are professors. (The author, who has been teaching for more than a decade, must defend his own guild.) But the very fact that they have become ecumenical symbols *in their role as theologians* has resulted in a sense of theological rift between the two continents. In the academic study of the ecumenical movement the tensions which have resulted in the theological rift prove so interesting that the faith in which all Christians are united sometimes tends to be overlooked. Yet it binds together the theologians already mentioned as well as the administrative leaders of the churches—Oxnam and Sherrill, Boegner and Dibelius— and all the delegates and visitors who bow together in worship at any ecumenical conference.

Because the disciples of our Lord in different parts of the world need to know one another at the depths of faith, the purpose of this book is to set forth the spirit of American Christianity as manifested in the religion of the people. This chapter therefore is not an exposition of the systems of our leading contemporary theologians; other books have been written in that field. It deals, instead, with the currents and countercurrents which are the major movements of Christian thought and with the deeper levels of popular faith.

THE TRADITIONAL FAITH

Before charting currents and crosscurrents, it is well to consider the sea of faith as it was before the streams of Christian thought which are now significant began to move beneath the surface.

At the beginning of the nineteenth century most American Christians subscribed to the traditional faith. They believed in Almighty God, in salvation from sin and hell to righteousness and heaven, through the death of Jesus Christ, revealed as the incarnate Son of God in an inspired Bible. American faith was, for the most part, Calvinistic. But throughout the century there arose a series of protests against the stern doctrine of predestination as it was then understood and preached. Many a frontier democrat who cherished his individual rights and believed that "one man is as good as another" rebelled against concepts of election and reprobation which elevated his neighbor to heavenly bliss but sentenced him to damnation without appeal. Baptist and Presbyterian preachers whose eloquence was kindled by the awfulness of their theme spoke with a vividness against which the children of darkness could only rebel: a typical assertion was that "the streets of hell are paved with the skulls of infants not a span long." Many voices cried out against such barbarous interpretations of the gospel. Methodists, Unitarians, Universalists, Transcendentalists, General Baptists, and Disciples of Christ were a few of the movements which called into question one phase of Calvinism or another. Even within the churches which stemmed from Geneva a general softening of the harsher dogmas took place.

The various protests against Calvinism may be considered as waves swelling on the surface of the ocean, but as the last quarter of the nineteenth century began, the sea of faith was much as it had long been. However they interpreted predestination, most American Christians subscribed to the traditional orthodoxy, believing in an infallible Bible, practicing a pietistic type of devotion, observing such requirements of Puritan morality as Sabbath-keeping and total abstinence, rejoicing in the victories of the revivalists. Our religion was still dominated by the outlook and customs of rural America.

But new winds were blowing and disturbances rising from the depths of the sea. The reader will recall the processes suggested in the first chapter: urbanization, which brought a greater sophistication, an increase in education, and the need for a settled ministry with professional training; immigration, which broke up traditional patterns of American life and brought us some intellectual radicals, along with Roman Catholics, Orthodox, and Jews; industrialization, which was attended by new social problems of great urgency. But, with all their difficulties, these trends were considered phases of "progress." Americans could hardly help believing in that alluring doctrine after the amazing achievements of a single century. But they were not alone. Victorian optimism was the mood of the times throughout the civilized world.

Of equal importance to Christian thinking were certain intellectual trends. The growing prestige of science, impressing itself on the popular imagination by its triumphs of healing and invention, led many to call in question various assumptions of the traditional faith. The works of geologists on the age of the earth provided abundant ammunition for free-thinking debaters who wished to challenge the preachers still clinging to an infallible book laced up with Bishop Ussher's chronology. The theory of evolution shook the old presuppositions even harder. How was Genesis to be reconciled with science? Meanwhile, the trek to the German universities had begun in the late nineteenth century. Brilliant young American students returned to their native shores imbued with the spirit of German scholarship. Suddenly "higher criticism" became a major concern of thinking Christians. So from another front the traditional view of the Bible fell under attack. How did the churches respond to these various forces and influences? What were their answers to these vexing problems?

LIBERALISM

The New Theology which emerged in the 1890's was one response. Under the name of "liberalism" it became a major movement in American Christian thought. It is a current which has been moving through the second depth of our sea of faith from that time to this.

The simplified theology of liberalism, brought into accord with the suppositions of science, commended itself to the free and enlightened people whom Americans consider themselves to be. As a summation of the cardinal elements of Christian doctrine, "the Fatherhood of God and the brotherhood of man" proved easily comprehensible to the man in the street. The emphasis on ethics and the high place given to the Sermon on the Mount appealed to the Puritan strain in our make-up, the conviction that religious profession ought to express itself in a superior morality. The view that God is immanent in the processes of nature, of history, and of human experience seemed to validate the concept of the essential goodness, worth, and perfectibility of man. That optimism regarding human nature was attractive to men of idealism living in a democracy. It also exerted a profound influence upon the theory of religious education during the time, early in the present century, when the old Sunday-school movement, largely conducted by laymen, was developing into a new sort of enterprise with professional leadership and with professors of religious education taking their place on the major theological faculties. The theology of immanence, laying hold on the idea of progress, made for a Christian utopianism. Liberals eagerly responded to the idea of the social gospel and called men to labor for the coming era of good will, brotherhood, and peace, which would be the Kingdom of God.

The recovery of Jesus. The exaltation of Jesus was the most attractive element of liberal thought. The recovery of the "Jesus of history" by the biblical scholars of the late nineteenth and early twentieth centuries enabled preachers to present him as a winsome and challenging human figure—the Ideal, the Master, the Man of all men. Extreme liberals or modernists sometimes stopped there, confining the significance of Christ to his humanity and reducing him from the role of Savior to that of supreme Martyr, but such a view never prevailed among any significant proportion of American Christians. It is true that the great Pauline affirmations of the pre-existence of Christ, the Johannine doctrine of the Logos, the records of the Virgin Birth, and the Nicene formulations were de-emphasized during the liberal era. They were interpreted as efforts to explain him rather than as authoritative definitions of dogma. Most liberals, however, thought of themselves not as emptying the person of Christ of divine significance, but rather as recovering his human significance. The simple Galilean kindled their affections and called forth their commitment. It was precisely because the ancient Christological symbols had so little to say about the Man of Nazareth that the liberals found them uninteresting. They frequently pointed out that the Apostles' Creed jumps from the Virgin Birth to the crucifixion under Pontius Pilate, with nothing but a comma between. The liberals were most attracted by what comes in that gap—the ideal manhood, the ministry, and the teaching of our Lord. To celebrate these values they wrote new creeds.

Only as men of a later generation and another ideology see the liberal doctrine of Christ positively rather than negatively can they understand its great appeal to many of the best minds and choicest spirits of American Christianity across half a century. In a theology of transcendence the human figure of Jesus is relatively unimportant, perhaps even irrelevant; our salvation derives from the irruption of the Wholly Other into time and history, by the Incarnation, and from the "mighty acts" of Crucifixion, Death, Resurrection, and Ascension. From such a standpoint the emphasis on the Jesus of history seems to have been dealing with a side issue. But in a theology of immanence, the interest falls on Immanuel—God with us—rather than on *Deus absconditus*. And the Nazarene is the supreme revelation of God. The liberals adored him in all the manliness and winsomeness of his personality; witness Charles Edward Jefferson's series of sermons issued under the title *The Character of Jesus*. They rejoiced to think of freeing the Master from the emaciated representations of the artists and the otherworldly preachers; they spoke of taking him out of the mosaics and the stained-glass windows and letting him walk once again, in flesh and blood, the dusty trails of Galilee. This Man, who went about doing good, who spoke as never man spake, who had compassion on the multitudes, who was tempted in everything like ourselves but without sin, died in faithful obedience to the will of his Father and allegiance to the Law of Love. But death could not hold him. By the experience of the Resurrection the apostles were convinced that he is alive forevermore. His Spirit still moves among men, inspiring them to live as children of God and saving them from the misery and folly of sin.

American revivalism, for more than a century, had emphasized the preaching of Jesus Christ and him crucified. The evangelists had spent little time elaborating the subtleties of

Trinitarian theology; the "dying love of Jesus" was their most powerful appeal to men to forsake a life of sin and accept the forgiving grace of God. The result was the "simple faith" that focused in the "centrality of Christ." Now that New Testament scholarship had harvested the fruits of the quest for the historical Jesus, the liberal preachers were able to present him as a convincing earthly figure, clothed in the lineaments of our flesh, and gathering up in his own person the fairest dreams of all mankind. Thus the liberal proclamation of Jesus continued, with a different emphasis, a tradition already well established in American Christianity, rooted in its pattern of devotion, enshrined in its hymns, formulated in popular slogans such as "Jesus only," "No creed but Christ," "For Christ and the Church." A gracious and heroic Galilean now marched through sermons and inspirational addresses, appeared in the literature of religious education, and adorned the pages of such a book as Harry Emerson Fosdick's *The Manhood of the Master*. This Christ spoke compellingly to the hearts of youth and purified the purposes of men and women in their maturer years.

Jesus was held up as the supreme revelation of God and the criterion by which every idea presented in the Bible must be judged. The concept of evolution as running through the entire pattern of human existence suggested the principle of progressive revelation, which brought to generations schooled in the old biblical literalism a glorious sense of release from problems created by the primitive conceptions in the Old Testament. No longer was it necessary to wrest the text or strain one's conscience in trying to reconcile the attributes of Jahweh with those of the God and Father of our Lord Jesus Christ. Our Quaker poet, John Greenleaf Whittier, had already struggled with the problem and had concluded:

> Nothing can be good in Him
> Which evil is in me.

The principle of progressive revelation now frankly asserted that the picture of a God of vengeance set forth in the Old Testament or the Book of Revelation is not authoritative and

must be judged by the character of Jesus himself. Even difficult passages in the Synoptic Gospels, such as those couched
in eschatological terms, were explained in the same manner:
Jesus was above his reporters. The Scriptures thus became
the record of man's search for God and of its fulfillment in
Christ. If the Bible lacked its former authority, it was prized
as a treasury of religious insights, and the Gospels were de-
votedly read.

Negative aspects. Certain emphases of the "old-time religion" were either explicitly repudiated or quietly de-
emphasized in liberal preaching. The "types and prophecies"
of the Old Testament, the "blood atonement," the cataclysmic
Second Coming proclaimed by premillennialists, and eternal
damnation struck the liberals as intellectually untenable or
spiritually offensive. The miracles, which had once been the
trustiest weapon in the armory of the apologist, suddenly became an embarrassment in a scientific age of natural law; the
liberals tended to rationalize them or to take an agnostic attitude toward them. The doctrines of the church as the
mystical body of Christ and of the sacraments as the means of
grace now had little appeal. Liberals pointed out how often
through history ecclesiastical institutions had betrayed the
spirit of Jesus. They conceived the church as the fellowship
of those who follow him, as the Beloved Community dedicated to the furtherance of the Kingdom of God.

The liberals regarded their mission as one of allegiance to
truth, as an effort to retain intellectual honesty in religion and
yet to maintain the essence of the Christian faith. In stripping
away the primitive and prescientific elements in the Bible they
found that all was not lost; they still were left with God as
Father, with the Law of Love, with Jesus as Lord, with the
Kingdom of God. These great doctrines they could preach as
a faith for free men, speaking to the modern mind in terms
and categories that it could understand and accept. If the
modern mind repudiated miracles, this was thought to be
under the compulsion of scientific truth, and the liberal was
prepared to see them go. What had the coin in the fish's

mouth or the stilling of the tempest to do with the Kingdom of God?

The appeal of liberalism. The new theology commended itself to laymen because of its constant effort to relate Christianity to practical problems. As early as the 1880's Henry Ward Beecher, considered our greatest pulpit orator, popularized the practice of preaching on "topics of the times." The heyday of liberalism in the 1920's and 1930's found ministers all over the country discussing every sort of contemporary issue, intellectual, social, or psychological. The liberal outlook was such that a preacher would draw upon all the resources of modern knowledge as well as upon the Christian tradition and the spirit of Jesus for help in dealing with a particular problem; in some cases the sermon might not even contain a biblical text. The question may well be asked: what was the normative Christian element in such discussions? But in asking the question we must also recognize the high degree of idealism, stemming from their Christian discipleship, which characterized the liberals and the moral courage which many of them showed in attacking entrenched evil or even in standing trial for heresy because they espoused higher criticism, evolution, or some other heterodox doctrine. And their inspiration was their faith in Jesus.

Among my ministerial friends is a liberal, now come to the age of retirement, who has had two long pastorates and is beloved throughout his state. Thirty years ago he was in a notable ministry with an important church when he was surprised by a visit from several officers of his congregation. The Ku Klux Klan was at the height of its power, and these men were members. They proposed to their pastor that he join this "one hundred per cent American" organization; if he did so they would make him famous throughout the country. He also knew that if he refused their invitation, his ministry in that place was at an end and his life possibly in danger.

After some discussion, he asked, "Gentlemen, do you want my answer tonight?"

"We're not in any hurry," one of them replied.

"I might as well give it now," he said. Whereupon he

reached for his Bible, turned to the Gospel, and read the story of the temptation of Jesus, concluding with the simple statement, "That, gentlemen, is my answer."

Within a few days that minister had been deprived of his pulpit and his salary. For a time he took up secular work to support his family, until he was called to another church unaffected by the poison of the Klan. In recent years Europe has had hundreds of Christian heroes who have sealed their faith with their own blood and thousands of others who have kept it at the risk of their lives. It is well to remember that many American liberals have found within their commitment to Jesus Christ, and his faithfulness to them, the resources to bear steadfast witness to their faith.

Limitations. The insufficiencies of liberalism have been so thoroughly aired during the past two or three decades that they need not here be discussed at length. Its optimism concerning human nature and the certainty of progress now appears naïve, and it was dominated far more than it realized by the spirit of the times. For example, it now seems clear that much of the vocal pacifism of the twenties and thirties, which all but vanished at our entrance into World War II, may have been an expression, in religious categories, of the isolationism then prevalent rather than of immutable Christian truth. Liberalism tended to disregard too easily the historic faith and to minimize the sterner aspects of the Christian tradition. Although there is validity in the effort to commend Christianity on pragmatic grounds, there is also a dual danger in asking people to accept the Christian ethic because "it works": they may merely undertake to keep certain portions of a religious law without a basic commitment to the will of God, or they may conclude that whatever seems to "work" is Christian. The gravest weakness was the outright humanism of some liberal theologians. I will not say with some critics that the surrender of theism is the logical outcome of the liberal position, but in the day of its greatest supremacy that was the tendency of its intellectual leaders. Richard Niebuhr has indicated the denatured faith of the more "advanced" liberals in a withering characterization: "A God without wrath brought men without sin into a kingdom without judgment through the ministrations of a Christ without a cross." [2]

What were the results of liberalism? To answer that question it is necessary to consider two other major movements of Christian thought and to plumb the depths of the popular faith.

FUNDAMENTALISM

Liberalism had no more become a clearly defined current of religious thinking than a violent countercurrent began to flow, a militant reaction of traditional orthodoxy at the extreme of biblical literalism. The movement took the name of "fundamentalism," adapting it from the general title of a series of books, *The Fundamentals*, which first appeared in 1910. Like most "antiheretical" movements in the history of the church, it derived its primary emphases from the denials of its opponents. So fundamentalism vigorously affirmed the doctrines which liberalism questioned or rejected. Each of these issues became a symbol, charged with emotion, certain to precipitate religious argument.

Essential emphases. The Virgin Birth of Christ was a primary emphasis, for it was the great miracle, the irrefutable answer to humanism, the unique guarantee of the deity of our Lord. His substitutionary death upon the cross as the perfect sacrifice in satisfaction for our sins was a second major item of faith: Christ was not a Martyr, but the Savior, redeeming man not by "moral influence" but by the shedding of his blood. The "blood atonement" was the phrase used to summarize this essential element of the fundamentalists' creed. The bodily resurrection of Jesus from the dead was a third insistence in their doctrine of Christ. They constantly taunted the liberals for holding a spiritual view of the Resurrection and decried the hopelessness of a faith which left the body of Jesus moldering in a Syrian grave. A corollary was the fundamentalists' doctrine of our Lord's bodily ascension, and the final element in their Christology was his imminent Second

[2] H. Richard Niebuhr, *The Kingdom of God in America* (New York: Harper & Brothers, 1937), p. 193.

Coming on clouds of glory to set up his Kingdom and to reign on earth for a thousand years.

Fundamentalism based itself on the Bible. It proclaimed the verbal inspiration and absolute inerrancy of the Scriptures as literally read. Consequently it denied many of the teachings of biblical criticism, especially the documentary hypothesis concerning the composition of the Pentateuch, the belief in a Second Isaiah, and the tendency to assign the authorship of certain New Testament books to the post-Apostolic period. On the basis of Genesis, fundamentalists vigorously campaigned against the theory of evolution and succeeded in getting the state legislature of Tennessee to enact a law (still on the statute books) forbidding the teaching of that doctrine in the public schools. When John T. Scopes was placed on trial for violation of the statute, he was defended by Clarence Darrow, the greatest criminal lawyer of the time. But William Jennings Bryan, celebrated orator and former secretary of state, represented the prosecution and won a conviction. The "monkey case" was front-page news across the land. It dramatized the determination of fundamentalists to insist upon the scientific and historic accuracy of the Bible.

The fundamentalists' loyalty to the Scriptures led them to make much of the miracles, from Elisha's floating axhead to the resurrected saints walking the streets of Jerusalem at the time of the Crucifixion. Nothing was involved except the question of faith; if a man found it impossible to accept any one of the miracles recounted in the Scripture, he simply did not believe the Word of God. A test question was, "Can a man be a Christian without believing that Jesus raised Lazarus from the dead?" Likewise on biblical grounds, fundamentalists continued to proclaim a fearsome Last Judgment and a literal hell of fire and brimstone for the damned, to all eternity.

The period of controversy. At the very time, then, that liberals were embarrassed by certain biblical concepts and were seeking to minimize their importance in order that Christianity might come to terms with the "mind of the twentieth century," fundamentalists seized on those very concepts which seemed so offensive and proclaimed them to be essentials of the faith. Reacting negatively to modernism, they also set themselves against the social gospel, on the ground that it tried to save men without the blood of Christ, by passing laws or getting rid of slums. The old phrase of the evangelists whereby a convert was asked to accept Christ as his "personal Savior" took on a new connotation: that salvation was purely interior and had nothing to do with the social order. As some fundamentalists denounced modernists for meddling in politics and business instead of preaching the old-time religion, certain men of affairs became generous financial supporters of the theology of reaction. In many quarters, fundamentalism allied itself with the old Puritan mores and thus found itself in controversy with liberalism in the realm of private conduct. Even the layman who was ignorant of theology could classify a certain church as modernistic because its young people were not forbidden to dance or because its minister smoked cigars.

During the first generation of our century there was violent controversy between liberals and fundamentalists in local congregations and denominational conventions. Whereas liberals tended to work quietly and not to disturb the minds of persons who had not yet become concerned about the questions at issue, fundamentalists carried the battle to the people at large. They feared a modernist conspiracy to undermine the faith. Consequently they warned the laymen in as many congregations as possible, released test questions for discovering the new heresy, and issued descriptions of a "modernist preacher" so that none of the unwary might be taken by surprise. One of our respected church historians affirms that fundamentalism failed to capture any of the major denominations.[3] Yet certainly it is the prevailing view among Southern Baptists, Churches of Christ, and the Pentecostal bodies. Fundamentalist-liberal tension has caused grave internal problems for the American (Northern) Baptists and the Disciples of Christ, and on a lesser scale for Presbyterians and Methodists. Its appeal has been strongest where the traditional view

[3] Winthrop S. Hudson, *The Great Tradition of the American Churches* (New York: Harper & Brothers, 1953), p. 12.

of the Bible has remained unchallenged by social and intellectual forces breaking down the old conservative structures of life and thought.

An appraisal. From the perspective of mid-century it is becoming clear that fundamentalism was a determined effort to retain the transcendent element of the historic faith. It saw plainly enough that a purely human Jesus, whatever moving tributes might be paid to him, is not the Savior of the world in the terms of the Christian gospel, that man's sin is a dread reality which has separated him from God and demands a salvation far beyond the power of moral resolution to achieve, that to eliminate the possibility of miracle is to reduce the Eternal God to the measure of man's mind, that to seek the Kingdom through rearranging the outer circumstances of man's life and trusting in human progress is a vain delusion, that to reduce the Bible to a human story of man's groping toward God and a collection of noble religious insights is to divest it of authority and to leave the Christian perilously close to subjectivism. Perhaps because of their theological position, perhaps because of their zeal (if the two can be separated), the fundamentalist churches have been carrying the greater burden of Protestant evangelism during the past two decades as compared with the liberal churches. The clarity of its Christian insight at the points here mentioned and the devotion with which it has continued to win men to Christ should have earned for fundamentalism a larger measure of gratitude and respect than it has been accorded by theologians and historians of other schools of Christian thought. Their general tendency is to dismiss its arguments with a wave of the hand and a superior laugh—or a sigh of regret that so many people who do not know better have been misled by them.

Yet fundamentalists have vitiated their witness by their pugnacity. They have circulated controversial and often scurrilous material about the most respected leaders in American Protestantism. They have brought accusations of modernism and of communism against the National Council of Churches and the World Council of Churches and have sought to hamstring the ecumenical witness because some men considered liberal hold membership in churches belonging to the councils and have been elected to posts of leadership. Many fundamentalists are grieved by the noisy negative tactics of a few of their colleagues and would prefer a more positive evangelical approach to the issues. But not a few Christians have rejected fundamentalism because of its militant wrath in an age that prizes tolerance and the gentler virtues; to many it has appeared as a kind of ecclesiastical McCarthyism.

There is, however, a deeper reason for the failure of fundamentalism. It has never really come to grips with the problems which brought liberalism into being. Actually, the issues seem never to have involved most of the fundamentalists in any existential struggle. The difficulty raised by science with respect to the traditional reading of Genesis, the moral issue of the imprecatory Psalms, the problem of the authority of the Bible in the light of what is known about its composition—none of these questions seems ever to have troubled the fundamentalist thinker in the depths of his own being. He was able to accept the authority of a literal Bible; anything therefore which disagreed with its words was wrong and need not be considered seriously. For minds that could accept his own presuppositions, he could answer the arguments of the liberals, but they were never real issues for him—only targets. There has been little real encounter between liberal and fundamentalist thinkers; they move in such different realms of thought that their minds rarely meet. Few fundamentalist theologians attempt to speak to the religious world at large, and even fewer succeed. One exception is Carl F. H. Henry; in *Fifty Years of Protestant Theology* he describes the main issues which have arisen in the twentieth century. While he is gratified by the neo-orthodox rejection of liberalism, he finds the new school no more acceptable than the old. He rejects the neo-orthodox concept that revelation consists of the acts of God and insists that Christian truth is *propositional*, that the Word is made known in actual language, that "the living God . . . has spoken . . . has inscripturated His revelation." [4] With a few exceptions, fundamentalism has not produced thinkers who were seriously concerned with the contemporary intellectual problems. As a movement it has been authoritarian, not intellectually critical. The leading publishing houses associated with the movement devote much energy to reprinting the works of nineteenth-century biblical commentators and theologians; its scholarship has been almost entirely apologetic rather than constructive. The zeal engendered by fundamentalism and its success among the people in certain areas (especially the popular response to the preaching of Billy Graham) have won it the right to more serious attention than it has received from those outside the fold. Yet by its naïveté and its essentially negative character it has forfeited the opportunity of intellectual leadership in the Christian world.

THE NEW ORTHODOXY

In our analogy of the sea of faith, liberalism and fundamentalism can well be designated as major movements during the first half of our century, and one may quite accurately be considered the countercurrent of the other. It is difficult, however, to describe the present situation in theology, either in terms of our oceanic analogy or in systematic ideological terms.

It is clear that a change has taken place. Although many a pastor or director of religious education still encounters persons with intellectual problems arising from the old biblical literalism, the fundamentalist-liberal discussion is passé in theological circles. The most stimulating authors and professors in the major seminaries have struck a new course, rejecting the methods of fundamentalism and various presuppositions of liberalism. Much is heard now of neo-orthodoxy, or realistic theology, or dialectical theology. If there is not one clear and inclusive name to designate the new trend, even less is there one coherent set of ideas. Sometimes the only point in common among the so-called neo-orthodox thinkers is their

[4] Carl F. H. Henry, *The Drift of Western Thought* (Grand Rapids: Erdmans, 1951), p. 158.

antipathy against liberalism. This does not arise, however, from any inclination toward fundamentalism, for they hardly regard it as deserving their attention; but most of them began their intellectual pilgrimage in the liberal tradition and are painfully conscious of certain defects in their former way of looking at God and man. How may the new orthodoxy be described?

Characteristics of American neo-orthodoxy. To begin with, it is not Barthianism. There is very little of that, in the thoroughgoing sense, in the United States. Except in churches with strong Continental ties—primarily the Lutheran bodies— few American ministers read German, and Barth did not appear in an English translation until the publication of *The Word of God and the Word of Man* in 1928. It was another five years before *The Epistle to the Romans* and *The Resurrection of the Dead* appeared in our language. The second part of the first volume of the *Church Dogmatics* did not come from the press till 1956, and further volumes are appearing; but even yet the bulk of the *Dogmatik* is, to most of us, a closed book. The spiritual mood in America differed so markedly from that of Europe in the twenties that our first reaction was violently negative. The theological stature of Karl Barth is now so towering that our students in seminary learn something of his system; there is an increasing interest in and knowledge of his works, largely confined, however, to academic circles. His earlier writings, at any rate, took such sharp issue with attitudes inherent in our American spirit that there is no present sign of his being about to attain among us the standing which he enjoys on the Continent. While many Europeans regard him as a prophet, our scholars are interested in him more as a major influence.

Partly influenced by Barth, but more particularly by those forces of world history which challenged the optimism of the social gospel, a group of Christian thinkers in America began during the thirties to re-examine the assumptions of liberalism. Two of the major revisionists—Professor Edwin Lewis at Drew University and Professor John C. Bennett at Union Theological Seminary—were dogmatic theologians, but some of the most penetrating and persistent questions were raised by professors in other fields, by pastors and editors. In 1937 the famous liberal preacher, Harry Emerson Fosdick, published a sermon entitled "The Church Must Go Beyond Modernism." In the same year Charles Clayton Morrison, crusading editor of the *Christian Century*, returned from the World Conference on Faith and Order at Edinburgh a convert to a much higher doctrine of the church than he and his early liberal associates had held; his Lyman Beecher Lectures entitled *What Is Christianity?* created a sensation at Yale in 1939. Meanwhile Reinhold Niebuhr, professor of social ethics at Union and most influential of all the critics of liberalism, was pouring forth books and articles; his work on *The Nature and Destiny of Man*, the Gifford Lectures of 1940, has become a classic of the new orthodoxy. But, limited by the bounds of his own teaching field, he has not published a major theological treatise on the doctrine of God. Other leading dialectical theologians have likewise confined their writings to particular realms of thought—Professor Paul Tillich of Harvard to philosophical theology, Professor Paul S. Minear of Andover-Newton Theological Seminary to biblical theology, Professor H. Richard Niebuhr of Yale Divinity School to historical theology. There is no American Barth: no one towers in influence like Mont Blanc above his contemporaries, no one has produced a major *Dogmatik* to give comprehensive and systematic expression to the new emphasis in Christian thought. Any effort therefore to characterize this movement must be recognized as a series of general and approximate statements.

The note most frequently sounded by neo-orthodox thinkers is the sinfulness of man, his sin arising not from his finitude but from his pretense that he is not finite. Because no human act, however virtuous, is free from sin, man constantly stands in need of redemption, but in this life he is redeemed only in principle; never is he able to transcend his sinful nature. "Realistic theology" is a theology of justification rather than of sanctification. If man is sinful as an individual, his own personal evil is multiplied in every social structure; even the family is corrupted by self-interest and uses its power selfishly, while the demonic elements in the labor union, the organization of manufacturers, of the nation are even more apparent. Far more than an individual, it is impossible for any social body to live by the requirements of the Law of Love.

If neo-orthodoxy in America started with a doctrine of man and society, it has been moving on to other realms of theology. Its teaching about God clearly rejects the naturalism of the more advanced theologians of the liberal era; yet the emphasis among us has not shifted to the stark transcendence of the Wholly Other as in Europe. Revelation, as over against the idea of discovery by a religious genius, has again become a compelling category of Christian thought, and a new interest in biblical theology has come to birth. The recognition of religious myth in the Scriptures has enabled our interpreters to approach with a new seriousness passages which liberals rejected as primitive or prescientific; when a portion is considered mythologically, however, the tendency is to regard it as a source of insight rather than as legalistic authority. (In arriving at a doctrine of the relation of man to woman, for example, few of us would appeal to Genesis 2 as some students in other parts of the world have done. To argue whether woman's creation from man's rib means that she must therefore be subordinate or that she is therefore his equal strikes us as a fundamentalist approach.) The most notable effect of the new biblical theology has been the espousal by certain leading thinkers of the concept of eschatology, calling into question the secular idea of progress and enunciating a "Christian philosophy of history." Such thinking, however, is by no means preponderant, even in our theological faculties, though the Second Assembly of the World Council has come to Evanston and gone.

The influence of neo-orthodoxy. Indeed, in terms of our analogy, the neo-orthodox trend is still largely a phenomenon of the surface level. There is no doubt that an important current is gathering force, but at present it is primarily a movement of theological professors, seminarians, and intellectuals among our younger ministers. It has not yet become a mighty stream in the life of the churches, nor has it pervaded our preaching, hymnody, or Christian life. The subtlety and sophistication of the dialectical process of thought, its delight in paradox, make it difficult to present to the popular mind. No great pulpit voice has become the national symbol of neo-orthodoxy as Fosdick became of modernism, although most of our thoughtful preachers show some effects of it in their sermons. Certainly it will be more difficult for the man in the street to accept neo-orthodoxy than it was to embrace liberalism. The dark view of human nature espoused by the realistic theologians does not come easily to a nation which has heard its politicians say for generations, "You can count on the good sense of the American people," and which has not suffered greatly nor experienced firsthand the horrors of twentieth-century evil. Our typical citizen is still more likely to attribute the demonic aspects of the Nazi and Communist terrors to the power of propaganda wielded by an evil totalitarianism than to an inherent perversity in human nature.

Among our working clergy who came out of seminary two or three decades ago the new orthodoxy has aroused irritation and resistance, although no theologian of major stature has emerged to halt its progress. Many preachers decry its "pessimism" and suspect that the young theologues who recite the current watchwords are merely latter-day fundamentalists. Their fears may not be wholly groundless, for the neo-orthodox criticism of liberalism has been so constant, so merciless, and at times so distorted that students of a younger generation may very well be left unmindful of its historical necessity, which Barth himself recognizes, and of the services which it has rendered. Our leading neo-orthodox theologians passed through the liberal stage in their own thinking, and they assume some of its principles as axiomatic; Charles Clayton Morrison even maintains that neo-orthodoxy is an extension of liberalism.[5] It is not yet possible to predict whether or

[5] *Christian Century*, June 7, 1950, p. 697.

not the young men who hear of liberalism only as a betrayal of Christianity will proceed from these same axioms. So the men of the older school, accustomed to "translating" the Christian message into current psychological or sociological categories, shudder at the revival of biblical language. They know that the theologians are employing many of the ancient terms in a mythological fashion but are not sure that the hearers understand this; they raise charges of theological double-talk and fear a resurgence of fundamentalism.

The typical American distrust of speculation, the attachment to a "simple faith" which finds expression in practical action, has aroused concern at the overwhelming interest in theology as such which now prevails in the seminaries. A minister of forty years' experience recently commented that earlier emphases in American religion—revivalism, pietism, religious education, the social gospel, pastoral counseling—were all practical and dealt with the experience of the layman, but that the present shift toward a sophisticated type of theology is beyond the grasp of anyone not tutored in the field and may well leave the layman cold and bewildered.

The comment leads to a more serious question: in the new orthodoxy, is the message of salvation sufficiently clear? Fundamentalism has an unmistakable word of redemption. Liberalism also speaks with confidence concerning the joy and the significance and the transformation of a life committed to Christ and to the service of his Kingdom. But to many ears the gospel of neo-orthodoxy does not sound like good news; it demonstrates clearly enough man's hopeless plight but, instead of getting him out of it, speaks merely of the "earnest" of a great joy after the consummation of all things. This may be all that can be said. But it is not the triumphant language of the New Testament. When Americans heard Professor Edmund Schlink of Heidelberg say at Evanston, "Whenever . . . people speak of the coming Christ as the *hope* of the world, they are always speaking of the *end* of the world," his word seemed to speak of hopelessness rather than of hope. The further question may well be raised whether neo-orthodoxy may not be dominated by the mood of its time (pessimism) just as liberalism unwittingly imbibed the spirit of its age (optimism). Perhaps neither school of thought has succeeded in taking a truly independent, Christian stand; perhaps no theology can ever transcend the outlook of its own generation, for it is produced as the gospel enters into encounter with the mind of that generation.

Whatever the limitations of the new orthodoxy, however, its much-needed service to the field of theology must be gratefully recognized. To the extent that it is humanly possible it has sought to help Christianity find its own norms once again; it endeavors to bring life and thought in any field under a specifically Christian criticism, more incisive than the idealistic common sense with which liberalism tended to come at a problem. Realistic theology has helped to disabuse us of an undue optimism about human nature and social progress; if for the moment it has left us less hopeful than as Christians we ought to be, at least it has removed the rose-colored spectacles from our eyes. We have been reminded again of the transcendence of God. Those of us who have read the Scriptures and listened to the words of Jesus in the light of the doctrine of immanence which liberalism emphasized have been led to many precious insights which we cannot abandon, but American neo-orthodoxy reminds us of the tension in which these two aspects of the divine nature—immanence and transcendence—must ever be held. Perhaps most important of all, the new orthodoxy is bringing a return to biblical theology. After decades of essential, but technical and sometimes spiritless, work in higher criticism, the positive message of the Scriptures has become once more the major concern of biblical scholars. Prophetic and priestly and apostolic categories of thought are once more being taken seriously. At the moment there is a tendency to indulge in a plethora of first-century imagery that is utterly foreign and well-nigh incomprehensible to the modern mind; some of the recent documents of the Faith and Order movement must seem like pious gibberish to one who has not been nurtured from infancy in biblical concepts and must strike as sheer literalism even those believers who have not been let in on the mythological secret.

But if Christianity is a religion of revelation, then the recovery of confidence in the Scriptures which has taken place within our generation is an event of major importance. If the full truths of the biblical authors are allowed to modify and to round out the emphases of the emerging neo-orthodoxy, and if a generation of preachers arises who can proclaim biblical theology with clarity and pertinence, a movement of major significance may well develop in American Christian thought.

THE FAITH OF THE PEOPLE

While the storms have lashed the waves on the surface of the sea and new currents have gathered force and moved across the middle stratum of the ocean, what has been happening in the great deep? What is the faith of the ordinary Christian who worships in the pew and walks humbly with his God during the week, but does not read books on theology or write a systematic outline of his convictions? Of course, it is impossible to select the "average man" in any situation, much less the "average believer" in a milieu so diverse, culturally and denominationally, as is the United States, but some general remarks may be made.

Where untrained ministers or fundamentalist preachers have glorified the old-time religion, the congregations have in many cases changed very little from the traditional faith described at the beginning of the chapter. Not all devoted laymen have seen the need for the militancy of their fundamentalist pastor, but if he has insisted on the inerrancy of the Bible they have taken his word for it and gone on living according to the faith of their fathers. Some university students and independent thinkers in such churches have drifted away into a mild agnosticism or perhaps have discovered a liberal minister who could meet their problems; others have continued in their old church, dividing their minds into compartments, with the section assigned to religion well insulated from that belonging to science.

Where liberalism has been preached for two generations, what has been its effect on this popular faith?

Certainly the faith of the people has been affected, both by the factors which called liberalism into being and by liberalism itself. As one listens to the speeches of politicians and other laymen who occasionally give forth a public utterance with a religious cast one concludes that liberalism has had far more influence on the popular mind than has fundamentalism, for one hears the familiar phrases about the Fatherhood of God and the brotherhood of man, the Golden Rule, the Sermon on the Mount, and even the Law of Love. But it would be a mistake to conclude that the people of the United States have embraced modernism lock, stock, and barrel, that their present faith is merely a form of humanism hallowed by a few traditional phrases. The description may suit the belief of many who have come under the Christian influences in our culture but have made no personal commitment. Of our active church members and of our pastors, however, probably not 5 per cent would give assent to a theology of naturalism. Yet their faith has been profoundly influenced by the liberal movement. It might be described as a liberal evangelicalism.

Along the eastern coast of Brazil where the Amazon River empties into the Atlantic Ocean the muddy water flows with such force that its course may be traced for miles out at sea. Ultimately, however, the alien waters mingle; the one is present in the other but can no longer be discerned. In some such manner the sea of faith received the movement of liberalism, for a time distinguishable from it, and finally accepted it into itself. Our traditional Christianity has incorporated much of the spirit and the emphasis of liberalism without the humanistic denial of the gospel.

The average American Christian has retained his belief in Jesus Christ as the revelation of God, as the crucified and risen Savior, as the Giver of Eternal Life. At the same time, however, he welcomed the liberal emphasis on the Jesus of history as Example and Teacher and was thrilled by the challenge to "Jesus' way of living" and to "building the Kingdom of God." He responded to the emphasis on the Gospels as the key portion of the Bible, for he could understand them reasonably well without benefit of courses in ancient history and could derive inspiration for living from nearly every chapter.

When he became a Christian he thought both in the traditional terms of personal salvation, perpetuated in the language of worship and of many hymns, and also of personal commitment to the cause of Christ, to which the liberal preacher invited him. This combination of certain liberal emphases with the basic positive elements of traditional religion is the faith of most of our people, as of most of our ministers. Many classify themselves as "liberal," meaning not at all that they are humanists but that they accept the principle of biblical criticism, the concept of evolution, the social responsibility of the churches, and the ecumenical movement, and that they are not fundamentalists. Indeed, to most working pastors, that sentence would be a fairly accurate definition of what they mean by liberalism. Many persons reared in the traditional faith are still fighting their way from an essentially fundamentalist outlook to a "liberalism" of this sort. It is the faith of such well-known religious leaders among us as E. Stanley Jones, Bishop G. Bromley Oxnam, Bishop Gerald Kennedy, Ralph W. Sockman, Robert J. McCracken, and many another. In view of this fact, the majority of our preachers do not quite know what is meant when they hear more "up-to-date" theologians preaching the funeral of liberalism as though it had already passed off the scene. When neo-orthodoxy puts itself forward in opposition to liberalism, there is an understandable fear that important values are being placed under attack.

It is quite probable that the neo-orthodox movement as it develops will influence the sea of faith in much the same way. There is as yet no sign of a violent struggle against the new orthodoxy such as fundamentalism set in motion against liberalism; rather, it will probably be absorbed as a needed corrective into the general ocean of popular belief. In that case we shall see the emergence of a chastened liberal evangelicalism—essentially the traditional faith of the Christian church, incorporating certain liberal concepts and certain neo-orthodox correctives. Such theologians as Richard Niebuhr, Charles Clayton Morrison, Nels Ferré, Georgia Harkness, and Daniel Day Williams reflect such a faith. Paul

Scherer, George A. Buttrick, Robert E. Luccock, and Charles
E. Templeton proclaim it from the pulpit. Our preachers in
general speak more of the Holy Spirit, of the Trinity, and
of heaven than they did twenty years ago; in the deepening
spiritual mood of our time they are finding new resources, not
so much in the existentialist philosophers or even in the neo-
orthodox theologians but in the Scripture and the historic
confessions of the church, which bear common testimony to
the abiding Word of God.

The neo-orthodox emphasis on biblical categories of
thought and on the importance of the theological venture itself should mitigate one of the dangers within American
Christianity. Lacking a closely articulated dogmatic structure,
the average church member is perhaps inclined to give first
place in his spiritual life to morality, to emotional religious
experience, or to the sense of belonging to a satisfying "church
home." The result has been not only a moving across the lines
of the traditional denominations of the center but also a slid-
ing off into Unitarianism, Mormonism, spiritualism, or the
bizarre cults. No great numbers of American Presbyterians
or Baptists drift beyond the bounds of classical Protestantism,
but some persons do. That such changes occur with no overwhelming sense of being converted, or of rejecting one's
former theological position, is evidence of the need for
clearer doctrinal lines in our religious life. That so few are lost
in this way indicates the cohesive power of the popular faith
in Christ, unsystematic though it is.

To return once more to our oceanic analogy, it distinctly
emphasizes one point: the great deep constitutes more of the
sea than does the surface. And the vast depth of the popular
faith is a major phenomenon which both the theologians, with
their intellectual sophistication, and the church historians,
preoccupied with institutions and "decisive" movements, tend
to overlook. The analogy calls attention to this massive
phenomenon, the faith of 100 million Christians. When every
allowance is made for inflated statistics and for the mere
formality which the religious profession of a sizeable proportion of "church members" undoubtedly is, the faith of mil-

lions still remains. (And we may well ask what genuine religious motivations, however feeble, are present, along with those of cultural conformity, tradition, and the like, which actuate an American to make even a merely formal profession.) When every critic has scored the limitations of this vast popular faith—the moralist for its ethical shortcomings, the theologian for its unexamined assumptions and amorphous doctrinal content, the social gospeler for its introversion and limited range of application, the churchman for its individualism and inadequate sense of the body of Christ, the liturgist for its banal and sentimental expression, the denominational executive for its insufficient stewardship, the local minister for its halfhearted devotion—it is still the major fact to be considered in the study of American Christianity.

By this faith hundreds of Christians in every county across the land live their daily lives.

In this faith they perform their daily work.

To this faith they turn for illumination of their most perplexing problems.

Upon this faith they draw for resources in meeting their sorrows, troubles, and fears.

From this faith they derive the inspiration which lifts their lives above the merely animal, the sordid, or the selfish and which lures them to the realization of their nature as spiritual beings.

In this faith they find the assurance of forgiveness and the power of moral renewal.

To this faith they turn for the sanctifying of life's supreme experiences—the hallowing of marriage and of birth, the enshrining of family affection, the commitment to lofty ideals.

Upon this faith they understand the most precious values of their society to be founded—freedom, justice, liberty, their "way of life," the great tradition of Western civilization.

In response to this faith they pour out a remarkable proportion of their time, interest, money, and concern to sustain the life of their churches and the manifold activities of the Christian mission.

By this faith they die and to it they cling for assurance in their last hour.

This faith centers in Jesus Christ.

For all its variety of institutional expression, it is fundamentally Christocentric. Its common element—devotion to Jesus Christ and confession of him as Lord and Savior—provides a powerful bond of spiritual union. It enables two-thirds of American Protestant and Orthodox Christians to co-operate in the National Council of Churches and offers an even broader basis of mutual understanding among individual believers. This common faith of American Christians is a major fact which our bewildering variety of doctrinal systems and sectarian institutions must not be allowed to obscure. The theologians themselves might well inquire more deeply into the significance of this fact.

It is at the deep level of faith, rather than on the surface of theological disputation, that the Christian really lives—not only the humble man in the pew hungering for the Word of Life, but also the preacher himself, and the theologian. A blessed memory recalls an evening hour spent in the company of Stephen E. Fisher who for more than thirty years had served as minister of the University Place Christian Church at Champaign, the seat of the state university of Illinois. Through the years the spiritual glow and the intellectual vigor of his preaching, and the faithfulness of his pastoral ministry, had attracted increasing numbers of townsmen and of students. Twice during his long pastorate it had been necessary to erect a new building, larger than its predecessor, to house the growing congregation, and the church which was completed in 1936 was considered one of the most beautiful structures of its time. For an hour the aging man of God conducted me about the building, commenting on one room and then another and recalling experiences from his long ministry. At last we came to his study. As one would expect, the shelves were crowded with books in many fields of interest, and those dealing with religious subjects indicated a liberal inclination. We turned to the minister's favorite chair. On the table beside it lay his Bible. He picked it up affectionately and said, "In the years I have been preaching to university students I have read many books, but I keep coming back to this Book. It has outlasted all the others." In the circumstances I had expected some brilliant comments on life and thought; instead, I heard an intimate testimony of faith.

A similar experience was mine on a memorable afternoon at Basel when some of us sat with Karl Barth, hearing him and asking him questions. He discussed great intellectual issues with authority and conviction. Yet his manner revealed him not primarily as a brilliant mind of the first magnitude, who has wrought a revolution in the spiritual life of a continent, but rather as a humble—one is compelled to say simple—believer bearing witness to his faith. His open Bible lay before him. Now and again he picked it up to read an illuminating passage, and it was apparent that as he listened he heard the Word of God.

The storms rage over the surface of the sea. The waves dance in the sunlight. Below, the great currents move with power. Liberalism, fundamentalism, neo-orthodoxy, or whatever—they flow in contrary and sometimes bewildering courses. But far beneath all such movement and conflict lies the great deep of personal faith in the God and Father of our Lord Jesus Christ. At that level those who have named the Savior's Name meet and find that they are one.

VII.

The Christian Life

A few weeks before the Lund Conference, Dean Stephen J. England and I sat in a restaurant in Italy with the pastor of a Waldensian church. As partakers of a common faith, we were grateful for the opportunity of Christian fellowship, and our host seemed encouraged by our visit. We had talked of many things when, at last, he said with an air of wistfulness, "Tell me about your church people in America. Are they really spiritual?"

"What do you mean?"

"Are they really devoted to the Christian faith?"

Our answer was qualified. We had to admit that on the roll of every church are the names of some who rarely appear at worship, that in every congregation may be found listless and halfhearted members whose religion is more a form than a force. (Such an admission would have to be made in most parts of the Christian world during most periods of the church's history.) But then we proceeded to tell him about faithful believers in congregations to which we had ministered, earnest disciples in all walks of life who work and serve in devotion to their Lord. And we assured our host that such devoted Christians are to be found in thousands of congregations, rural and urban, across the United States.

"I am encouraged to hear you say so," the Waldensian confided. "A professor in my congregation who taught in America for a year surprised us by telling us the same thing.

Now I am glad to have the same report from you. We do not ordinarily think of you as a religious people."

If Europeans have not been made aware of the deeper spirit in American life, it is not surprising. The Old World knows us primarily through Hollywood films, the hurried, carefree visits of tourists, and the presence of United States troops. Superficial as such contacts are, yet because they are frequent and repeated it is from them that widespread impressions of America are derived. Persons who are subsequently given deeper and more accurate insights into our life and thought sometimes find it difficult to accept factual evidence which does not accord with the preconceived stereotype. Surely the American Christian they have encountered must be a rare exception!

More than one European who has had intimate contact with our soldiers has commented to me, invariably with surprise, about their wholesome friendliness, their love for children, their eagerness for companionship, their pride in their families, their open and natural interest in religion. It always strikes me as strange, on listening to such a report, that the European should consider it so unusual for an American boy to talk about his home and his church. Our armed forces include a cross section of the youth of our nation. If some of our soldiers are arrogant or sensual or vulgar, we confess with shame that some of our people at home are too, and that some soldiers always have been, especially when in a foreign land, but we do not consider these the norm. We know that other men in our forces are courteous and upright and serious, like many of the young leaders in our pews who have come back to us from the military service with a deep concern for a world in need of the spirit of Christ. In recent years we have seen our theological seminaries crowded with earnest and able ex-servicemen, determined to give their lives to the ministry, and we know that in our armed forces now are many other young Christians of the same caliber.

An American minister from Montana recently spent a winter in Geneva with his family, having been granted a leave of absence in order to study at the Ecumenical Institute. Seven young men from his church were serving in Europe in different branches of our armed forces, and he invited them to come to his house during the Christmas holiday. From various parts of Europe all seven of them came, five of them during the holiday season. The incident is significant. It manifests more than the desire to be in a home or to visit a fellow countryman, more than a response to a good pastor. It reveals an attitude of American Christian youth, a love for the church, for the friendships associated with it, and for the life it symbolizes.

It seems appropriate to set forth at this point an account of the Christian life as it is lived in the United States today, to recount the sort of information which the Waldensian pastor and other European Christians have welcomed eagerly when America was being discussed.

THE WORSHIP OF GOD

More people are going to worship in the United States than ever before in our history. Twenty years ago the general experience of ministers was that one-third of their members would be present on an average Sunday, that two-thirds would attend at least occasionally during a year's time, and that one-third no longer put in an appearance at all. Today the proportion of members present on a given Sunday is nearer one-half, and in some cases even more. A good many churches conduct two identical services on Sunday morning and have found that the additional "early" congregation often approaches in size that which assembles at the traditional hour of eleven o'clock.

What does the dramatic increase in church attendance during the past fifteen years mean? Does it represent a merely quantitative gain? Spiritual results are always difficult to assess, especially by statistical standards. Yet it would seem that the increase in churchgoing among us is equally as significant as other missionary gains in the long Christian past. It has been accompanied by a growth in church membership. And most ministers sense an earnestness in their congregations which is at least as intense as that of earlier periods in America.

Doubtless some persons still come to church for social purposes or business ends or other inadequate or unworthy reasons. But most of them come, I am convinced, seeking God and longing for a Word of Life.

The order of worship in our Protestant churches, except the Lutheran and Episcopal, would doubtless strike most Europeans as informal. This would be especially true in most of our smaller congregations and in rural areas; but in many large urban churches also the revivalistic mood still predominates and the service moves with little order in an air of easy informality, the tone being set by the spirit of the gospel songs and the friendliness of the minister. The prayers, for the most part, are spontaneous and, except on Communion Sunday in certain denominations, any portions of the historic liturgies are totally lacking. It must not be inferred, however, that such worship is barbarous or irreverent; it has nurtured the soul of a people in simple communion with God throughout our history and can certainly seem no more foreign to a European observer than the High Mass of the Church of Sweden or Anglican evensong would seem to a Baptist congregation in Iowa.

Meanwhile, an increasing number of our congregations, both urban and rural, are feeling the effects of the so-called liturgical movement. In American Protestantism this movement has not resulted in the imposition of the ancient liturgies upon our services; rather has it recalled the churches to a realization of the importance and meaning of worship. For a generation now our theological students and our ministers have given themselves to a serious study of the subject and to an effort to raise the standards of public devotion in our churches. In the early days of the movement there were some false starts—an ill-starred emphasis on "enriching" the services culturally with operatic arias and secular poetry and aesthetic dance, an inclination to manipulate the congregation psychologically so as to induce various "moods," an effort to "restore" the historic liturgies by attempting to import them into the life of a people whose whole religious tradition was not only alien to but incompatible with the ancient forms. In spite of such slips, however, our liturgical movement has made for a deepening understanding of worship and for a new dignity and integrity in our congregational praise. Setting their studies in a context of liturgical history, such writers as Vogt, Sperry, Palmer, Blackwood, Seidenspinner, and Coffin have recognized as valid the essentially "free" type of worship characteristic of American Protestantism and have helped develop it, in its own right, as a worthy vehicle of corporate devotion.

Among our churches generally (excepting the Episcopalian and the Lutheran with their fixed forms at one extreme and the "ecstatic sects" at the other) the liturgical movement has had increasing influence, especially in culturally sensitive congregations served by ministers from the theological seminaries. If you should go to worship in such a church—it might be Baptist, Methodist, Presbyterian, United, Disciple, Evangelical United Brethren, Church of God—you would find, with minor variations, a type of service which is emerging as more or less standard, not by the decree of any ecclesiastical council but out of the common experience, critically examined, of American Christians.

You approach a new, or recently remodeled, church building which, unless it is in the center of a city where real estate prices are high, is set back from the street on unwalled, "landscaped" ground. While some recent buildings are Georgian or Spanish in design, you are more likely to find a "modern" structure, spare and functional in appearance, with a few reminiscent Gothic lines and a graceful spire to proclaim its character as a church. In contrast to most European chapels, the newness of the building and the freshness of its paint seem almost harsh; but if it fails to convey an impression of ancient wisdom mellowed by the joys and tragedies of centuries, it is bright and clean and evidently holds a meaningful place in contemporary life. On passing through the open doors, only two or three steps above ground level, you enter a capacious foyer where you are greeted by a husband and wife serving as "hosts" for the day. If it is wintertime, they direct you to a cloakroom where you will leave your coat and hat, for the building is centrally heated. A friendly usher, after conducting you to your pew, hands you a printed or stenciled bulletin containing the order of service.

You find yourself seated in a sanctuary accommodating three hundred to five hundred worshipers. The place gives an impression of spaciousness yet intimacy. Its lines are clean and uncluttered, and the subdued tints of the walls are bright with sunlight; our architects have eliminated the "dim, religious light" from our churches. The room is divided by an aisle leading to the elevated communion table or altar. Until this generation the central pulpit dominated our Protestant churches, and the table was often all but lost on the floor below; today most of our churches set the pulpit to one side, with a lectern on the other. But pulpit, altar, and lectern are elevated essentially for the sake of visibility: they are not *separated* from the congregation by undue height nor removed by deep distance within the chancel; this is a "people's church." Behind the communion table there may be a symbolic stained-glass window or a reredos of carved wood; more likely there is a dossal curtain of deep-hued velvet over which is hung a cross of burnished brass.

The people enter quietly, but not in the absolute silence the minister would like; the tradition of the church as a friendly meeting place is still with us. *Fellowship* is more meaningful to the worshipers than *awe*, and most of them smile greetings at their friends and even carry on subdued conversations. We do not kneel in our churches, for the most part, nor do we know the custom of standing for a moment with bowed head on entering the pew. But as the time for the service draws near, people read through the bulletin to familiarize themselves with the order of service, and an increasing number bow their heads for meditation and prayer. You will note that the sanctuary is soon well filled, and you will be impressed by several characteristics of this congregation: the large number of men, probably not quite half of the attendance, but a large proportion; the way in which whole families come in together; the many young married couples (the church maintains a nursery for tiny children so that mothers and fathers may worship together); the number of children over six and of young people in their teens and early twenties, including university students and men in military uniform. Here is a cross section of our population, although on any given Sunday there are more persons outside our churches than in them.

A meditative prelude on the organ hushes the spirit of those just arriving. Perhaps two young girls in robes may enter bearing tapers to light the candles on the communion table. The full-throated organ announces the processional hymn, the congregation rises expectantly, and the choir enters singing, "Joyful, Joyful, We Adore Thee." The prevailing sort of vestment for our choirs is a robe cut on academic lines; the most common color is blue or wine red trimmed with a gold or silver stole. An increasing number of our ministers wear a plain black pulpit gown.

The minister takes his place at the lectern and leads the congregation, still standing, in an introit and invocation, followed by the Lord's Prayer. The people are seated for a meditative type of anthem and for the Scripture lesson read from a modern translation, most likely the Revised Standard Version. A quiet hymn is sung, such as "Dear Lord and Father of Mankind," followed by the pastoral prayer, which contains elements of praise, confession and assurance of forgiveness, thanksgiving, and intercession. The minister may read the prayer, but if so he will do it in a natural tone of voice, and it will be a prayer he has prepared with the specific needs of his own people in mind. At its conclusion the choir sings a response. If he has not already done so, the minister extends an informal welcome to all who are present, invites visitors to linger after the service, and asks everyone to register his name, address, and other information on a card provided in the pew. The cards, which are collected by the ushers, keep the minister informed as to visitors, newcomers, persons interested in church membership, and others in special need. Next comes the offering; as a worshipful expression of their stewardship, the people reverently place their contributions on the plates, the choir sings an anthem of praise, and as the ushers carry the gifts to the chancel the congregation stands and joyfully sings:

> Praise God, from whom all blessings flow;
> Praise Him, all creatures here below;
> Praise Him above, ye heavenly host;
> Praise Father, Son, and Holy Ghost.

After a quiet interlude the minister ascends the pulpit. The sermon remains the high point of American Protestant worship. It tends to be more pointed, practical, personal than European preaching, less a formal discursive essay on a theological problem and more a quiet conversation about God and the way in which the gospel meets some particular need in the life of the hearers. Generally speaking, an American pulpiteer subdues his individuality less than does a Continental preacher; he knows that the hearers tend to think of the service largely in terms of the sermon, and he tries to make it interesting and appealing, for he wants them to come back. At the same time he is mindful of his obligation to proclaim the Word of God and mediate his revelation. Frequently he is constrained to utter unpopular convictions, but American congregations admire a minister who delivers his soul in courage and in love. Our members exercise the responsibility imposed by the priesthood of believers by insisting that the preacher speak without fear or favor, and they are likely to answer a complaint that a sermon has been too pointed by quoting a proverb: "If the shoe fits, wear it." Indeed, the appeal to conscience, spoken from the pulpit, has become the chief means of maintaining discipline in our churches which, with neither compulsory confession and penance nor the old practice of solemn excommunication by the congregation still uphold a high standard of morality. Few of our sermons fail to strike an ethical note. Yet the minister does not exhort his hearers to be nice. He proclaims the gospel, urges the claims of Christ upon the life of every hearer, and seeks to win a response of submission to our Lord. In the tradition of evangelism, an American preacher strives to move his hearers, and the sermon usually reaches its climax with at least an implicit appeal for commitment to the will of God.

The sermon concludes with a prayer of dedication. There is a hymn of personal consecration, during which persons wishing to make a profession of faith may be invited to "come forward." The benediction follows, the choir sings an "Amen," and the service ends.

Attendance at worship over a period of time indicates that our American pattern tends to be more flexible and varied than the historic liturgies. In the service just described the only materials recurring week in and week out are the Lord's Prayer, the Doxology, the Gloria Patri, and the choral responses. While the general structure of the service is relatively stable, the use of varying materials each Sunday and the fact that these are not officially prescribed imparts a freshness of spontaneity within a general framework of dignity and reverence. Paradoxically, however, much less Scripture is read than in a liturgical service or in the worship of a Reformed church in Europe.

Unlike the European liturgical movement, its American counterpart has not agitated for the restoration of the Eucharist to a central place in worship. Perhaps one unconscious reason is that the denominational service books tend toward much "higher" liturgical practice in their suggested orders for communion than for the ordinary morning worship, and many Americans would resist the repetition of such formalities week after week. Also on "Communion Sunday" the sermon is often crowded out of the service, and our people do not want regular worship without preaching. Disciples of Christ, Churches of Christ, and the Church of the Brethren observe the communion every Lord's Day as the center and climax of their worship, but because of the simplicity of their tradition there is still time for the sermon. But whether at the pulpit or the altar, American worship at its best seeks to bring the congregation into communion with the living God. The growing attendance at our churches would seem to indicate that most of the time, for all our failures, the hungry sheep look up and *are* fed.

CHRISTIAN EDUCATION

Religious education is a distinctive and creative element of American Christianity. The Sunday school did not originate in the United States, but in England, and many other countries have contributed to its development. But religious education has flourished uniquely in American church life for at least three reasons: (1) From the beginning of our national history the churches had to assume the burden of imparting religious knowledge to youth, without the assistance of the state. (2) The "free" churches which predominated in American Protestantism, having for the most part no official catechisms, sought other and less stereotyped methods of teaching the young. (3) In sparsely settled rural areas, with an inadequate supply of ministers, the Sunday school provided an ideal means for faithful laymen to form little Christian communities and to study the Bible. From these peculiar roots American religious education has grown into a large and flourishing plant.

In the late nineteenth and early twentieth centuries the Sunday school was permeated by the mood of revivalism. Among a population largely unattached to the church it served as a primary agency of missions. Every effort was put forth to reach children and adults "outside the fold." Aggressive Sunday-school superintendents constantly introduced new devices to increase attendance and sponsored endless series of contests between the "Reds" and the "Blues" or among the various classes, awarding prizes for new members, for "gains over last year," and for every other tangible achievement. At county conventions the young "scholars" demonstrated their biblical learning, preachers delivered inspirational addresses, and banners were presented to schools with the best record. Organized classes flourished, with activistic names like Willing Workers, Loyal Bereans, Hustlers, and Kum-Join-Us. Attendance at Sunday school usually exceeded by 50 per cent that at the corporate worship which followed, though teachers directed at the pupils their regular closing chant: "Stay for church." While numbers and enthusiasm were the virtues chiefly publicized, devoted teachers imparted to youth a knowledge of the Bible and a love for Jesus Christ, and ministers prized the Sunday school as their right arm in evangelism.

Early in the twentieth century a new spirit manifested itself. Religious education became an academic discipline; the theological faculties appointed professors to lecture in the field, and their graduates went forth as professional directors of religious education to join the staff of many a large church alongside the minister. The psychology of religion was a subject exciting attention, and liberalism was the ascending mood in theology. The professors generally espoused these new interests, oriented their theory toward them, and created a technical terminology for their field of specialization. Reacting against the flamboyance of revivalistic methods, against the process of biblical indoctrination, and against the limitations of unsophisticated lay leadership, they sought to harmonize their work with the new philosophy of secular education. Decrying contests and the emphasis on numbers, they stressed the importance of personality development. The psychological terminology employed by religious educators and the humanistic outlook of a few gave to some of their writings a secular tone; unfortunately it is the works of this sort which are best known to those European theologians who inveigh against religious education.

But what was happening in our churches as a result of the religious education movement? The academic abstractions and such humanistic theorizing as there may have been made little impression on the lay leadership of our church schools, but their work was greatly strengthened on the practical side through the labors of the professors and directors of religious education. Every major communion produced a carefully planned curriculum of study, from infancy to adulthood, and church schools set up departments and classes graded according to age. Standard courses for the training of teachers through interdenominational co-operative schools were developed and improved, and many books and magazines with guidance for teachers appeared. Great strides were made in the publication of religious pictures, of "activity materials"

for the use of children, and of audio-visual aids. Superintendents learned to give less attention to contests and awards,
while emphasizing the teaching function of the church school
By discussing the "objectives of Christian education," [1] many
schools raised themselves considerably above the level of regarding a big attendance as a sufficient virtue in itself and of
viewing their teaching as a process of formal indoctrination.
The churches learned much from the professors, and the professors, checking their theories against a generation of practical experience, learned much from the churches.

The result has been a deepening evangelical concept of religious education. The late Professor Nevin C. Harner set it
forth succinctly in a definition: "Christian education is a
reverent attempt to discover the divinely ordained process by
which individuals grow toward Christlikeness, and to work
with that process." [2] The church thus becomes concerned
about the total experience of each person, about the varied
needs and interests of every pupil, about ministering to the

[1] The objectives were given classic statement, after a nation-wide survey,
by Professor Paul Vieth of Yale in his book, *The Objectives of Religious
Education* (New York: Harper & Brothers, 1930). They were first stated as
follows: "To foster in growing persons a consciousness of God . . . and a
sense of personal relationship to him. To lead growing persons into an
understanding and appreciation of the personality, life, and teaching of Jesus
Christ. To foster in growing persons a progressive and continuous development of Christlike character. To develop in growing persons the ability
and disposition to participate in and contribute constructively to the building of a social order embodying the ideal of the fatherhood of God and
the brotherhood of man. To lead growing persons to build a life philosophy
on the basis of a Christian interpretation of life and the universe. To
develop in growing persons the ability and disposition to participate in the
organized society of Christians—the church. To effect in growing persons
the assimilation of the best religious experience of the race, as effective
guidance to present experience." Later, an additional objective—"to develop
in growing persons an appreciation of the meaning and importance of the
Christian family, and the ability and disposition to participate in and contribute constructively to the life of this primary social group"—was added.
Religious educators are now engaged in a new analysis and restatement.
The original group of objectives became known to many pastors and
superintendents of Sunday schools through a warmly written practical
book edited by James Asa White, *Christian Education Objectives* (West-
wood, N.J.: Fleming H. Revell, 1932).

[2] Nevin C. Harner, *The Educational Work of the Church* (Nashville
and New York: Abingdon Press, 1939), p. 20.

particular condition of each individual. The entire program of the congregation is caught up in this concern and is directed by a pastoral sense of responsibility for the guidance of every personality touched by the church. Christian education is more than formal instruction in a class or from the pulpit: it includes fellowship, evangelism, worship, personal counseling, service, and all those activities for which American Christianity is so well known. But these activities are not ends in themselves. They are, in Professor Harner's phrase, phases of "the divinely-ordained process" by which needy men and women and children are brought into encounter with God and are enabled to grow in grace.

The focus is on persons. From the pulpit the minister looks upon faces, one by one, and speaks to waiting hearts. His pastoral prayer unfolds from his knowledge of intimate needs. The scores of lay teachers in the church school give themselves, each one, to a ministry of helpful guidance centering on perhaps a dozen boys and girls. The men and women who go out to do evangelistic calling are seeking other men and women for whom Christ died. The chairman of the board names a new member to serve on a committee, not to take some work off his own shoulders but because the recent convert needs to render some personal service to his Lord. The various classes and groups within the church provide numerous occasions of wholesome fellowship, not simply because young people like picnics, certainly not as "bait," but because every person needs a sense of "belonging" to a group of like-minded persons who are interested in him. Our preachers urge the practice of stewardship, not just to get more money for the church but because every Christian needs a sense of partnership with God and because, as a rule, those who give generously prosper spiritually. Perhaps no church succeeds in keeping the ideal of a person-centered ministry clearly in control of every activity. The bane of institutionalism steals imperceptibly upon us, and we fall into sin by thinking of persons as means to our institutional ends—increasing the attendance or underwriting the budget. But then we remember that our institution is ordained of Jesus, who came to be ministered unto but to minister, and we repent. Our church goes forward in his spirit, who, when he saw the multitudes, was moved with compassion for them.

An American congregation conceives of its mission in such concrete and personal terms, and the religious education movement of the past half century has helped us both to clarify the concept and to give it effective expression in our corporate life. We do not think of the church primarily as a liturgical community obediently repeating offices to the glory of Christ until he comes. We do not conceive its task as being essentially the instruction of the members in sound theology from the pulpit. We do not regard it as chiefly a priestly establishment to celebrate the mysteries of birth and marriage and death, of national crisis and victory. We do not see it basically as an instrument for the amelioration of social conditions. Doubtless the church ought to be performing all these functions. But we conceive its fundamental mission to be the finding of men and women and children, one by one, in their particular need, and bringing them into redemptive relationship with Christ and the transforming fellowship of the Christian community. We consider the measure of our love to our Lord the degree to which we strive to feed his sheep. This is the reason for the many activities that go on in an American congregation.

The church school remains the basic agency of Christian education among us. Almost universally the sessions are conducted on Sunday morning, in most cases before the corporate worship. The program lasts for at least an hour, while that for the younger children is often continued in an "expanded session" that extends through the time of the church service. There is a department or class for every age group and, while our growing population is continually overflowing our best-planned "educational buildings," the churches strive to provide each class with a clean, well-lighted room, with furniture suited to the size of the pupils, with Bibles, workbooks, blackboards, additional audio-visual aids, and other necessary equipment.

Teaching methods are flexible and creative. If a teacher of

young children tells a story dealing either with a biblical event or with present-day experience, she makes use of beautifully printed pictures in color and leads them in appropriate songs; or the pupils themselves may act out the story. Many lessons are taught through carefully planned activities—coloring pictures, constructing a model of a Palestinian house, making paper baskets to hold flowers for a sick friend—which enable the children to participate in the expression of a Christian ideal. Worship is an element in every session. It is planned as part of the "total experience" of the morning, so that thanksgiving grows out of a lesson on "God's Loving Care" or an occasion for personal commitment arises from a study of "Jesus Appoints Twelve Helpers." Such worship is not a repetition of a liturgy used in the church service, but expresses in appropriate words, songs, and acts the spiritual mood of the age group. Often it derives so naturally from the activities of the session that the pupils almost spontaneously break forth into a song of praise or offer a series of personal prayers.

Many problems confront us in the work of our church schools. An hour a week is insufficient time for religious education, and the weekdays of our children are pre-empted during most of the year by activities of the public schools. A partial solution has been the use of the summer holiday, through vacation church school with daily sessions of two or three hours for two or more weeks, or, more recently, through a "day camp," to which a church takes its young children between breakfast and supper for Christian experiences of learning and outdoor play. Following the lead of the Presbyterian Church in the U.S.A., most of our major communions have developed a curriculum of religious education which seeks to involve the home along with the church school in the systematic spiritual nurture of children, but such an effort will be successful only with those families most deeply concerned. With other families, the attendance of children at Sunday school tends to be irregular, so that the pupils who are most in need of the ministry of religious education receive it only in smatterings. A constant problem is the maintenance of a full staff of qualified teachers, and it becomes ever more difficult with the increasing fluidity of American life. My own congregation of nine hundred members, with an average attendance of three hundred and fifty in its nineteen church-school classes requires a force of thirty-three teachers and twenty-two officers, prepared and on the job every Sunday morning. A constant program of recruiting and training is necessary to maintain such a staff of volunteers. Yet our churches do so and, while many teachers have limitations, here is a remarkable "lay ministry" that enlists the consecrated service of an army of faithful men and women.

In nearly every congregation will be found a nucleus of devoted teachers who have held their posts loyally through the years, who have kept themselves prepared by continued personal study and by attendance at "leadership training schools," conventions and conferences, who have maintained a personal, almost pastoral, interest in the spiritual growth of their pupils, and who have become an inspiration to many. Until her recent untimely death, a Christian housewife in a Southern town had been the teacher and adviser of the young people in her church for more than thirty years. During all that time she was faithful in attendance, she kept herself in-formed about developments in youth work, she taught in state-wide conferences and camps, she set a winsome example of Christian living and loyalty to the church, she was a loving and understanding counselor of scores of young men and women; a large proportion of the present congregation looks back with gratitude upon her friendship and her teaching as a major spiritual influence during the years of their youth. Not every church is given a teacher so richly endowed with per-sonal gifts, so radiant with Christian grace, but our church schools have called forth a glorious host of earnest disciples who have gladly sung

> In the service of the King
> Every talent I will bring

and have poured out their energies in a ministry to boys and girls and men and women, to the glory of God.

Noteworthy in the American church school are the classes for adults. Normally, there are about four of these in a school, each with an age span of roughly ten to fifteen years: in effect, the "young married people," the parents of school-age children, the men and women of mature years, and the retired. The present emphasis is on husband and wife attending the same class: a generation ago there were huge men's classes and women's classes, which concentrated on developing "class loyalty" and enthusiasm. At that time church-school attendance usually exceeded that at morning worship; today a balance has been attained or the situation slightly reversed. Most of the adult classes are organized, with a roster of officers; they hold regular meetings for fellowship in addition to the Sunday morning study hour, and they carry on certain projects of service and of giving to Christian causes. The church school is the largest agency of adult education in the United States: of 49 million adults pursuing some form of organized study, 15 million are in Sunday schools. While many adults engage in little or no private study of the lesson and depend entirely on the lecture of the teacher for knowledge and inspiration, others do put forth some personal effort.

Although our church schools leave much to be desired as a means of serious study, they play an important role. The Sunday-school class is a small and intimate fellowship centering in the Christian life, and it is a primary agency of bringing persons of all ages to Christ and the church.

An important phase of the work of Christian education in our churches is the program for young people. Among us the term "youth" denotes an earlier period of life than in some other parts of the world, namely, the ages from twelve to twenty-three; normally we have three departments, corresponding to the system of public education: intermediate, or junior high school (ages twelve to fourteen), senior, or high school (ages fifteen to seventeen); college and working young people (ages eighteen to twenty-three). In all three departments the same general type of program is followed, growing out of some seventy-five years of experience since the rise of the Christian Endeavor movement (1881). Besides the church-school class which meets on Sunday morning there is almost universally a Sunday evening youth meeting for at least an hour of worship, study, and discussion, the young people themselves taking the lead under the counsel of an adult adviser. In many churches the evening session is expanded in time to include also a period of recreation (directed play), a time of group singing, and a light supper. So the Sunday evening meeting becomes a happy and inspiring experience in the lives of young people, week after week, enriching the instruction of Sunday morning (which, whatever our intention, tends to be more formally didactic) with pleasant and interesting activities in an atmosphere of purposeful Christian fellowship.

Beyond the congregation the most notable feature of our work with youth is the program of camps and conferences. In the various states every denomination conducts a series of camps for youth during the summer, with attendance running from sixty to two hundred in each. The customary program lasts about a week, providing classes in the Christian faith and life, group worship and private devotion, discussion of personal problems, directed play, and experience in living together as Christians. Many of the conferences end with a solemn service of personal consecration. A sizable minority of our Christian young people, especially our leaders, attend church camp through a full course of four to seven summers; this group provides a core of earnest and intelligent workers in most of our congregations and a large portion of our recruits for the ministry.

Under the auspices of the United Christian Youth Movement, an arm of the National Council of Churches, a number of interdenominational conferences are held each year; outstanding young people from the various communions in a state are brought together for a week of intensive study and discussion in an ecumenical setting. Pioneered by the Friends and the Brethren, the "work camp" has become an important means of transforming idealism into service and of enabling youth to gain a Christian insight into social problems over a period of several weeks.

In the earlier development of our work with young people, especially under the auspices of the Christian Endeavor movement, mass meetings held an important place. County rallies brought together hundreds, state and national conventions assembled thousands, for programs of inspirational addresses. In the past thirty years, as denominational boards have developed separate youth programs and as the educational emphasis has shifted to leadership by the young people themselves rather than listening to speeches by eloquent adults, mass meetings have diminished in importance. During World War II, however, the "Youth for Christ" movement revived the mass meeting under fundamentalist auspices, carrying on its work independently of the denominational programs. There are still large Christian Endeavor conventions in some states, and at four-year intervals the United Christian Youth Movement has sponsored an interdenominational Christian Youth Conference of North America with several thousand young people in attendance. But most of our young people find their decisive Christian experience in the intimate fellowship of the group in their own church or the intensity of a week in summer camp, rather than in the enthusiasm of great mass meetings.

Students who have come to America from abroad have been impressed by the program of Christian activities on university campuses. In some private and church-related colleges, where a spiritual purpose dominates the life of the institution, religion is an integral part of the student's educational experience: professors present their subjects as men of faith and many extracurricular events are pervaded by a Christian purpose. Our state universities, however, are by law religiously neutral, and these are our largest and fastest growing schools. The YMCA, YWCA, and other student Christian movements work on such campuses, and the various denominations have undertaken to follow their own students to the university.

The pattern of work which emerged in the generation just passing has centered in a "house"—Wesley House, Westminster House, Pilgrim House—where students may come together for informal and directed activities. The Sunday evening program includes worship, recreation, and discussion on a university level. In addition, the house serves as a meeting place for small groups during the week, and its director is an understanding counselor of students. In some instances the house serves as a hostel, where a small number of young people may live. While most such Christian student centers regularly reach only a minority of the students of the sponsoring denomination, they succeed in evangelizing some, and most of them constitute a nucleus of intense Christian devotion in a somewhat secular and impersonal environment. Unfortunately, the plurality of "houses" near most of our universities emphasizes the fact of our sectarian divisions, not from any desire to do so but because they are sponsored by denominations. They do much work together, but in only a few instances have the communions pooled their efforts to erect one worthy and well-equipped center of Protestant religious life on a campus and to contribute their workers to a common staff carrying out a united religious program.

In recent years some leading workers have expressed a fear that, while the student house is an arm of the denomination, it tends to become a substitute for the local congregation. An effort is now being made to tie the work of house and church more closely together or even to move the scene of all religious activities to the church building. When the latter is near the campus of the university, such efforts are usually successful; in other instances they may result in a surrender of the Christian mission to a doctrinaire principle.

We are mindful of many limitations in our work with young people. Our influence as churches on the formation of ideals is often secondary to that of television, radio, motion pictures, and the popular magazines. Our efforts to implant the high and difficult standards of Christian morality do not always meet with success. We often fail to give, even to some of our committed young disciples, a systematic understanding of Christian doctrine. But as a general rule the young people whom we reach regularly during their high school and college or early working years remain loyal to Christ and the church. Such young men as these maintain a spiritual concern during their military service. As a rule, our leading laymen are "graduates" of our Sunday schools and youth organizations, as are nearly all of our ministers. Ten years ago my wife helped organize a Sunday evening program for a new group of about ten "intermediates" (younger adolescents). They followed the usual round of activities—worship, discussion, recreation, singing—in an atmosphere of Christian dedication and friendliness. Sometimes they had picnics or played ball on our lawn. That summer several of them went to their first Christian camp and came home with a new vision of service and a deeper loyalty to their church. Three of those boys are now finishing their course in theological seminary and one of the girls is engaged in Christian social work. Many advisers of young people in our churches could report similar experiences.

In the life of the church as a whole, and not just with young people, fellowship is cultivated as a major activity. Weekly church dinners during the winter and monthly class picnics during the summer help members to know one another as Christians. Such dinners are not held for the meal alone—often the food is quite simple—but as a popular and convenient means of bringing people together. Nearly always there is an explicit educational or inspirational purpose. Some churches present at their weekly dinners a course of lectures which brings to their people outstanding Christian personalities and guidance on major spiritual issues. "Family camping" is a growing movement in religious education, bringing parents and children together for experience of worship, play, study, and Christian fellowship.

So with purpose and imagination our churches try to enlist persons of all ages in all those processes which contribute to their growth toward Christlikeness. Christian education, for all its limitations, becomes a major and many-sided enterprise which enriches the quality of life and inspires many who have been redeemed by our Lord to follow in his steps.

THE PROGRAM OF A CHURCH

A typical American conviction is that a church should not merely exist: it should have a "program." The activism of our nature tells us that a congregation is of little worth unless it is "doing things" and that every member ought to carry his share of these activities. The entire "program" is motivated by a congregation's sense of mission, and members are enlisted in its manifold responsibilities as a part of their own growth in the Christian life.

The program of a church may be defined as the specific work which it undertakes to do during a set period of time. "Program planning" involves the congregation in a discussion of its particular mission and in the process of agreeing upon specific goals for the coming year. Such an experience raises many basic questions about the life of a church and sets the people to thinking seriously about their common obligations. The denominations provide guidance for such exploration. A committee of the Congregational Christian Churches, for example, recently set forth certain criteria for an effective rural church:

1. an adequate church plant [building and equipment]
2. systematic financing
3. a prospect list [for evangelism]
4. an organization adapted to the parish area
5. an indigenously planned program
6. good community relations
7. the responsible functioning of laymen
8. an adequate theological base.

More specifically, a program is outlined for each of the major areas of the church's concern—worship, evangelism, membership development, stewardship and finance, missions, Christian education, social action. For each of these areas a committee or department is appointed to lead the congregation in the achievement of the goals. In such a way a large portion of the membership is enlisted to engage in the Father's business. Dwight L. Moody, the nineteenth-century evangelist, used to counsel ministers: "It is better to put ten men to work than to do the work of ten men." As a matter of policy, many congregations allot to every member some particular responsibility for the church's task. Even large congregations attempt to approximate this goal. The Northwood Christian Church in Indianapolis, for example, increases its number of elders, deacons, and deaconesses as the membership grows; with 1,600 persons on its roll, it elects 185 to its official board, each of whom is assigned to a major department or "functional committee." Moreover, it is a policy that no one shall be immediately re-elected to an office at the expiration of his three-year term. The planning and execution of the annual program thus becomes an important means of educating the membership in the church's work, of expressing in practice the democracy inherent in the concept of the priesthood of believers, and of providing for many ordinary Christian men and women an opportunity for significant stewardship of time and talent.

A major enterprise in nearly every American congregation is the work of the women, combining elements of service, devotion, fellowship, and study. It is not a substitute for the regular program of the church and the corporate worship on Sunday. Rather is it an effort to enlist all the women of a congregation in activities of Christian service. So it has become a means of redeeming the leisure time of many women and directing it into channels of eternal significance.

Even in frontier days, our Christian women were leaders in the temperance and missionary movements: their "dues" from their "butter-and-egg" money or whatever other slight funds passed through their hands helped send some of the first nineteenth-century missionaries. In many rural communities they met to piece quilts or to put up fruit and vegetables for needy families or charitable institutions. During times of economic depression they have served dinners at a small profit to help pay off the indebtedness on the church building. They have explored every honorable means by which the devotion and labor of willing hands might be turned into cash for enterprises of the Kingdom. Today the effort is to enlist every woman belonging to a congregation in the work of its women's auxiliary or society of Christian service. Ordinarily each woman is assigned to a group of twenty or thirty members who meet regularly in one of the homes for fellowship and missionary study. Usually there is also a general monthly meeting for planning and inspiration.

The women of our churches still raise sizable funds by their service and by extra giving. In the congregation to which I belong the Christian Women's Fellowship in a recent year raised $4,600, much of which came from direct giving and half of which as a matter of policy was dedicated to missions. This came from about 175 active women (out of a large group of 420 on the rolls) and was "over and above" the contributions which they and their families made to the regular church budget. When one gets "inside" the life of an active congregation one is amazed to discover the hours of arduous and sometimes menial service which devoted women dedicate each month to the work of Christ.

The large-scale enterprise thus described is a supplement to the regular activities of the church in worship and Christian education. It is possible because our women are being increasingly freed from household drudgery and prefer to devote some of their daytime hours to Christian service rather than to television and cardplaying. But our women are not segregated from the regular life of the church. Undoubtedly one factor in the emergence of the ladies' aid societies during frontier days was the domination by the men of the affairs of the congregation. But today in most of our local churches women serve on the board of officers, sometimes in equal numbers to the men, and hold membership on all major committees.

"Men's Work" as an organized activity within the congregation operates on a less extensive scale than that of the women. One reason may be the traditional domination of men in the business of the church so that they have felt less need for separate meetings of "their own," but that condition is rapidly changing as women carry increasing burdens of leadership. A more important factor is the limited leisure time available to men except on Sunday. Many churches have a men's meeting one night a month for fellowship, inspiration, and the cultivation of "church loyalty." There is a growing interest in "prayer breakfasts": one morning a week men assemble at the church to eat and pray together before starting out on the day's work. The burden of organized personal evangelism has been carried by men, many churches having an Andrew Fellowship or other similar group which sets aside at least one night a month to call on the unchurched. On a spring Saturday a number of men may gather to paint the church building or to work on the shrubbery and lawn. The men especially like to do a good turn. When a farmer at Scott City, Kansas, was taken ill at wheat-sowing time, the Christian Men's Fellowship of his church planted his crop for him.

The emphasis is on prayer and good works. Few of our men's organizations undertake to raise funds, but try rather to encourage their members in stewardship and tithing to support the church. Our men have not carried as far as their European brethren studies in the Christian implications of particular vocations such as law, business, or farming. The pattern of our churchmanship was set in a day when being Christian in one's work was understood in simple terms of diligence and honesty and when young congregations being planted in the West needed the loyalty and leadership of men if they were to survive. We still tend to think of an outstanding layman as an upright believer who is a "wheelhorse" in the program of his church.

A major responsibility of many congregations in recent years has been the erection of a new building. Hundreds of parishes have been created in the past ten years as a result of missionary work in our expanding urban areas, and all of these have had to be housed. And many of our churches with buildings erected in the nineteen-twenties or earlier have had to replace them; until the present generation only a small portion of our buildings, especially in the West, have been constructed of expensive permanent materials. But ever since the late thirties there has been a building boom in churches; the high degree of national prosperity has favored the collecting of building funds and the erection of more expensive but more enduring structures of stone, brick, or steel and concrete. In 1940, $59 million was spent for new church construction; by 1953 the figure had increased to $474 million; in 1955 it reached $773 million. We are living through a period which may be compared to the great age of church building in the European Middle Ages: we are erecting few cathedrals but hundreds of effective parish churches. In the first five years I lived in Indianapolis, the congregations of my own denomination alone constructed (or remodeled on a large scale) thirteen buildings in that city. In our near neighborhood four churches of different communions instituted major building programs. Fortunately this era of tremendous construction comes at a time when popular taste in architecture and understanding of worship are relatively mature. Most of the sturctures being erected have been carefully planned, but with only a slowly increasing acceptance of contemporary architectural styles.

Except in areas which suffered heavy damage during the war, most European congregations worship in buildings constructed decades or centuries ago, part of their heritage from a long Christian past. The average Christian in the Old World has perhaps given little thought to the labor and dedication and dreams and prayer that go into the erection of a worthy house of God. By contrast, a large portion of American Christians have gone through a "building program," and few of our pastors have not been involved in at least one of the three stages—collecting a building fund, planning and constructing and dedicating the new building, paying off the building debt. Such a program is a large undertaking for a congregation. University Park Christian Church, to which I belong, recently completed the first unit of its building (adequate facilities for the church school are now under construction) at a cost of $300,000. Two-thirds of this amount was in hand, from gifts of the membership, at the time the building was dedicated. This left us with a debt of $100,000 on which we have been paying $1,000 a month. Meanwhile we have underwritten an additional $100,000 to make possible the beginning of construction of our education building. Ours is a congregation of 537 family units, most of whom shared generously in the undertaking; there are no "large givers" to underwrite the major portion of the cost. All this money has had to be raised in addition to the normal budget of the church, and missionary giving has increased each year.

Such an undertaking becomes a spiritual experience for those who pass through it; many learn for the first time the joy of giving in large measure out of love for Christ. A few critics among us have scored this great American era of church building as a supreme manifestation of selfishness on the part of Christian people, who, it is said, ought to have been pouring out these large funds in works of mercy and mission. For my part I am willing to take issue with the critics. Doubtless some congregations have indulged their corporate pride in an unjustifiable lavishness. But in most instances they have provided for the first time an adequate physical "plant" for the fulfilling of their mission. Moreover, since most of our buildings now being erected are relatively permanent, they represent nonrecurring expenditure. So the grace of giving on a large scale which many congregations are now learning may in the future be diverted to other worthy enterprises. The minister of Northwood Christian Church in Indianapolis, who had led his congregation through a major building program involving an expenditure of more than $600,000, recently challenged them to give $100,000 "for others" during the ensuing three years, over and above their regular missionary budget. The church voted to accept such a moral obligation even before their building had been completed.

Even when no building is contemplated or being paid for, the planning and execution of the "program" in an aggressive congregation of four hundred members or more is a large administrative task. Our ministers study "the art of church management" and devote long hours to an endless cycle of committee meetings. They are constantly engaged in the promotion of some "emphasis" in their local program or the life of their denomination. The burden of administration often demands a disproportionate share of their energy, at the expense of pastoral work or study for the pulpit ministry. Many a devoted layman also finds himself weighed down with responsibilities for the affairs of his church so similar to the details of his daily business that religion becomes for him a drain rather than an inspiration. Yet American Christianity has thrived on such organized activity. People want to belong to a congregation that is "doing things." Our pastors have popularized a slogan: "A Going Church is a Growing Church."

Back of all the activity, it must be remembered, is a spiritual motivation. Our people find satisfaction in "doing things" —not just in going through motions, but because they believe that "we are workers together for God." When the inner motives of the hardest working men and women in a congregation are analyzed, as well as those of the minister, it will be discovered that they serve their church because they believe that it is helping other men and women, that it is ministering to the needs of a troubled world, that thus it is doing the work of God. One measure of the influence of Christianity upon American life is the large proportion of the splendid energy of our young race which has been channeled into the flumes of consecration "for Christ and the church."

VIII.

The Haunting Question

The churches of the United States occupy a crucial place in the contemporary world. Our nation is one of the two major powers in international affairs, and among the great states of our time no other has such flourishing religious institutions as do we. By every standard of outward success, the American churches are prospering, with growing membership rolls, increasing attendance, rising budgets, impressive buildings, and widespread popular favor. If our Christianity exerts a significant outreach, if the faith of the populace manifests a truly redemptive effect upon the policies of government and of business, then the world should take hope at the prosperity of our religious institutions.

But those *ifs* are huge interrogation points. They raise the haunting question: is the present good fortune of the American churches a true revival of Christian spirituality? Are the lives of men and women being transformed after the likeness of our Lord? Is the mind of Christ permeating the culture? Are Christian principles determining the character of the common life? We cannot help asking these questions.

Our uneasiness is compounded when we realize that many Europeans and Asiatics look upon our nation with grave apprehension. They fear our economic power, they are uncertain about our foreign policy, they question the maturity of our judgment. Such uncertainties we can, in a measure, understand. But it comes as a shock to discover how seriously even our Christian brethren in other lands question the adequacy of our religion. They are by no means certain that just a little more numerical success on the part of our churches will assure the peace and well-being of the world. Undoubtedly much of the suspicion about our faith arises from insufficient knowledge of the religious situation here and misunderstanding of our corporate Christian life; this book has been written in an effort to impart a more adequate interpretation of the spirit of American Christianity. There is much that is positive in our tradition and a great deal that is encouraging in the present institutional vitality of religion. But our recognition of this fact must not blind us to the urgency of the haunting questions we have posed.

As a background for our consideration of the growth of our churches and its inner meaning, we must first consider a striking paradox in contemporary history—a world-wide resurgence of the historic religions, accompanied by a deepening secularization of society—and then a dramatic change that is coming over the American character.

RELIGIOSITY AND SECULARISM

On the world scene two countermovements are apparent with respect to religion. There is manifest, on the one hand, a striking revival of the historic faith in many parts of the earth; at the same time, the process of secularization continues to supplant religious constraints by other considerations in those areas where the significant decisions of modern society are being made.

In the new nations of Southeast Asia, India, and the Middle East the ancestral faiths of Buddhism, Hinduism, and Islam are experiencing a remarkable renewal of personal loyalty among the populace as well as institutional prosperity. One may attribute the revival of the historic religions, in part at least, to the deep spiritual need of mankind in every generation, accentuated by the atomic terrors and the mounting pressures of our time. Perhaps an even more significant factor in their resurgence is the identification of religion with the particular cultural heritage. To be a good Indian means to be a good Hindu, to be a good Arab means to be a good Moslem; so with us, to be a good American means to be a good Protestant or Catholic or Jew. It may be that a proper understanding of the renewal of religious interest in America must await a more thorough analysis of the resurgence of the ancestral faiths across the world.

Yet the widespread prosperity of religious institutions and the general indentification of twentieth-century men with the faith of their fathers must be seen against the background of increasing secularization. Though the formal manifestations of religion may be on the increase, religious considerations have less and less to do with the decisions that really determine events in contemporary society. The sovereign nation, the autonomous interests of massive blocs of economic power, the demands of science and technology—these are the really decisive forces. The revival of Hinduism is not producing a more distinctively Hindu culture in India. Rather, in a renewal of his devotion to Hinduism an Indian finds himself inwardly related to his own spiritual and cultural heritage. So for the Arab who finds roots in Islam. But the structure of the new society in India or Egypt, as in the United States, is increasingly determined, as are the decisions made within it, by the canons of contemporary technological and industrial civilization, not by the peculiar tenets of the traditional faith.

The fundamental test of true spiritual revival in the contemporary world is not the mere flourishing of institutional religion or even the increase of personal piety; it is the degree to which there may be regained for a transcendent faith the throne of decision which has been usurped by autonomous secular concerns. The test must be applied to the present flowering of Christian interest in the United States. But the problem is not ours alone.

AMERICAN SOPHISTICATION AND CONFORMITY

An understanding of the present religious trend in our country may be heightened by considering the alteration of the American character since the so-recent days of the frontier and the isolated rural community.

The frontier era of our history is regarded as having ended in 1890. In that year one-third of our population lived in cities, the proportion having doubled in a generation; by 1950 only one-sixth of our people were left on the farms, and the proportion continues to decline. Meanwhile rural life has become more urban in character as a result of consolidated schools, rapid means of travel, and the mass media of communication. The old stock types of country boy and city slicker are as archaic as the gun-toting cowboy. American culture has entered a new era of sophistication which is having its effect on the life of the churches and on the spirit of the people.

Various factors besides the removal of frontier isolation have contributed to the new sophistication.

The industrial progress of the United States, with its almost miraculous expansion of productivity, has come as the result of thousands of manufacturing enterprises across the land, each with its own highly complex processes of production. This development has demanded an almost infinite degree of technological specialization on the part of a highly skilled labor force, and a corresponding reduction in the number of unskilled laborers, "brothers to the ox." The technician who handles today's productive machinery has a sense of power, of respect for human capacity, of belief in the almost unlimited technical possibilities of human inventiveness, barring an atomic disaster: he is himself a man of power, of self-assurance, of education.

The international power of the United States is another factor in the new sophistication. In every American community are veterans of two world wars who have returned victoriously from campaigns in Europe, Africa, Asia, and the islands of the Pacific, in the great oceans, and in the air. These and many other Americans have traveled over the whole world as representatives of a powerful state and an advanced technological culture and have reached sometimes arrogant conclusions about the "superiority" of their way of life. American military, diplomatic, industrial, and educational leaders are constantly dealing with men from every part of the world and are making decisions which affect the lives of persons elsewhere.

The growing prosperity of the United States over a long period of time has made for sophisticated patterns of living. Memories of the Great Depression have pretty well faded. Prosperous executives, white-collar workers, and skilled laborers practice the "gracious living" of suburbia, their lives marked by gentility and self-assurance as they enjoy every convenience and resort to new luxuries.

The sophistication with which we are dealing represents both a new sense of power and status and a sense of conforming to the patterns of behavior expected of persons of such status. Standardization has become, therefore, a conspicuous mark of American life; it is rich and many-sided, not the standardized poverty of the Middle East or the standardized drabness of the Communist state store. Regional differences are fading, with little more than distinctive accents in speech remaining as a mark of differentiation. Towns across the United States look increasingly alike. The people read the same magazines, go to the same movies, and watch the same TV programs in their living rooms.

Just as surely as the millions assaulted by the mass media have learned to "Brush Your Teeth with Colgate's" or to "Live Modern," so they have, sometimes unconsciously, but often deliberately, taken their mores and their ideals from the great centers of the communications industry. Within memory, the Puritan behavior standards of rural American Protestantism have virtually disappeared from the scene: the old prohibitions against play or commerce on Sunday, against cardplaying, theatergoing, dancing, smoking, gambling, and drinking, are wholly or largely disregarded. The triumphant reports that 60 per cent of our population claimed membership in some church had just been published when an Indiana newspaper carried the intelligence that 60 per cent of the population of our state drink beer. These two groups of persons are not identical, but if the figures are correct, at least a third of the church members are also beer drinkers. The propriety of beer drinking is not the point at issue, but rather

—when due allowances have been made for churches which have never espoused Puritan mores—the disappearance of the old, accepted, outward, formal signs of the difference between Christians and non-Christians. In our increasingly standardized society, Christianity represents the accepted cult according to which the people celebrate the rites of worship; it does not necessarily provide the controlling standard of conduct.

In the newly sophisticated America a florescence of mass culture has brought an appreciation of the arts to large segments of the population. Classical music is played by scores of local orchestras; leading soloists and musical organizations appear on concert series in hundreds of communities presenting symphony, opera, and ballet; classical record clubs send out recordings every month to thousands of hi-fi enthusiasts. Book clubs flourish by the dozen, some of them specializing in the classics; the Great Books Seminars have become a recognized phase of adult education; publishers have struck a new gold mine with paper-back editions of scholarly and literary titles. Art museums throughout the land take pride in their acquisitions; many individuals own fine oil originals; publishers have found a growing market for expensive books with full-color reproductions from the great painters; and a minor industry has grown up to provide hotels with copies in oil of famous paintings. In our more sophisticated culture, familiarity with the arts is a sign of status.

Yet the new American sophisticate is not characterized by independence of thought. Ours is a sophistication of manners, not of mind. For all our universal public education, our unbelievable expansion of colleges and universities, even for all our publication of serious books, it may be seriously questioned if as a people we have the vigor of intellectual dissent from prevailing patterns which characterized earlier periods of American life. Such vigorous and unorthodox thinkers as Paine, Jefferson, Emerson, Channing, Beecher, Ingersoll, Mencken, and Fosdick all enjoyed a popular following, vocal supporters who engaged in countless local debates. By contrast, ours is an era of conformity, with little of the color of dissent.

Various reasons may be suggested for the decline in independent thinking. The day of vigorous independent journalism has passed, with vast fortunes now required to launch even a successful local paper, to say nothing of a national magazine. Liberal arts education has not kept pace with the vast growth of the technical schools; science has its place among the liberal arts, and it prompts men to ask questions, though apparently not the ultimate ones. In many schools, certain of the liberal arts which were calculated to stimulate independent thought, namely, philosophy and classical studies, have declined absolutely even as faculty and student body have multiplied. Doubtless the power and prosperity of the nation discourage the mood of radicalism which characterized an earlier and a leaner generation. Perhaps even more influential is the advent of the new ethic of conformity, which David Riesman has so tellingly described. The contemporary sophisticate lacks transcendent standards; his goal is acceptance by his peer group. He is in a constant state of uneasiness unless he is certain of approval; consequently individualism in thinking is an ideal he will not cherish. Doubtless also there is a new mood of humility before the potential terrors of the atomic age; there is little confidence in sheer humanism. Men are groping for belief, and skepticism is muted among writers, teachers, and students.

Reflections of the new sophistication in American culture are apparent in the life of our churches. Greater decency, dignity, and formality characterize our public worship, new propriety and comfort mark our church buildings (provided with chancel, nursery, and parlor). The quality of our hymns has improved, and they are led by vested choirs and robed ministers. Preaching is more restrained and less bombastic than in the past. New churches are established in elegant properties and respectable buildings which commend themselves to suburbanites. Church pageantry and drama are more sophisticated than formerly.

From the Christian standpoint not all has been gain. While worship has gained in dignity, it has often lost in intimacy. The art of *ex tempore* prayer bids fair to disappear from the public worship of many congregations. Meanwhile, the extra services where the members came together in informal fellowship to pray for one another—the Sunday evening service, the midweek prayer meeting—have generally been disbanded. There is still much informality, but it is at church dinners and other dominantly social affairs.

Another obvious reflection of the new sophistication is the vast growth of theological education. Three years of graduate theological education for the ministry (leading to the Bachelor of Divinity degree) have become standard in the denominations which grew out of the great American frontier revivals as well as those which derived from Europe. The growth of multiple staffs in local churches indicates a desire of the laity to have specialized, well-educated leadership. Laymen, moreover, are showing a new interest in theology; not that they are concerned about mastering full-orbed systems, but they are searching for answers to ultimate questions.

Yet the religious manifestations of the new sophistication in the American culture do not include genuine theological maturity or even well-informed Christian thought on the part of American laymen. Most of them have little awareness of the direction of biblical scholarship, whether critical or theological. Indeed, liberal ministers who have hesitated to plunge their congregations into some of these problems, now that religion is again a popular interest, find their people uncritically accepting fundamentalist assumptions. The lack of well-informed religious thinking parallels the shortage of independent thought in the culture as a whole. So, paradoxically, as the number of nominal Christians in America increases, the number of informed Christians appears to be declining. Relatively few laymen outside the fundamentalist churches could pass an examination on the content of the New Testament or the rudiments of Christian doctrine as contained in a catechism. Few popular writers today have the large following that Harry Emerson Fosdick or Sherwood Eddy or E. Stanley Jones served in their fearless works of doctrinal exposition and Christian social criticism a generation ago. A few intellectuals have been profoundly stirred by the reading of Niebuhr and Tillich, but the religious authors most generally known among us are Billy Graham and Norman Vincent Peale, who make no pretense of facing intellectual issues regarding the faith.

It is against the background of the new sophistication in manners and culture but not in thought that we must consider the remarkable growth of religious interest and of ecclesiastical institutions in recent years.

THE "RETURN TO RELIGION"

A generation ago piety was not a popular pose in the United States. Well-known authors wrote articles for magazines on "Why I Do Not Go to Church" and similar subjects, wiseacres in the universities referred with condescending skepticism to the historic faith, the traditional methods of evangelism seemed to have lost their appeal, and, despite the faithfulness of multitudes in pew and in pulpit, the churches found themselves working in a vast field of popular indifference.

Today the mood has changed. Ever since the United States became involved in World War II there has been a growing popular interest in religion. Church attendance has spectacularly increased. Books with Christian themes have become best-sellers. Pseudo-religious motion pictures and popular songs have led the "hit parade." A wistfulness for faith has become evident in the common life, as has also the willingness to witness to personal convictions. Some observers have seen in these events the signs of imminent revival. Others have dismissed them with cynicism. The true meaning is difficult to assess.

Much of the new interest in religion betrays the longing for serenity in an age of anxiety and frustration. The titles of some of the most widely read nonfiction of recent years illuminate the groping for security: *The Return to Religion* (1936) by Henry C. Link, a consulting psychologist; *Peace of Mind* (1946) by Joshua Loth Liebmann, a Jewish rabbi; *Peace of Soul* (1949) by Fulton J. Sheen, the best-known Roman Catholic preacher in America today; *Peace with God* (1953) by Billy Graham, the celebrated evangelist; *The Power of Positive Thinking* (1952) by Norman Vincent Peale, popular Protestant preacher and television personality. The past two decades have also witnessed an increase of sermons on similar themes—"How to Keep from Feeling Frustrated," "How to Overcome an Inferiority Complex," "How to Find Inner Peace"—with Dr. Peale as the best-known exemplar of preaching in this vein. While the "cult of serenity" has come in for much searching criticism and its oversimplifications have been parodied in the Christian press—"You Too Can Be a Big Booming Success," "Take up Your Cross and Relax"— the response of congregations all over the country to sermons on interior problems indicates that the gospel is meeting one of the deep needs of our times.

The popular interest in religion manifests itself in many other ways. During World War II people thronged the churches on occasions of national intercession and thanksgiving, culminating in "V-E Day" and "V-J Day." More recently the American Legion, our most powerful veterans' organization, has launched a "Back to God" movement, employing the various channels of advertising and publicity to encourage church attendance and Bible reading. Religious appeals in public discussions and political addresses seem to be on the increase and cannot be entirely dismissed as a lure to catch the "church vote." President Eisenhower's baptism after his election but before his inaguration and his unaffected resort to prayer on certain occasions, as well as the Wednesday morning "prayer breakfasts" attended by a number of officials in Washington and the recent completion of a prayer chapel for congressmen in the Capitol Building, all indicate that leaders in our public life feel their need for the resources of religion.

To judge from the topics announced in the press and from published sermons, American congregations are hearing the central message of the gospel more clearly than in the twenties and the thirties. The vogue for discussing from the pulpit various questions of passing interest, of reviewing books, of appealing to the public fancy, which characterized some popular preachers in those days has yielded before a resurgence of biblical and doctrinal preaching. The new trend does not avoid contemporary problems, as the preaching on psychological subjects shows, nor is it chained to a formal pattern of biblical exposition: after the Evanston Assembly, Dr. Harold Bosley preached a series of sermons on the theme *What Did the World Council Say to You?* and he even has a discerning sermon on "A Christian Interpretation of the Kinsey Report." But our pulpits are reflecting the deepening theological mood of our times and the recovery of a clearly Christian standpoint as a basis for the criticism of life.

One of the strangest phenomena of the new interest in religion is a sentimental type of "popular song" inanely "plugging" some spiritual truism or celebrating faith or prayer or church. Over radio and television, on automatic coin machines, even on dance floors, one hears pseudo-religious ditties making familiar references to God and assuring everyone that everything will be all right. It is difficult to know what to make of such music. Some of it is doubtless written and produced by sincere believers of limited taste and theological insight; some of the rest is ground out by cynical tunesmiths with an eye to the current demand of the "market": the writer of one recent song is reported to have said, "It had a kid in it, and God. It had to be a hit." Meanwhile, if some people like these tunes for the moment, they are to be heard for the most part outside the churches.

Increasingly favorable religious statistics, especially the steady growth of church membership, have received considerable publicity in the secular and religious press, both here and abroad. The total number of adherents to all religious bodies in this country in 1955 was 100,162,529 persons, or 60.9 per cent of the total population. As recently as 1900 the proportion was only 36 per cent; not till 1940 did it reach 49 per cent. Thus, while it took four decades to increase the population from one-third to one-half, only fifteen years were required to go from one-half to three-fifths of a rapidly expanding population. Other statistics are equally imposing. Contributions of 49 Protestant and Eastern Orthodox churches in 1955 totaled $1,687,921,729. The estimated value of new construction in religious buildings ran to $736 million.

These are impressive figures and deserve a serious explanation. The quantitative gains are not lacking in positive Christian significance. At last the American churches are reaping the fruit of two hundred years of revivalistic effort. Probably never before in church history has such a concerted evangelistic enterprise been conducted on so vast a geographical scale over so long a period of time as that put forth as a continuous part of their program by American congregations since the Great Awakening in colonial days. Beginning with less than 10 per cent of the population at the start of our national life, the churches have exerted a major portion of their effort to win the unchurched; indeed, in many congregations the primary emphasis in every service of public worship is still evangelistic (and the lion's share of the numerical gains are made by the revivalistic denominations). All this prodigious effort has gained results, and progress is at an increasing rate; the stronger the churches become numerically the more concentrated is the fire on the dwindling proportion of the populace still religiously uncommitted. While new dangers arise for Christianity when it becomes the prevailing cult rather than a self-conscious minority, the situation is historically inevitable when the Christian mission is successful. And it cannot be denied that in many instances spiritual gains have come with the numerical growth. An Anglican bishop from India who visited the United States in 1954 said, "This country is much more sane and much more concerned with religion than I had realized."

BUT IS IT REVIVAL?

Yet, when the situation is examined qualitatively as well as quantitatively, grave reservations need to be entered. Thoughtful critics have raised questions about every aspect of our much-heralded "return to religion." Dean James Pike of the Episcopal Cathedral in New York has loosed some pointed barbs at the "great increase . . . in official piety" which expresses itself in religious language and ceremony but is much more difficult to discern in our international policies. President Henry Pitney Van Dusen of Union Theological Seminary has observed that, while church membership has reached a "new high" in our history, so has our crime rate; the loudly trumpeted revival of religion has not effected a new birth of morality in the body politic. Another commentator remarks that in all our current talk about religion we have too many preachers and too few sinners, that everyone is speaking the language of piety but no one is making confession. Others note with perturbation that almost unconscious blending of religion with nationalism: the increasing tendency to include appeals to the Deity in the insignia of government or the exhortation to attend church because it is "the American Way." It may also be noted that the thought-world of our philosophers and intellectuals generally has scarcely been penetrated, much less permeated, by the insights and concerns of the historic Christian faith. The revivalists and the personal evangelists are once again attracting the masses toward the churches and the atomic scientists are proclaiming the need of a spiritual mastery over physical power, but our theologians are being heard almost exclusively in Christian circles: neo-orthodoxy has made little impression on the secularism of the intelligentsia, or, at any rate, has not mastered it.

The inanity of the religious "message" in the popular songs, as in some "peace-of-mind" sermons, has elicited a spate of criticism. Much of it has come from American preachers themselves, who rightly deplore a tendency to turn the Christian faith into latter-day magic, devoid of ethics or of judgment; the acid comments of D. W. Brogan, the perceptive Englishman who wrote in the *Manchester Guardian* on "God and the Juke-Box," really made no points which had not already been sounded from scores of our pulpits.

The core of our problem seems to lie in the fact that the churches have succeeded in establishing themselves within the acceptable pattern of American life just at the time when the pressure to conform has become such a powerful factor in behavior. One cannot be sure whether an applicant for church membership is seeking salvation or social respectability. Indeed, whereas former revivalists frightened men into the church with the fear of hell, it would appear that the fear of being different is now a larger consideration. Uneasiness gnaws constantly at the man who is not "in tune with" his peer group, who is a member of Riesman's *The Lonely Crowd*. (The irony of it appears when Billy Graham exhorts the thousands in Madison Square Garden "Be not conformed to this world" and castigates conformity as a major sin of our time, while it is unquestionably a determining factor in his success.) So another paradox emerges: the revivalistic churches which once insisted on the "new birth," on the commitment of responsible believers who took their stand over against the prevailing pattern of society, though they still use the old vocabulary and may think they are winning the same kind of "decisions for Christ" are actually calling people out of the minority into the majority; they have become almost indistinguishable from paedobaptist churches in the fact that membership in both tends to become automatic, a feature of belonging to a Christian civilization. Affiliation with a church may be an accepted formality rather than the decisive experience of one's life, fraught with violent inner struggle. Yet the evangelists still use the heroic and extravagant language of the earlier revivalism to describe the process.

In effect, Christianity (along with Judaism) has become the prevailing cult in America, and receiving baptism may be a great deal like the ancient Roman's burning incense to Caesar —a routine act of social conformity. A recent survey of American college students, for example, reveals the cultic rather than the ethical nature of the new religiosity:

There is a "ghostly quality" about the students' religious beliefs and practices. Normally they express a "need for religion," but they do not expect this religion to guide and govern decisions in the secular world; such decisions are to be "socially determined." [1]

---

[1] William Kirkland, "Fellowship and/or Freedom" (reviewing *Changing Values in College* by Philip E. Jacob), *Christian Century*, April 17, 1957, p. 490.

The new religion is not the sovereign on the throne, but the court chaplain who invokes upon the undertakings of the king the blessings of God and brings him spiritual solace. An example is the routine custom whereby public meetings are opened with prayer by a local clergyman; the practice is followed at the gatherings of the white citizen's councils upholding racial segregation, with little sense of incongruity.

But there is something in the popular religiosity besides conformity to a cult. For a striking fact about Protestant Christianity in the 1950's, though this may be a passing phase, is its reversion to the "old-time religion" of biblicism, pietism, and revivalism. The dominance of the fundamentalist and traditionalist churches on the religious scene cannot be ignored: Southern Baptists, Missouri Synod Lutherans, the Churches of Christ, the various Churches of God, the Holiness churches. These are the communions making the real inroads on the unchurched element of our population. Theirs is the viewpoint heard over the radio hour after hour on Sunday broadcasts and represented in the major new religious journal to be launched in recent times, *Christianity Today*. They are the people whose language Billy Graham really speaks.

In the presumably "emancipated" churches at the center of American Protestantism little protest is heard against the popular reversion to fundamentalism. One cannot believe that no laymen have serious questions about all this; perhaps the pressure to conform keeps them silent. Meanwhile, some of the real gains, as well as certain insufficiencies, of the liberal movement seem to be going by default. The Christian concern for social action has sharply declined; a discouraged alumnus in his mid-thirties reports that the last social action group at the Yale Divinity School recently disbanded. Our pulpits have not succeeded in communicating to the people the insights of a century of biblical criticism or the more recent perception the revelation was in the Event and in the Person, not in the words. The appeal of the evangelist is still "The *Bible* says . . . !"

This reversion to the unquestioning affirmations of the "old-time religion," precritical and uncritical, seems a strange anomaly in the face of the new sophistication in American culture. But may it not be explained by the suddenness with which the American people have been catapulted into an advanced technological civilization, the responsibilities of world leadership, and all the complexities of contemporary life? Sophisticated as they think they are, they are not yet at home in the new world; they find status but not solace in chrome and picture windows and hi-fi and modern art. The easiest way to "go home," to find "peace of mind," is to return to the "old-time religion," to the simplicities and assurances of "the little brown church in the vale." So thousands of New Yorkers cuddle up cozily within the spine-tingling warmth of sentimental gospel songs and crowd Madison Square Garden for a type of revivalism which urbanites a generation ago had dismissed as an outmoded holdover from our rural past. The "other-directed" man of our conformist culture is never at ease, Riesman points out, for he can never be certain that he is really attuned to the expectations of his peer group. Out of his deep anxiety he grasps for assurance, and doubtless he finds a satisfying measure of it in the heaven-or-hell preaching of the fundamentalist evangelists.

Thus our continuing gains in adherents to the church may also represent a loss—not the courage of individual commitment to the will of God which our evangelism has sought in the past, but rather a deep sense of uneasiness until one has become identified with the church as a mark of being civilized.

The confusion of Christianity with American culture is seen in the increasing tendency toward a tacit "establishment" of religion in our public life, even though the separation of church and state is scrupulously maintained. While our politicians have always known how to include an appeal to divine assistance in their speeches, they seem in recent years to have become much more open—and, one must add, apparently quite sincere—in their practice of religion and their use of religious language. There can be little doubt that one major reason for the high regard in which the people hold President Eisenhowever is his unaffected but unconcealed piety and the moralistic, almost sermonic, tone of many of his public utterances. In 1956 Congress adopted as the official motto of the United States the words "In God We Trust." This slogan is now being inscribed on all coins and currency and on those denominations of postage stamps most frequently used. But the affirmation seems to reflect a sense of satisfaction with ourselves as we are and the belief that God is similarly satisfied with America, rather than any sense of humiliation and dependence upon him. The Christian faith seems to have been taken over as the American tribal cultus, and the forms of Christian worship are used in public ceremonies as appropriate national rites. When a political leader sees the nation under the judgment of the Christian God as Lincoln did in his Second Inaugural, this sort of sociological (as over against legal) "establishment" may be a wholesome thing. But is there not some danger that we are merely inviting God to march in our parade?

American Christianity is prospering in its environment, but there is little convincing evidence that it is challenging the culture in any radical way. The religious concepts of our leaders in public life, as of most American laymen, tend to be naïve and uncritical of our society. Much of the religious expression in popular songs and best-selling books, which is so widely heralded as signifying a revival of the spirit, is incredibly shallow; it represents primitive magic or superstition dressed up in Christian terms rather than any adequate understanding of the gospel ("Somebody up there likes me"). Outside the ranks of the clergy we have few intellectuals or authors with a mature grasp of the Christian faith and the ability to speak it incisively into the present, to compare with T. S. Eliot, C. S. Lewis, Dorothy Sayers, Christopher Fry, Graham Greene, Sir Walter Moberly, and others of similar stature in England. Doubtless our lack of a vigorous theological tradition in large measure accounts for the intellectual incoherence of our laymen with respect to the faith (as over against their highly commendable religious devotion). Another likely factor is the decline of the Christian college and university in the proportion of students reached in the world of higher education.

Little sense of divine judgment disturbs contemporary American religion. For two decades now we have considered ourselves as a nation arrayed on the side of the angels of light in the struggle against the demonic hosts of dictatorial darkness—Nazi, Fascist, Communist. But we tend to forget that we too are sinners. Few searching questions are asked in our churches about the perils of our unprecedented wealth and almost unlimited power. There is little moral uneasiness about racial segregation. If our increase in church attendance constitutes a revival, it is a revival without repentance. People are joining the church not because they regard themselves as sinners in need of cleansing but because they consider themselves respectable folk who should consequently belong to church. The preaching of the old-line revivalists deals for the most part with the "traditional sins," so that their forthright morality has a certain archaic tone. Across the land generally, "the fear of the Lord" is a phrase we do not use or understand.

Too much of the popular interest in religion is seeking after a nostrum. Christianity is held in esteem as a potential bulwark against communism or as the foundation of the American Way of Life or as an accessible resource for peace of mind. We are loving God for our sakes rather than for God's sake.

Far too many of our church members lack a sense of mission. They love their church, enjoy participating in its life, find inspiration in its services, and give with relative generosity to its support. But in their thinking it tends to be an end in itself. It sanctifies and improves the good life they are living and brings release from tension. But they do not see it as challenging their way of life or the culture of which they are a part; they do not think of themselves as a people set apart from the world with a mission of service and redemption to men and nations around the globe.

GRACE AND FORGIVENESS

One who takes a long, hard look at American Christianity must be deeply disturbed by such signs as have just been discussed. Yet if he knows the church—or any congregation—well, he recognizes that these are generalizations. When he looks at the picture in the large, he tends to form sweeping and discouraging judgments; when he considers a particular group of Christians he realizes that there are noteworthy exceptions, scores of devoted disciples whose first and highest loyalty is to the will of God and who seek to understand their mission as Christians in the world.

For my own part, while I am disturbed by the limitations in American Christianity, I cannot be skeptical about its significance or its possibilities for great good. For all across the United States at the heart of every congregation are Christians of unquestioned commitment who are giving themselves to the witness of evangelism, who are sharing generously of their means for the upbuilding of their own church, for missions and for works of mercy around the world, who are striving in their daily walk to render faithful obedience to Jesus Christ as Lord. And there is a growing ministry, more adequately educated than ever before in our history, exercising an effective leadership in the practical concerns of church administration but with an increasing theological awareness and with few illusions about the status of the church today. For the members and the ministers to whom I refer know that the church must be judged not by its material prosperity but by its spirit and its faithfulness to God.

Furthermore, if the current enlargement of our religious institutions has not yet produced a genuine revival, we must recognize the opportunity which is present. This may be the church's great chance, when men and women are looking to it, unashamed of their spiritual need and willing to be taught. Certainly there is significance in the open but humble identification with the church on the part of the leaders in our national life—President Eisenhower, Vice-President Nixon, John Foster Dulles, Harold Stassen, Sam Rayburn, Lyndon Johnson, Adlai Stevenson, Brooks Hays, and many others. A Christian friend from a Communist nation has spoken to me more than once with deep feeling about the fact that these men prominent in public life are willing to be known as members of the church.

So it may be some comfort to the rest of the world to realize that America is a country with a Christian tradition, growing Christian institutions, and a high degree of Christian commitment among many of its people, that leaders of our nation, whatever the wisdom of particular decisions, are disciples who seek to guide their policies by the principles of their faith, that we have a vocal Christian community which speaks boldly on current affairs from the pulpit, the church press and convention platform, that we have millions of believers who order their lives by prayer and obedience to the will of God as they understand it.

The signs of the times do not yet indicate a revival of religion in contemporary America in any thoroughgoing Christian sense. What they do reveal—and almost every sensitive pastor could bear corroborative witness at this point—is the great heart-hunger of men and women in our day. At a time of the greatest material prosperity in our history, our people are manifesting an inward loneliness, an awareness of Another, a longing—as yet unsatisfied—for the living God. This heart-hunger is perhaps only half-recognized, and many are seeking to satisfy it with that which is not bread. Our so-called "return to religion" may be only a resurgent primitivism which would silence doubt and fear with the magic of faith, invoking a divine blessing upon the American Way rather than devoutly seeking the will of the Eternal God for America. A shallow and selfish religiosity, neither rooted in doctrine nor flowering in ethics, is not to be confused with revival.

Yet surely the task of the church is clear—to proclaim to a people suddenly become "very religious" the judgment and the grace of the Unknown God whom they worship in ignorance. It has become fashionable in some quarters to delight in expressions of cynicism about the current trend in our religious life. There are perils in a complacent piety, soothing itself with the balm of Gilead, taking its ease in Zion, and forgetting the wrath of God. But there is also a danger in the theological sophistication and moral superiority complex of the professionally religious, who thank God that they are not as other men. If we are inclined to discount too skeptically the present religious interest because, forsooth, it is not as mature as our own Christian faith, perhaps we need to go to school to the priests. While not forgetting the prophetic lessons of righteousness and judgment, we may need to learn anew the priestly insight into the mercies of God, who makes himself accessible to all, high and low, and who hallows the common life by simple tokens and sacramental signs of his all-inclusive grace.

The apostolic admonition warns us against self-confidence: "*Let no one boast of men*" (1 Cor. 3:21). As American Christians we dare not worship ourselves. Rather, we must ask whether our faith and our obedience are sufficient to the needs of this dread hour. We must seek the grace of penitence and of submission to the guidance of God.

One of the hymns most frequently heard in our churches is the prayer of our Quaker poet, John Greenleaf Whittier. The mood of that hymn is the only safe note on which to end this book, in the hope that it truly reflects the heart of American religious life today:

> Dear Lord and Father of mankind,
>   Forgive our foolish ways!
> Reclothe us in our rightful mind,
> In purer lives Thy service find,
>   In deeper reverence, praise.
>
> In simple trust like theirs who heard
>   Beside the Syrian sea
> The gracious calling of the Lord,
> Let us, like them, without a word,
>   Rise up and follow Thee.
>   . . . .
> Drop Thy still dews of quietness,
>   Till all our strivings cease;
> Take from our souls the strain and stress,
> And let our ordered lives confess
>   The beauty of Thy peace.

Breathe through the heats of our desire
   Thy coolness and Thy balm;
Let sense be dumb, let flesh retire;
Speak through the earthquake, wind, and fire,
   O still, small voice of calm! [2]

[2] John Greenleaf Whittier, *The Complete Poetical Works* (Boston: Houghton Mifflin, 1894), p. 450.

Bibliographical Note

GENERAL

As an interpretation of American Christianity, the present work delineates important influences from the past, but it is not a formal history. Several recent introductions by competent church historians may be mentioned as useful. William Warren Sweet, *The Story of Religion in America* (New York: Harper & Brothers, 1942) gives more extensive treatment to the earlier period. Jerald C. Brauer, *Protestantism in America: a Narrative History* is a brief and colorful account, with nearly one-third of the attention given to developments in the twentieth century. Winfred Ernest Garrison, *The March of Faith: The Story of Religion in America since 1865* (New York: Harper & Brothers, 1933) vividly characterizes the major movements of seven decades which saw the passing of the frontier and the emergence of new problems and opportunities. Vergilius Ferm (ed.), *The American Church of the Protestant Heritage* (New York: Philosophical Library, 1953) presents historical essays on twenty-one major communions, each written by a member of the body involved.

Several previous interpretations of American religion merit attention. Willard L. Sperry, *Religion in America* (Cambridge University Press, 1945), is an urbane essay written for English readers in wartime; the focus is on New England and on the more sophisticated centers of our religious life. Also addressed to an English audience is William Warren Sweet, *The American Churches: an Interpretation* (Nashville and New York: Abingdon Press, 1948), a series of topical studies developed historically with authority and insight. Daniel Jenkins, *Europe and America: Their Contributions to the World Church* (Philadelphia: The Westminster Press, 1951) presents the sympathetic and responsible observations of an English Free Churchman who knows the

American churches well and develops his comparisons within an ecumenical setting.

I. THE AMERICAN SPIRIT

From the time when the United States achieved nationhood, travelers from abroad have exercised their literary skill in commenting on the American character. A useful anthology of their observations is Henry Steele Commager (ed.), *America in Perspective: The United States Through Foreign Eyes* (New York: Random House, 1947; available also, abridged as a paperback Mentor Book, published by the New American Library, New York). More recent discussions by Europeans include D. W. Brogan, *The American Character* (New York: Alfred A. Knopf, 1944) and André Siegfried, *America at Mid-Century* (New York: Harcourt, Brace and Company, 1955). An illuminating series of essays by an American historian is Arthur M. Schlesinger, *Paths to the Present* (New York: The Macmillan Company, 1949), the first chapter of which takes its title from Crèvecoeur's question, "What then is the American, this new man?" and is particularly revealing. Later chapters deal with urbanization, immigration, and other factors.

The thesis that the frontier was a major factor in shaping the American character and institutions is set forth in Frederick Jackson Turner, *The Frontier in American Life* (New York: Henry Holt and Company, 1920) and a sizable body of subsequent literature. While some would qualify the emphasis on the frontier and would draw attention to subsequent developments, the "Turner thesis" has gained wide acceptance among American historians; the study of the West has become a recognized branch of historical scholarship. I am deeply indebted for insights here presented to courses in the West under Dr. E. E. Dale of the University of Oklahoma and Dr. Dan E. Clark of the University of Oregon. See Dan Elbert Clark, *The West in American History* (New York: Thomas Y. Crowell Company, 1937), for ordered historical treatment and Turner and Merk, *List of References on the History of the West* (Cambridge: Harvard University Press, 1922) for comprehensive topical bibliographies. Authors who have traced out some implications of the Turner thesis for church history include William Warren Sweet, *Religion in the Development of American Culture 1765–1840* (New York: Charles Scribner's Sons, 1952) and Winfred Ernest Garrison, *Religion Follows* the Frontier: A History of the Disciples of Christ (New York: Harper & Brothers, 1931). See further Sweet's four volumes of source materials under the general title, *Religion on the American Frontier: The Baptists, 1783–1830* (New York: Henry Holt and Company, 1931), *The Presbyterians 1783–1840* (University of Chicago Press, 1936), *The Congregationalists* (*ibid.*, 1939), and *The Methodists* (*ibid.*, 1946). Also important is Richard C. Wolf, "The Middle Period, 1800–1870, The Matrix of Modern American Christianity," *Religion in Life*, XXII (Winter, 1952–53), 72 ff., for its contention that the first seven decades of the nineteenth century—the period of the great growth of the Western "people's churches"—rather than the colonial period were truly formative for contemporary American religion. For a moving and discerning analysis of the influence of frontier conditions on the formation of character, read the early chapters of Carl Sandburg, *Abraham Lincoln: The Prairie Years* (New York: Harcourt, Brace and Company, 1926). See also my *Ely Vaughn Zollars, Teacher of Preachers, Builder of Colleges: a Biography* (St. Louis: Christian Board of Publication, 1947). An earlier work, one of the first in church history to reckon with the "Turner thesis," and still suggestive, is Peter G. Mode, *The Frontier Spirit in American Christianity* (New York: The Macmillan Company, 1923).

An illuminating account of the influence of immigration on American life and character is found in Carl Wittke, *We Who Built America: The Saga of the Immigrant* (New York: Prentice-Hall, Inc., 1939). For special reference to the religion of the immigrants, their children, and their grandchildren, consult Will Herberg, *Protestant–Catholic–Jew, an Essay in American Religious Sociology* (Garden City: Doubleday & Company, Inc., 1955). A disturbing though deceptively selective, description of the effects of mechanization is Robert Jungk, *Tomorrow Is Already Here*, trans. Marguerite Waldman (New York: Simon and Schuster, 1954).

II. A Free Church and a Free State

The fundamental work on the theme of this chapter is Anson Phelps Stokes, *Church and State in the United States* (New York: Harper & Brothers, 1950), an authoritative survey in three large volumes. An illuminating document from the formative period is James Madison, "Memorial and Remonstrance against Religious

Assessments, 1785," to be found in Saul K. Padover (ed.), *The Complete Madison: His Basic Writings* (New York: Harper & Brothers, 1953), pp. 299–306. Important treatments of the origin of the American conception of freedom include Clinton Rossiter, *Seedtime of the Republic: the Origin of the American Tradition of Political Liberty* (New York: Harcourt, Brace and Company, 1953), Carl Becker, *The Declaration of Independence: a Study in the History of Political Ideas* (New York: Harcourt, Brace and Company, 1922), and Alice Mary Baldwin, *The New England Clergy and the American Revolution* (Durham: Duke University Press, 1928). Oft-quoted observations on the separation of church and state are those of James Bryce in *The American Commonwealth*, 2d. ed. rev. (New York: Macmillan and Co., 1891, chapters CII and CIII).

A persuasive exposition of the principle and discussion of issues deriving from it is Charles Clayton Morrison, "The Separation of Church and State in America," in *International Convention of Disciples of Christ: Annual Assembly, Buffalo, New York, 1947* (Indianapolis: International Convention of Disciples of Christ), pp. 101–118. Much publicized protests against the exclusion of religious teaching from the curriculum of the public schools are George Arthur Buttrick, *Faith and Education* (Nashville and New York: Abingdon Press, 1952) and Henry Pitney Van Dusen, *God in Education: A Tract for the Times* (New York: Charles Scribner's Sons, 1951). Important recommendations of responsible public educators for the presentation of information about religion as an element in the cultural heritage and for the development of morality are found in *The Relation of Religion to Public Education: The Basic Principles*, by the Committee on Religion and Education (Washington, D. C.: American Council on Education, 1947), and *Moral and Spiritual Values in the Public Schools* by the Educational Policies Commission (Washington, D.C.: National Education Association, 1951). A vigorous discussion of the investigation of religious leaders by congressional committees is G. Bromley Oxnam, *I Protest* (New York: Harper & Brothers, 1954.

A stirring historical defense of the separation of church and state as having contributed to the vitality of religious institutions and to the permeation of the culture by Christian principles is Winthrop S. Hudson, *The Great Tradition of the American Churches* (New York: Harper & Brothers, 1953). Interesting observations of a German on the influence of religion without establishment appear in the essay by Francis J. Grund, "Religion and Morality Preside over Their Councils," in Henry Steele Commager (ed.), *America in Perspective* (New York: Random House, 1947). For the guidance of Christian principles in public life, see Catherine Marshall (ed.), *The Prayers of Peter Marshall* (London: Peter Davis, 1955), Part Two: The Senate Prayers.

III. PROFILE OF A FREE CHURCH

The literature of stewardship consists largely of exhortation and methodology. A recent historical study is George A. E. Salstrand, *The Story of Stewardship in the United States of America* (Grand Rapids: Baker Book House, 1956). For fundamental principles as expounded by an American Lutheran see T. A. Kantonen, *A Theology for Christian Stewardship* (Philadelphia: Muhlenberg Press, 1956); by a Disciple of Christ, Orval D. Peterson, *Stewardship in the Bible* (St. Louis: Christian Board of Publication, 1952). A European Christian who has also served the church in Indonesia comments on American stewardship (and other practices discussed in this chapter), with serious reservations, in H. R. Weber, "A Greenhorn's Impressions of The People of God in North America," *The Ecumenical Review*, IX (April, 1957), 267–278.

Useful historical introductions to American evangelism include William Warren Sweet, *Revivalism in America: Its Origin, Growth and Decline* (New York: Charles Scribner's Sons, 1944), Charles A. Johnson, *The Frontier Camp Meeting: Religion's Harvest Time* (Dallas: Southern Methodist University Press, 1955), and Timothy L. Smith, *Revivalism and Social Reform in Mid-Nineteenth Century America* (Nashville and New York: Abingdon Press, 1957). The traditional ethos of American evangelism is well expressed in the sermons of George W. Truett, such as *A Quest for Souls* (New York: Harper & Brothers, 1917). Principles of theory and practice are set forth by the long-time director of evangelism for the Federal Council of Churches and the National Council of Churches in Jesse M. Bader, *Evangelism in a Changing America* (St. Louis: The Bethany Press, 1957). An excellent example of the way in which Roman Catholicism has adapted to the American situation is John Anthony O'Brien (ed.) *Winning Converts* (New York: P. J. Kenedy & Sons).

For historical studies of the ministry in the United States, see

Sidney E. Mead, "The Rise of the Evangelical Conception of the
Ministry in America (1607–1850)," and Robert S. Michaelsen,
"The Protestant Ministry in America: 1850 to the Present," both
in H. Richard Niebuhr and Daniel D. Williams (eds.), *The
Ministry in Historical Perspectives* (New York: Harper &
Brothers, 1956). An account of the economic situation of the
ministry in one denomination without strong central government
is William Martin Smith, *For the Support of the Ministry: A
History of Ministerial Support, Relief, and Pensions among
Disciples of Christ* (Indianapolis: Pension Fund of Disciples of
Christ, 1956). A charming fictional evocation of ministerial ex-
periences and of church life in late nineteenth-century rural
America is Edgar DeWitt Jones, *Fairhope: The Annals of a
Country Church* (New York: The Macmillan Company, 1919).

IV. EXPRESSIONS OF OUR FAITH

The characteristics discussed in this chapter emerge not so
much in the major scholarly works on American church history
as in the biographies of religious leaders and in the histories of
a given denomination in particular states. In these sometimes art-
less accounts appear scores of incidents which illustrate the points
made in this chapter and reflect the common life within the
churches.

A useful interpretation of activism in terms of its influence on
theology is the final chapter in Sweet, *The American Churches*.
The appearance of these traits within the Roman tradition, and the
problems created, may be noted in Theodore Maynard, *The
Story of American Catholicism* (New York: The Macmillan
Company, 1941). Influential Christian thought on social issues
may be studied in the writings of Walter Rauschenbusch and
Reinhold Niebuhr. See also H. Richard Niebuhr, *The Kingdom
of God in America* (New York: Harper & Brothers, 1937). In-
sight into the "simple faith" is best acquired through the reading
of representative sermons; e.g., John S. Sweeney, "The Simplicity
That Is in Christ" in *Sweeney's Sermons* (Nashville: Gospel Ad-
vocate Publishing Company, 1892), Charles Edward Jefferson,
The Character of Jesus (New York: Thomas Y. Crowell, 1908).
Edgar DeWitt Jones, "The Light on the Lord's Face" in *A Man
Stood up to Preach* (St. Louis: The Bethany Press, 1943) and
"The Most Unforgettable Person I Know" in *Sermons I Love to
Preach* (New York: Harper & Brothers, 1953).

V. The Search for Unity

The classic study of American religious divisions, in terms of social and cultural factors, is H. Richard Niebuhr, *The Social Sources of Denominationalism* (New York: Henry Holt and Company, 1929). A complete collection of current statistics on all denominations and councils of churches, as well as articles on important trends, will be found in the *Yearbook of American Churches;* the edition used herein is Benson Y. Landis (ed.), *Yearbook of American Churches: Information on All Faiths in the U.S.A.*, Twenty-Fifth Issue—Annual (New York: National Council of the Churches of Christ in the U.S.A., Edition for 1957, Issued September, 1956).

A brief account of unity movements in the United States, along with chapters on the ecumenical interests of various denominations, is Robert S. Bilheimer, *The Quest for Christian Unity* (New York: Association Press, 1952). See also Donald Herbert Yoder, "Christian Unity in Nineteenth Century America" in Ruth Rouse and Stephen Charles Neill (eds.), *A History of the Ecumenical Movement, 1517–1948* (Philadelphia: The Westminster Press, 1954). An important theological and pragmatic critique of the denominational system and proposal for unity by merger on a broad scale is Charles Clayton Morrison, *The Unfinished Reformation* (New York: Harper & Brothers, 1953). See also Winfred Ernest Garrison, *The Quest and Character of a United Church* (Nashville and New York: Abingdon Press, 1957).

Brief introductions into important aspects of the problem in America, with important bibliography, will be found in a guide written in preparation for the North American Study Conference on Faith and Order, by Paul Minear, *Ecumenical Conversations on the Nature of the Unity We Seek* (New York: World Council of Churches, 1956).

A reporter's account of developments toward racial inclusiveness in congregational life is Robert Root, *Progress against Prejudice: The Church Confronts the Race Problem* (New York: Friendship Press, 1957).

VI. The Sea of Faith—the Currents and the Depths

Several surveys of American religious thought deserve mention. Two important symposia, with chapters covering the various disciplines of Christian scholarship, are Samuel McCrea Cavert and Henry Pitney Van Dusen (eds.), *The Church through Half a Century: Essays in Honor of William Adams Brown* (New York: Charles Scribner's Sons, 1936) and Arnold S. Nash (ed.), *Protestant Thought in the Twentieth Century: Whence and Whither?* (New York: The Macmillan Company, 1951). Helpful elementary expositions of major contemporary theologians may be found in William Hordern, *A Layman's Guide to Protestant Theology* (New York: The Macmillan Company, 1955), Daniel Day Williams, *What Present-day Theologians Are Thinking* (New York: Harper & Brothers, 1952), and David Wesley Soper, *Major Voices in American Theology: Six Contemporary Leaders* (Philadelphia: The Westminster Press, 1953).

Classics of warm and constructive liberal thought are the devotional studies prepared by Harry Emerson Fosdick: *The Manhood of the Master* (New York: Association Press, 1913), *The Meaning of Prayer* (*ibid.*, 1915), *The Meaning of Faith* (*ibid.*, 1917), and *The Meaning of Service* (*ibid.*, 1920). A stirring account of the early theological struggles of the twentieth century by the leading preacher of "modernism" is Fosdick's autobiography, *The Living of These Days* (New York: Harper & Brothers, 1956). An autobiographical account of the encounter with the Ku Klux Klan, which is mentioned in this chapter, appears in Frank Elon Davison, *Thru the Rear-View Mirror* (St. Louis: The Bethany Press, 1955).

Significant surveys of the theological scene from the fundamentalist standpoint are two books by Carl F. H. Henry: *Fifty Years of Protestant Theology* (Boston: Wilde, 1950) and *The Drift of Western Thought* (Grand Rapids: Eerdmans, 1951). A survey of recent ecclesiastical controversies, in which fundamentalism was a large factor, is Ralph Lord Roy, *Apostles of Discord: A Study of Organized Bigotry and Disruption on the Fringes of Protestantism* (Boston: Beacon Press, 1953).

Two critiques of "the faith of the people," especially its lack of adequate dogmatic content, written from the prevailing theological mood (though Anglican rather than truly neo-orthodox in slant) are W. Norman Pittenger, *The Historic Faith and a Changing World* (New York: Oxford University Press, 1950) and Theodore O. Wedel, *The Christianity of Main Street* (New York: The Macmillan Company, 1953).

VII. The Christian Life

For a generation an important stream of books on worship has made manifest the rethinking of theory and practice within the American "non-liturgical" churches. An important pioneer was Von Ogden Vogt, *Art and Religion* (New Haven: Yale University Press, 1921). Significant successors include Willard L. Sperry, *Reality in Worship: A Study of Public Worship and Private Religion* (New York: The Macmillan Company, 1925), Albert W. Palmer, *The Art of Conducting Public Worship* (New York: The Macmillan Company, 1939), Andrew W. Blackwood, *The Fine Art of Public Worship* (Nashville and New York: Abingdon Press, 1939), Clarence Seidenspinner, *Form and Freedom in Worship* (New York: Harper & Brothers, 1941), and Henry Sloane Coffin, *The Public Worship of God* (Philadelphia: The Westminster Press, 1946). J. Paul Williams surveys the liturgical practice, as well as the central doctrines, of the various denominations in *What Americans Believe and How They Worship* (New York: Harper & Brothers, 1952).

A comprehensive symposium on the theory and practice of religious education is Philip Henry Lotz (ed.), *Orientation in Religious Education* (Nashville and New York: Abingdon Press, 1950). Two manuals representative of the ideals of the religious education movement as held by informed leaders in the congregations, before the recent emphasis on theology, are Nevin C. Harner, *The Educational Work of the Church* (Nashville and New York: Abingdon Press, 1939), and *Youth Work in the Church* (*ibid.*, 1942). The theorists of religious education have in recent years been engaged in a radical theological criticism of the liberal presuppositions on which the movement was largely based. H. Shelton Smith, *Faith and Nurture* (New York: Charles Scribner's Sons, 1941) was one of the pioneering books of reevaluation; Lewis J. Sherrill in *The Gift of Power* (New York: The Macmillan Company, 1955), constructively reorients religious educational theory in terms of neo-orthodox theology. Randolph Crump Miller presents guidance in theology for teachers of the various age groups in *Biblical Theology and Christian Education* (New York: Charles Scribner's Sons, 1956).

Most of the material on the program of the church is to be found in handbooks prepared for pastors and committee chairmen by the boards of the various denominations. Orman Leroy Shelton, *The Church Functioning Effectively* (St. Louis: Christian Board of Publication, 1946) sets forth basic principles and procedures. H. Richard Niebuhr (in collaboration with Daniel Day Williams and James M. Gustafson) considers the total program of a congregation and the demands it makes upon contemporary leadership in *The Purpose of the Church and Its Ministry: Reflections on the Aims of Theological Education* (New York: Harper & Brothers, 1956).

VIII. THE HAUNTING QUESTION

The secularization of modern society is presented on a world scale in James Hastings Nichols, *History of Christianity, 1650–1950: Secularization of the West* (New York: The Ronald Press Company, 1956). See also Clarence Tucker Craig (ed.), *The Challenge of Our Culture* (New York: Harper & Brothers, 1946) and J. Richard Spann (ed.), *The Christian Faith and Secularism* (Nashville and New York: Abingdon Press, 1948).

For the emergence of the new "conformist ethic," see David Riesman, with Nathan Slazer and Reuel Denney, *The Lonely Crowd: a Study of the Changing American Character* (Garden City: Doubleday, 1953). Also important is William H. Whyte, Jr., *The Organization Man* (New York: Simon & Schuster, Inc., 1956).

Important efforts have been made to convey contemporary theological and biblical insights to lay readers. The Westminster Press is now engaged in the publication of a Layman's Theological Library, Association Press has brought out a new series of low-priced "Reflection Books," and various publishers are issuing important religious titles in paperback editions. Other titles worthy of mention include Archibald M. Hunter, *Interpreting the New Testament, 1900–1950* (Philadelphia: The Westminster Press, 1951) and M. Jack Suggs, *The Layman Reads His Bible* (St. Louis: The Bethany Press, 1957).

Index

Activism, 83–90, 183, 194–201, 230
Adams, John, 6, 45
Adams, John Quincy, 6
Administration, 200. See Program
Adult classes, 190
Africa, 83
African Methodist Episcopal Church, 120, 131, 139
African Methodist Episcopal Zion Church, 131
Ainslie, Peter, 118
Akron Plan, 72
Allegheny Mountains, 5
Amazon River, 168
American Baptist Convention, 120, 131, 137, 141, 157. See Baptists
American Council on Education, 36, 228
American Evangelical Lutheran Church, 131
American Friends Service Committee, 40
American Legion, 211
American Red Cross, 78
"American Way," The, 20, 32, 171, 214, 219, 221
Amsterdam Assembly (WCC, 1948), 145
Amsterdam, Classis of, 98
Anglican. See Church of England; Protestant Episcopal Church
Anticlericalism, 53, 77, 106
Anti-Saloon League, 129
Apostles' Creed, 149, 150
Appalachian Mountains, 3, 27, 84
Architecture, ecclesiastical, 72–73, 178–79, 199, 208
Arizona, v, xi
Arkansas, v, xi
Arts, 87, 207, 208
Asbury, Francis, 92, 104
Asia, ix, 22, 83, 202, 203
Assembly of God, 62, 119
Athenagoras, Archbishop, Metropolitan of Thyatira, 1, 102
Athens, 13
Atlantic seaboard, 5, 27, 77
Atonement, 152, 155
Augustana Evangelical Lutheran Church, 131
Augustine, St., 74

Bader, Jesse M., 229
Bahai, 117

Baker, William G., xi
Baldwin, Alice Mary, 228
Baltimore, Lord, 29, 44
Baltimore, Maryland, 18, 104, 118
Baptism, 65, 102, 138, 215
Baptists, 8, 30, 65, 90, 98, 114, 117, 118, 130, 140, 147, 177, 178, 227. See American Baptist Convention; Southern Baptists
Barth, Karl, 114, 115, 144, 146, 161, 164, 173
Becker, Carl, 228
Beecher, Henry Ward, 92, 153, 207
Beecher, Lyman, 52, 84, 92
Bennett, John C., 110, 161
Berggrav, Eivind, 1
Bible, 34, 44, 45, 56–57, 64, 81, 83, 89, 91, 92, 98, 100, 132, 146, 147, 148, 151–52, 154, 156, 158, 159, 163, 165, 166, 170, 172–73, 182, 183–85, 209, 216, 233, 234
"Bible Belt," x
Biblical criticism, 148, 149, 151–52, 156, 160, 209, 216, 234
Biblical theology, 162, 163, 165, 166–67, 170, 216, 233
Bilheimer, Robert S., 231
Bill of Rights, 28, 30
Blackwood, Andrew W., 178, 233
Board of Church Extension (Disciples of Christ), 86
Boegner, Marc, 1, 146
Boehm, John Philip, 98
Boggess, S. F., 86
Bologna, Archbishop of, 107
Boniface, St., 74
Boninsegna, Giuseppe, 107
Bosley, Harold A., 92, 212
Bossey, Château de. See Ecumenical Institute; Graduate School of Ecumenical Studies
Boston, Massachusetts, 18
Boy Scouts, 79
Brauer, Jerald C., 54, 225
Britain, 9, 76, 90
British immigration, 2, 18
Bro, Margueritte Harmon, 105
Brogan, D. W., 214, 226
Brooks, Phillips, 92
Brotherhood, 148, 149, 168
Brotherhood of the Kingdom, 108
Brunner, Emil, 114, 144
Bryan, William Jennings, 156
Bryce, James, 33, 52, 228
Buckner, George Walker, Jr., xi
Buddhism, 117, 203

Building of churches, 58, 85, 91, 172, 196, 198–200, 213
Bunyan, John, 91
Bushnell, Horace, 92
Butler University School of Religion, xi
Buttrick, George A., 36, 92, 115, 170, 228

Caesar, 215
Calhoun, Robert L., 146
California, 40
Calvin, John, 144
Calvinism, 146, 147
Cambridge, Massachusetts, 2
Camp, 188, 191, 194
Camp meeting, 62
Campbell, Alexander, 92
Canada, 9
Canterbury, Archbishop of (Geoffrey Fisher), 1
Carey, William, 56
Cartwright, Peter, 90, 92
Carver, George Washington, 23
Cavert, Samuel McCrea, 232
Cayuga, Indiana
First Christian Church, v
Champaign, Illinois, 35
University Place Christian Church, 172
Channing, William Ellery, 92, 207
Chaplaincy, 40–41, 132
Character, American, 1–26, 83–116, 148, 161, 204–10, 226
Charlemagne, 84
Cherokee Strip (Oklahoma), 85–87, 100
Chicago, Illinois, x, 19, 34, 67, 69, 85
Chinese, 128
Christ Unity Science Church, 119, 120
Christian Century, The, 39, 131, 162
Christian Churches (Kentucky), 119
Christian education, 63–64, 65–66, 70, 87, 96, 113, 130, 132, 133, 149, 151, 165, 183–97, 233. See Colleges and universities; Sunday school
Christian Endeavor, Society of, 130, 190, 192
Christian Men's Fellowship, 198
Christian Methodist Episcopal Church, 131, 139
Christian Women's Fellowship, 197
Christian Youth Conference of North America, 192

235

239

241